FATE OF THE NATION

FATE OF THE NATION

Three Scenarios for South Africa's Future

Jakkie Cilliers

Jonathan Ball Publishers

Johannesburg & Cape Town

© Text Jakkie Cilliers 2017
© Published edition 2017 Jonathan Ball Publishers

Originally published in South Africa in 2017 by
JONATHAN BALL PUBLISHERS
A division of Media24 (Pty) Ltd
PO Box 33977
Jeppestown
2043

ISBN 978-1-86842-797-0
ebook ISBN 978-1-86842-798-7

*Every effort has been made to trace the copyright holders and to obtain their
permission for the use of copyright material. The publishers apologise for any
errors or omissions and would be grateful to be notified of any corrections that
should be incorporated in future editions of this book.*

Twitter: www.twitter.com/JonathanBallPub
Facebook: www.facebook.com/JonathanBallPublishers
Blog: http://jonathanball.bookslive.co.za/

Cover by publicide
Design by Triple M Design
Editing by Mark Ronan
Proofreading by Alfred LeMaitre
Index by Sanet le Roux
Printed and bound by CTP Printers, Cape Town
Set in 10.25/18pt Minion Pro

To Paul and Pierre –
and in loving memory of SP and Betsie

Contents

Scenarios past and present

Men make their own history, but they do not make it as they please ... The tradition of all dead generations weighs like a nightmare on the brains of the living.

– Karl Marx[1]

Many efforts have been made at forecasting the future of South Africa. In fact, predicting South Africa's implosion, decline and inevitable collapse – the gloomy prognosis adopted by many – has spawned something of a cottage industry.

The historian RW Johnson leads this negative storyline by a long chalk with his 2015 best-seller, *How Long Will South Africa Survive?* – although there have been valiant efforts by other authors. That South Africa has been in the five-minutes-to-midnight territory for several decades, in the eyes of many, is reflected in the fact that Johnson published an earlier book with the exact same title – back in 1977. The 38 years that passed between Johnson's two books indicate that either South Africa has an unexpected level of resilience or that there has been faulty analysis.

Although this sense of impending crisis is unlikely to change, I don't believe the projections of these doomsday merchants will actually materialise. It is not a question of whether South Africa will survive or not. Of course it will! The question is rather, will we become more prosperous and less divided as a nation, or will we remain at variance, hugely unequal and generally poor? Will investors have confidence in our future trajectory and will local professionals stay in the country and invest, or will many of the increasingly multiracial cohorts of professionals who are trained locally at great expense continue to escape to cold, wet and dark places, such as the United Kingdom, Canada and New Zealand?

The purpose of this book is to present likely scenarios for South Africa's future. These have been modelled as far as 2034, a year when national elections are due. A scenario, however, is not a prediction; it is a coherent story about the future – a sequence of events that unfold over time and are internally consistent and plausible.

Economists love the phrase 'path dependency', meaning the past inexorably determines the future. According to this view, we have little control over our future because the past has set us on a particular pathway. By contrast, if you are working in the field of scenario planning, you do not believe the future is predetermined even if the parameters of the possible are necessarily limited. You need the ability to think creatively about developments some years into the future, which requires an ability to step outside orthodoxy and groupthink, and to bend path dependency towards a desired outcome rather than merely accepting that our destiny is beyond our control.

This book therefore adds meat to the bone of forecasting, making the various scenarios that are posited realistic and understandable. The first three chapters analyse the Zuma presidency and the declining election prospects of the African National Congress (ANC). In Chapter 4, I present a set of detailed political forecasts, mapping out the potential results for the three main South African political parties, the ANC, the

Democratic Alliance (DA) and the Economic Freedom Fighters (EFF), during the 2019, 2024 and 2029 national elections. I leave it to the reader to speculate on the possible outcomes in 2034.

These political scenarios determine key economic and development outcomes, and the results of these are analysed in Chapters 5, 6 and 7. Chapter 8 presents an overview of the prospects for crime, violence and stability, while Chapter 9 looks at South Africa in a global context, seeking to unpack the impact of the different scenarios on the future. The book concludes with a set of recommendations to realise a more prosperous future.

However, as no one can predict the future, the only certainty is that things will unfold somewhat differently. We can debate and model the future, discuss probable developments and the like, but inevitably some, perhaps most, of the associated effort ends up being speculative. And the longer the time horizon, the greater the degree of uncertainty shrouding the forecast, because the margin for error increases exponentially with each passing year.

In 1988, I had resigned from the South African Defence Force (SADF) for political reasons and subsequently tried to contribute to the settlement process in my own way. I had served in the artillery (which left me partially deaf after several stints on the border between Namibia and Angola), but my studies on the Zimbabwe War of Liberation[2] and, later, a PhD on collective political violence in South Africa had served to open my eyes to broader events in South Africa and the region.[3]

In March 1990, I attended a conference in Lusaka with members of Umkhonto we Sizwe, the armed wing of the ANC, organised by the Institute for a Democractic Alternative in South Africa and, on my return, I established the Institute for Defence Policy, the forerunner of the Institute for Security Studies (ISS). With funding from the Anglo American and De Beers Chairman's Fund, and the Hanns Seidel Foundation, we worked on developing an appropriate vision and future for the armed forces of a post-apartheid South Africa. These were difficult times. I was constantly being monitored by military intelligence, my phone was tapped and my family and co-workers were intimidated.

Negotiations between the SADF, Umkhonto we Sizwe and other armed groups started only in 1993, as the National Party wanted to maintain the organisational coherence of its military should things go wrong with the multi-party negotiation process. In the end, South Africa narrowly escaped a coup d'état by the SADF and a very violent rupture when Constand Viljoen, former chief of the SADF and then leader of the Freedom Front, backed away at the last moment from seeking to violently split South Africa into two.

It was a time of both fear and euphoria. White South Africa was a highly militarised society, fearful of possible retribution yet also excited about a potential future of joint prosperity and growth. It was around then that I was introduced to the concept of scenario development as a tool for social change. In 1992, the Institute for Defence Policy used scenario development to try to provide a positive vision for a post-apartheid military. In the process, I engaged with all the various armed forces involved in the South African transition, including those from the homeland militaries in Transkei, Ciskei, Venda and Bophuthatswana.

More broadly, scenario development of various types has played an important part in South Africa's recent history.[4] Once the logjam of apartheid had been broken, a number of well-known analysts, including the doyen of scenario work, Pierre Wack (a former executive from oil company Shell, and one of the first to apply scenario analysis in the private sector), visited South Africa during the tumultuous transition years from

1990 to 1994. After leaving Shell in 1982, Wack had begun consulting for Anglo American, the South African mining corporation, in its efforts to globalise and had warned the company about the impact of the end of apartheid on the gold price. It was his work for Anglo American and his dealings with Clem Sunter, former chairman and CEO of a division of Anglo American, that brought him to South Africa.[5]

At the start of the transition process, banking group Nedcor and insurance giant Old Mutual developed a series of scenarios on the future of South Africa that were particularly influential and insightful. In 1992 Robin Lee, the project's research coordinator, and I presented these scenarios to Joe Modise and other senior leaders of Umkhonto we Sizwe. The Berlin Wall had collapsed a few years earlier and, with it, the communist orthodoxy in which the entire top ranks of the ANC had been ideologically schooled. Modise and his colleagues were in desperate need of an alternative framework to guide a post-apartheid South Africa – one that was not being presented by the National Party, white bureaucrats and others generally considered to be untrustworthy.

The Nedcor/Old Mutual scenarios (titled *The World and South Africa in the 1990s*) built on aspects of previous scenario analysis done by Sunter. Modise and his team were transfixed when they saw them. The presentation, initially scheduled for an hour, turned into a seven-hour meeting, during which we viewed and discussed the entire video set that had been compiled by the Nedcor/Old Mutual team.[6]

The market-friendly tone of these scenarios proved to be a perfect fit – after all, Modise was not averse to the profit motive himself: at the time of his death in 2001, it was widely speculated that he had benefited from key defence procurements after he was appointed as South Africa's defence minister in 1994.[7]

To me, this experience confirmed the potential that scenarios have:

they can shape thinking and open up disparate minds to alternative possibilities, encouraging a shared vision of the future. The Nedcor/ Old Mutual scenarios succeeded in focusing our minds on a common future, as opposed to dwelling on the differences between us. It was surprising and encouraging to realise how little difference there was in where the various actors in the transition, on different sides of the political fence, wanted to get to. Eventually, these efforts – together with the exposure of ANC leaders such as Nelson Mandela to chang- ing views on nationalisation – helped drive ANC policies towards the modern, post-communist world.

Mont Fleur and other efforts at scenarios

I was not involved in the other big South Africa scenario project at the time, the 1991/92 Mont Fleur scenarios (named after the hosting conference venue).[8] This brought 25 influential South Africans from diverse backgrounds together in a series of meetings – including the likes of Rob Davies, Saki Macozoma, Trevor Manuel, Tito Mboweni, Jayendra Naidoo, Sue van der Merwe and Christo Wiese – to develop alternative scenarios for a post-apartheid South Africa. The outcomes, four scenarios titled Ostrich, Lame Duck, Icarus and the hopeful and visionary Flight of the Flamingos, played an important role in shaping thinking about the future during a period of great uncertainty in South Africa.

It was during the Mont Fleur programme that the need for a social compact – a grand compromise between labour, business and government, a bedrock for future development – was born, encapsulated in the vision of the confident and graceful flight of a flock of flamingos. And that vision became reality, in the sense that, in 2017, South Africa is generally a much better country to live in than it was in 1992.

Key to the success of both these scenario processes was the credibility of the people involved, the consultative nature of the scenario development and the widely disseminated results.

These scenarios were developed just before the dawn of democracy in South Africa. Later, in 1997, the September Commission of the Congress of South African Trade Unions (COSATU) produced a set of scenarios on the future of the unions – The Desert, Skorokoro and Pap 'n Vleis and Gravy.[9] These three models portrayed the economic policies pursued by the ANC as potentially conservative, zigzagging or social-democratic. Looking back, it is clear that the vision that has emerged in recent years reflects the uneven and unequal scenario, Skorokoro (meaning an old banger of a car), with its associated social fragmentation and culture of entitlement.

It is ironic that, as it turned out, the main contributor to that unfavourable outcome was COSATU itself, particularly the way in which the labour confederation ended up constraining the country's ability to increase employment opportunities, thereby contributing to poverty and inequality. Initially, COSATU was the most powerful partner in the Tripartite Alliance, and its policies on labour and the economy largely determined ANC, and therefore government, policy.

Later, COSATU also played a key role in ousting President Thabo Mbeki when he tried to challenge their policy orthodoxy by moving away from the Reconstruction and Development Programme (RDP). The RDP was the policy-framework agreement in the pre-1994 alliance between the ANC, COSATU and the South African Communist Party (SACP). COSATU would not forgive Mbeki when he abandoned the RDP in favour of the Growth, Employment and Redistribution (GEAR) strategy in 1996, with the ANC just two years into government.

Thus began the revisionist history of the so-called 1996 class project

– South Africa's own version of fake news that sought to cast Mbeki and his finance minister, Trevor Manuel, as neoliberals in cahoots with the World Bank and the International Monetary Fund (IMF), sharing their conservative approach to fiscal policy.

Other efforts have been less successful in terms of formulating outcomes, although the analysis itself does remain useful. In September 2008, the month the ANC recalled Mbeki as president, the hitherto powerful Policy Coordination and Advisory Services (PCAS), a unit in the Presidency, released a report, *South Africa Scenarios 2025: The Future We Chose?*[10] The three scenarios contained in the report were called Not Yet Uhuru, Nkalakatha (the name of a popular song of celebratory energy and swaggering self-confidence) and Muvhango (the name of a TV drama series that chronicled the fortunes and misfortunes of a divided family torn apart by jealousy, betrayal and the quest for money and power).

The PCAS scenarios went down like a lead balloon. The country's ttention was firmly fixed on the drama, humiliation and ejection of Mbeki. Following the election of Jacob Zuma as ANC president at the party's Polokwane conference and the subsequent recall of Mbeki, these scenarios had no real impact, in part due to the subsequent restructuring of the Presidency. The thing is, in the scenario business, timing (and buy-in) is everything, and the PCAS scenarios had neither.

During the April 2009 elections, the ANC achieved a resounding victory at the polls and Zuma took over from Kgalema Motlanthe, who had kept the presidential chair warm as it awaited Zuma's grand arrival. During this period, a sense of crisis and drift made an impressively diverse group of South Africans from all political walks come together to develop the Dinokeng scenarios[11] (named Walk Apart, Walk Behind and Walk Together). The rationale for developing these scenarios was that, despite its many achievements, South Africa stood at a crossroads and faced critical social and economic challenges that were exacerbated by a constraining global environment – in 2008 the world had entered its most serious financial crisis for almost a century.[12]

The Dinokeng scenarios placed national reconciliation and the need for a social compact (or social contract) at the centre of their findings and recommendations. Each reflected a unified Rainbow Nation, a concept that had originally been popularised by the Mandela administration, despite the fact that Mbeki steadily backed away from the notion of non-racialism and unity.

Declining future prospects

In 2013, the IMF's country report on South Africa[13] provided the following projection for the short to medium term:

> The outlook is for continued sluggish growth and elevated current account deficits, reflecting global developments and important domestic factors. Absent structural reforms, growth will be insufficient to reduce unacceptably high unemployment. Risks are tilted firmly to the downside, especially from lower capital inflows, though the stronger implementation of the National Development Plan ... would improve the outlook.

Three years later, in July 2016, the IMF had become even more pessimistic about South Africa's future. In the press release that accompanied the results of its regular consultations with the South African Government, it noted that deep-rooted structural problems – infrastructure bottlenecks, skill mismatches, and harmful insider-outsider dynamics – are holding back growth and exacerbating unemployment and inequality. South Africa's vulnerabilities are elevated … The outlook is sobering with considerable downside risks …

Downside risks dominate and stem mainly from linkages with China, heightened global financial volatility, and domestic politics and policies that are perceived to harm confidence. Shocks could be amplified by linkages between capital flows, the sovereign, and the financial sector, especially if combined with sovereign credit rating downgrades to speculative grade.[14]

The IMF's prediction proved 100 per cent accurate: in the first week of April 2017, Standard and Poor's and Fitch downgraded the country's sovereign credit rating to junk status. South Africa is rapidly approaching the end of Zuma's lost decade. A new dawn may be approaching, but it will take hard work and several years to undo the damage wrought by the incoherence and squandered opportunities since the Zuma faction assumed power. Change is difficult and often painful.

Despite the uncertainties brought about by Brexit and the election of Donald Trump, global growth is accelerating. South Africa will benefit from that growth, although less than it ought to – largely thanks to the damage done to the country's prospects as a result of the ANC's incoherent policies, failure to implement its plans, wastage, corruption and incompetence under the leadership of Zuma.

Much will depend on the next two years, and particularly on the choices that will be made during the December 2017 national conference of the ANC and the outcomes of the 2019 national elections, particularly in Gauteng. Either a reinvigorated ANC or the rise of competitive multi-party politics might deliver improved prospects. But, either way, it's going to be a rough ride.

The three scenarios

The scenarios that are laid out and analysed in this book do not have the benefit of wide consultation nor the comprehensive approach associated with the Nedcor/Old Mutual and Mont Fleur scenarios. Nor are they underpinned by the impressive preparatory diagnostic review that preceded the National Development Plan.

Their more modest development path has come about from a series of publications that I have authored at the ISS since 2013, funded by the Hanns Seidel Foundation of Germany. The work presented here has, however, been substantially and comprehensively reworked and updated. The three scenarios are as follows:

❏ Bafana Bafana, named after our mediocre national soccer team, is the most likely scenario.
❏ Mandela Magic is the desired scenario.
❏ Nation Divided is the downside scenario.

Bafana Bafana is the familiar story of a perennial underachiever, always playing in the second division, even though the potential for interna-tional championship success and flashes of brilliance are evident for all to see. This scenario is essentially a forecast of 'more of the same', and in it South Africa steadily loses ground.

Mandela Magic, on the other hand, is the story of a country with a clear economic and developmental vision, which it pursues across all sectors of society. In this scenario, Team South Africa play to a single game plan and are consistent in execution during every match, refining and harmonising their strategy as they go along. In the Mandela Magic scenario, a new leadership and/or the impact of competitive politics could see a reinvigorated ANC. Alternatively, if the party crumbles, voters may turn in increasing numbers to opposition parties, in which case stronger opposition parties could deliver the same positive trends but with some delay.

The Nation Divided scenario reflects a South Africa that steadily gathers speed downhill as factional politics and policy zigzagging open the door to populism and further fracturing of the ANC. Nation Divided is an undesirable low road, entailing macro instability, high inflation, capital flight, currency depreciation and periods of negative economic growth for several years. For a country that already has high levels of public debt, these effects could prove disastrous.

In this scenario, concerned by the apparent rise of populist parties to its left, the ANC itself becomes more populist (a trend already well underway as this book goes to print) and adopts a raft of self-defeating policies that lower growth, increase unemployment and poverty, and generally lead to a shrinking economy with concomitant social turbulence. Violence in society increases as populist policies run out of fiscal space and all South Africans are the losers. As we will see, this is a scenario in which the ANC is likely to be forced into an alliance with the EFF which, in the process, could emerge as a kingmaker on the national stage before it succumbs to the contradictory policies that have condemned countries like Zimbabwe to ruin. However, South Africa is not Zimbabwe, and there is, in my view, no chance of populism becoming mainstream without the ANC and the EFF being punished at the polls.

Mandela Magic and Nation Divided might seem like typical best-case and worst-case scenarios. However, South Africa may do considerably better or worse than either.

The intention with each scenario mapped out in this book is to provide plausible combinations of events from antecedents. The elements that emerge fully formed in each scenario all have their roots in current reality. The election forecasts that are presented in Chapter 4 lie at the heart of the story told here. The ANC is central to all three storylines, although many other factors come into play to influence them.

South Africa's future is finely balanced between these three alternative pathways. That future will be determined by the raging succession battle being waged between the two dominant factions in the ANC. Either way, the impact of the policy and leadership choices that the party makes in its December 2017 conference, and that the public make in the elections in 2019, are likely to determine our future and that of the next generation.

I used the International Futures forecasting system (IFs) to model the impact of the scenarios. IFs is developed and maintained by the Frederick S Pardee Center for International Futures at the University of Denver, where I spent some time as a Fulbright scholar. The ISS and the Pardee Center have been working in partnership on various aspects of the future of South Africa (and Africa) for several years. Unless indicated otherwise, all currency figures are in 2016 values.

The genesis of the early work produced by the ISS is to be found in the settlement process that unlocked one of the world's most intractable problems, South Africa's unlikely transition from apartheid state to democracy. South Africa is once again at a tipping point, perhaps even set for another transition. And, like the context of Mont Fleur and Dinokeng in the early 1990s, this is an ideal time to turn again to scenario development to map out South Africa's possible futures.

CHAPTER 1

Zuma and the future of the ANC

The root cause is not the ANC, not the president alone, it's the state of capture.

– Bonang Mohale[1]

South Africa is fast approaching a decisive political turning point. This will be determined by the outcome of the struggle for power between two main factions within the ANC, which I describe as the Traditionalists and the Reformers. This struggle will come to a head in December 2017, when the party elects its leadership during the ANC's elective conference.

This chapter discusses the main divisions within the ANC and how the rift between them has led to policy confusion and even the development of a parallel security state.[2] It will also show how the actions of the Zuma administration – or lack of them – have compounded the impact of other developments, thus lowering growth, increasing poverty and threatening the fabric of society. South Africa is a laggard in a region that is expected to be among the most rapidly growing in the world, and it also lags behind its upper-middle-income peers globally.

When government is absent, distracted or incompetent, other agencies and actors move in to fill the void, and new political dynamics emerge.

The 2019 elections will most likely see further reductions in electoral support for the ANC and gains for opposition parties, unless the party can pull a very large rabbit out of the hat.

Government is being 'tested by mounting demands, but falls short in its response,'[3] said the Human Sciences Research Council in its 2016 *State of the Nation* report. A growing protest movement is calling for change across the areas of service provision, labour issues and un-employment, and university fees and staffing, and, most recently, for Zuma's resignation.

There is no doubt that Zuma has become a liability to the ANC as a result of his unashamed efforts at state capture, unethical behaviour, poor decision making and his proclivity to depend on the largesse of oth-ers – first in the form of businessman Schabir Shaik, and now the Gupta brothers, Ajay, Atul and Rajesh. Furthermore, his personal choices, in-ability to manage his personal finances and use of state resources for private gain, have sullied the reputation of the country, the Presidency and the ANC.

Beyond his role in helping to bring peace to KwaZulu-Natal, Zuma's major political success ahead of his campaign to oust Thabo Mbeki was to convert that province into an ANC stronghold. He did this by doing a deal with traditional leaders over land, which swung most of them away from the Inkatha Freedom Party to the ANC ahead of the 2004 general election.[4] 'This,' argues Nick Branson of the Africa Research Institute, 'came at the cost of genuine land reform and entrenched rather than dismantled apartheid-era divisions over land rights and ownership.'[5]

Beyond that double-edged achievement, the president maintains an indifference to economic policy, and a disdain for investor predictability and the need for policy stability. Indeed, his vernacular pronouncements to an exclusively ANC audience point to a lack of conviction in the constitutional democratic project, such as the statement that he could solve all of South Africa's problems if made a dictator for six months.[6]

The rule of law, good governance and the effectiveness of systems have all have suffered at the hands of Zuma. He clearly desires a very different type of society from the one reflected in the South African Constitution and Bill of Rights, preferring traditional 'big man' rule. Zuma acts like a traditional chief who is not bound by considerations of due process, the Bill of Rights or the constraints of an international economy that punishes countries that live beyond their means.

Accelerating a trend first evident under Mbeki, Zuma has undermined, or attempted to damage, the integrity and effectiveness of institutions such as the National Prosecuting Authority (NPA), the Constitutional Court, the Office of the Public Protector, the South African Revenue Service (SARS), the Treasury as well as the media. Under Zuma, all have been subjected to unprecedented levels of political interference as part of the ANC policy of cadre deployment. Recent revelations have revealed a much grander effort at state capture.

Originally, the most well-known were ventilated in the North Gauteng High Court, which found in April 2016 that the NPA's 2009 decision to drop 783 charges of fraud, racketeering and corruption against the president was irrational, a decision that opened the door to Zuma's prosecution by the NPA. Zuma and the NPA subsequently announced that they would appeal against the decision in a clear effort to continue to kick this particular can as far down the road as is legally possible.[7] At the time of writing, the obstacles to prosecution have steadily been peeled away and the case may proceed towards the latter part of 2017.

That the NPA has been subjected to manipulation and interference is public knowledge. The National Director of Public Prosecutions is appointed by the president for a term of ten years – but none has yet been able to complete a term because of corruption and ANC factional battles. Shortly after Shaun Abrahams, the most recent incumbent, was appointed, he launched a very public campaign to charge the then newly appointed, Minister of Finance and prominent member of the Reformist faction, Pravin Gordhan, of having established a rogue spy unit during his previous tenure in the same position. When Gordhan did not blink, Abrahams dropped the charges for lack of evidence.

Abrahams is the latest in a long list of Zuma appointees to the criminal-justice system. Each NPA director is, it seems, appointed by the president to serve a particular political purpose, and not for his or her competence. When fulfilling the role proves legally difficult or when seeking to pursue prosecutions too close to presidential comfort, such as charging Zuma on the so-called spy tapes[8] or Gordhan on the so-called SARS rogue unit, every legal loophole is exhausted (often at the expense of the taxpayer) and eventually the latest incumbent finds himself in hot water.

Abrahams was unable to pursue the charges against Gordhan, who was proving an obstacle to access to lucrative contracts linked to a proposed new nuclear power build, and deals relating to South African Airways and others. But, with Zuma steadily losing power, he may still survive.

Corruption and patronage have compromised the strength of many of South Africa's justice and law-enforcement institutions. To an extent, Zuma is following here in the footsteps of his predecessor. In 1999, Mbeki decided to appoint diplomat and struggle veteran Jackie Selebi as National Police Commissioner despite his lack of experience of policing. At the time, Selebi was the director general of the Department of Foreign Affairs and embroiled in a serious clash with his minister, Nkosazana Dlamini-Zuma. After a disastrous nine years as police commissioner, which steadily eroded the ability of the police to fight crime, Selebi was eventually forced out and convicted of corruption.[9]

In 2009, Zuma appointed the KwaZulu-Natal MEC for Community Safety, Bheki Cele, to the same position; Cele was, in turn, suspended in 2012 after a report by Public Protector Thuli Madonsela found a number of irregularities in building leases. Cele was replaced by Ria Phiyega, who was herself suspended after three years. At the time of writing, the South African Police Service (SAPS) has an acting commissioner who, although a career policeman, is under investigation by the Independent Police Investigative Directorate for fraud.

Instead of appointing competent career technocrats to lead the police, the NPA or the Hawks and the like, Zuma is compelled by the litany of ethical, legal and moral issues that enmesh him to seek protection in some form or the other. The only way for the president to stay out of court, and possibly even jail, is to control key appointments, to manipulate the system and to purchase loyalty through patronage.

Inevitably, political survival and staying out of prison have become Zuma's overriding preoccupation. This he does through a vast network of patronage – appointing loyalists to positions of influence in government and state-owned enterprises, although there are some exceptions in the Cabinet and elsewhere. Zuma's patronage politics and the lack of policy stability are destroying the ANC. Since he became president, he has expanded and reshuffled his Cabinet 11 times, averaging 8,6 months between reshuffles.[10]

This was probably to be expected, in part because Zuma assumed the presidency with little to offer in terms of policy or new ideas, except a burning desire to oust Mbeki and protect himself from prosecution for corruption. The result is a regularly changing (and large and expensive) Cabinet that pays lip service to the vision of the National Development Plan, numerous policy contradictions (look no further than policy on visas, management of state-owned enterprises, industry, energy, communications, land reform, etc.), and a government that is constantly having to defend the office of the president from one ethical and moral lapse after the other.[11] Zuma's ambitions changed when he met the Guptas.

The Gupta brothers first came to public attention in July 2010 when it was reported that they had hijacked Zuma's state visit to India, acting as gatekeepers for access to the president. (It would later appear that Essop Pahad, brother of Aziz Pahad and close confidant to Thabo Mbeki, had played an important role in helping the Guptas establish their first major venture in South Africa, Sahara Computers, for which he was rewarded by being made a director of the company.[12])

Duduzane Zuma, the president's son, and Khulubuse Zuma, his nephew, appear to have served as the link between the Guptas and their father. Duduzane was made a director of Sahara six months after Jacob Zuma became president of the ANC. In addition, he was also made a director of Shiva Uranium and Oakbay Investments, eventually resigning from the latter because of political pressure.[13] Khulubuse became a director of 11 companies owned by the Guptas.

By April 2013, the Guptas' influence was such that they were able to arrange for a passenger jet to land at Waterkloof Air Force Base, a national key point, carrying guests from India to attend the wedding of Vega Gupta, the niece of the Gupta brothers, at Sun City.[14] This deceit was facilitated by many, including the Indian High Commissioner in South Africa, who abused diplomatic channels by using Zuma's name, and presenting the visit as official.[15]

The family had relocated to South Africa from India in 1993, apparently with quite limited means but, by late 2016, Atul Gupta was listed as the seventh richest person in South Africa, with a net worth estimated at R10,7 billion. That organisations such as the ANC Umkhonto we Sizwe Military Veterans Association and the ANC Youth League emerged as defenders of the Guptas is no surprise. The Association was provided with R250 million in shares by the family, who also supported Youth League president Collen Maine to purchase an upmarket home in Woodhill, Pretoria.[16]

The Guptas launched a daily newspaper, *The New Age*, and in 2013 a news channel, ANN7, would follow – but this only after the brothers had tried to take control of the state broadcasting corporation, the SABC. Today ANN7 and *The New Age* are mouthpieces for the Zuma faction within the ANC, and are heavily subsidised by taxpayers through government advertising and breakfast meetings with senior ANC politicians.[17]

Then came Nenegate in December 2015, when Zuma fired Minister of Finance Nhlanhla Nene and replaced him with an ANC backbencher, David van Rooyen. This caused such a public outcry, and wreaked such havoc on the stock exchange, that Zuma was forced within days to replace Van Rooyen with Gordhan. It soon came to light that the Guptas had even tried to influence Cabinet appointments by, among others, offering then Deputy Finance Minister Mcebisi Jonas the position of Minister of Finance shortly before Nene was removed.

In response to these and other revelations, the ANC National Executive Committee (NEC) mandated Secretary-General Gwede Mantashe to investigate the allegations of state capture, but supporters of the president strong-armed the NEC into shutting the limp investigation down. To compound Mantashe's complicity, it also emerged that three of the country's top intelligence officials had met with him in mid-2016 to remind him of a 2010 report submitted to the Inspector General of Intelligence that detailed how the Guptas influenced the appointment of ministers and the awarding of government tenders – an investigation that eventually cost them their jobs.[18]

Ever since, South Africans have rightly been asking, who is really benefiting from key economic decisions, such as the procurement of aircraft, defence relations with India, companies through which the payment of social grants is channelled, and the provision of coal to Eskom and uranium for the proposed nuclear build?[19] Many of the answers to these questions were to be found in the report of outgoing Public Protector Madonsela, *State of Capture*, which called for a judicial commission of inquiry into the matter. The problem is that only the president can mandate such an inquiry. Inevitably, Zuma's legal team have challenged the report, and the matter is due to be heard in October 2017.

Many of the associated deals and tenders were done in the name of radical economic transformation, which in effect comes down to allocating state contracts to a coterie of well-connected businesspeople (including, of course, the Gupta family), all somehow aligned with the president's family and faction in the party.

In his 2015 organisational report, Mantashe said that ANC branches had become polluted by factional politics and that the party was at risk of being sold to the highest bidder. In a June 2016 report, the party lamented the extent to which

> the political life of the organisation revolves around permanent internal strife and factional battles for power [and] contestation for power and state resources, rather than differences on how to implement the policies of the movement ... These circumstances have produced a new type of ANC leader and member who sees ill-discipline, divisions, factionalism and infighting as normal practices and necessary forms of political survival.[20]

Speaking after an NEC meeting, which considered a motion for Zuma to step down in November 2016, Mantashe admitted that relations within the party were poisoned. A call for party unity was therefore prominent in the January 2017 annual statement of the ANC.[21]

Today, the party faces serious challenges to its unity. Divisive tendencies, gatekeeping and manipulation of internal processes, exist at all levels of the ANC and its associated leagues, and within the Tripartite Alliance. Government is preoccupied with infighting and does not pay sufficient attention to citizens' needs. But, in the words of well-known ANC analyst Susan Booysen, 'despite the strong disappointment with the government and its leaders, South Africans retain their faith in the democratic system and do not transfer their discontent to the ... ANC'.[22]

Still, all of these issues sap energy from a party that finds itself continually embroiled in a public, private and legal rearguard action to clean up after the president. Despite the millions of rands of taxpayers' money spent on the president's lawyers, corruption charges continue to hang over Zuma like the sword of Damocles. 'JZ is no longer Number One – he is the number one problem,' said former ANC supporter and now head of the Save South Africa campaign, Sipho Pityana, days ahead of the 2017 state of the nation address.

For the ANC to go into the 2019 elections with Zuma at the helm would therefore be disastrous. While ANC members will choose a new president at the party's national conference in December 2017, Zuma could technically stay on as president of the country until 2019. However, the longer he remains in power, the better the chances of other parties, such as the DA and EFF, faring well in the polls. This outcome is analysed in the scenarios later in the book.

But the transition from Zuma to a new political regime will not be without its challenges. South Africa has a long history of turbulent and disruptive leadership transitions. Except for the Mandela–Mbeki handover, each change of leader has set the country on a particular trajectory and has had long-term implications.

Looking ahead, the events and decisions leading to the choice of a successor to the current president of the ANC in December will determine the country's stability and growth prospects, as they will define the policy orientation and the coherence of the governing party.

How long will Zuma survive?

In its findings in March 2016 on the use of public money for upgrades at Nkandla, the private homestead of the president, the Constitutional Court delivered a unanimous judgment that Zuma had failed to 'uphold, defend and respect' the Constitution.[23] Schedule 2 of the Constitution binds the president to 'obey, observe, uphold and maintain the Constitution and all other law of the Republic'. Section 83 provides that 'the President . . . must uphold, defend and respect the Constitution as the supreme law of the Republic'.

Other than voluntarily stepping down, the president of the Republic of South Africa can be removed by a two-thirds vote in the National Assembly on the grounds of 'a) [a] serious violation of the Constitution or the law; b) serious misconduct; or c) [the] inability to perform the functions of office'.[24]

During the subsequent vote on impeachment in Parliament that was brought by the DA, the party discipline of the ANC in the National Assembly saved the president from what would have been a removal from office under normal circumstances, given the breach of his constitutional obligation.

The farce repeated itself in November 2016 following the publication of the Public Protector's *State of Capture*, which implicated Zuma in a litany of questionable dealings, abuses of power and ethical trans-gressions of the office of the president. The report finds, among other things, that Zuma has used his official position to 'extend preferential treatment to Gupta-linked businesses in the form of state contracts, business financing and trading licences'. It lists numerous breaches in the Executive Members' Code of Ethics, the Public Finance Management Act, the Prevention and Combating of Corrupt Activities Act and the Income Tax Act.

In a strongly worded opinion editorial published in the *Daily Maverick*, EFF leader Julius Malema laid down the political argument behind his call for Zuma to step down, which he based on the *State of Capture* report and the subsequent efforts to subvert its findings:[25]

Our Constitution has only two qualifications that any adult citizen must have in order to be president. It does not ask them to have a matric certificate or a PhD, it only asks them to be faithful to the Republic and obey the Constitution.

Jacob Zuma has violated the Constitution, in that he allowed a crime of corruption to take place in his home, in his name, for his benefit and did nothing, even when he was told [this in reference to the Nkandla saga]. Most importantly, as the Constitutional Court judgment states, his failure manifests from the substantial disregard for the remedial action taken against him by the Public Protector in terms of her constitutional powers.

The second respect in which he failed relates to his shared section 181(3) obligations. He was duty-bound to, but did not, assist and protect the public protector so as to ensure her independence, impartiality, dignity and effectiveness by complying with her remedial action. Such a person has disqualified himself to occupy the office of the president, even if voted by any majority, no matter how big or powerful that majority may be.

However powerful Malema's political argument may be, it does not pass constitutional muster. Only a majority of members of the National Assembly can remove the president by passing a vote of no confidence in him. The ultimate remedy lies either with the ANC or with the electorate, who may decide to punish the ruling party for their willingness to suffer Zuma's leadership.

In November 2016, a group of 101 ANC veterans added their voice to the general clamour for Zuma to step down. Once again, party discipline kept the detractors at bay and the subsequent motion of no-confidence in the president was defeated by 214 votes to 126, with one abstention. The NEC also met a few days later to discuss an ANC motion for Zuma to step down. The motion was tabled by the tourism minister, Derek Hanekom (subsequently fired on 30 March 2017), and, according to news reports, supported by the health minister, Aaron Motsoaledi, the Minister of Public Works, Thembelani Nxesi, and the ANC chief whip in Parliament, Jackson Mthembu. (It was later revealed that Zuma had, as part of his defence and in an effort to rally the troops, bizarrely told the meeting that foreign enemies had made three attempts to poison him.[26] This was apparently in addition to the almost successful attempt on his life by one of his wives, Nompumelelo Ntuli-Zuma, in 2014.)

The motion was also defeated and the subsequent focus was on re-establishing unity within an organisation that was feeling considerable pain. During the subsequent press conference, Mantashe set out the road map to the ANC's national conference in December 2017. As a sop to the veterans, the national policy conference in June 2017 was extended to allow for two days of self-reflection on the status of the ANC.

As these events were unfolding, Zuma was also having to protect himself from attacks on other fronts. With only four days left of the 2016 parliamentary session before the recess, Zuma referred the Financial Intelligence Centre Act (FICA) Amendment Bill back to Parliament, ostensibly on the basis that its provision for searches without a warrant (clause 32 of the bill) was unconstitutional, despite assurances from the Banking Association of South Africa and others to the contrary. The referral came just before a court deadline for the president to decide on the Bill, which had been awaiting his signature since May 2016.

South Africa became a member of the intergovernmental Financial Action Task Force (FATF) in 2003:[27] 'The objectives of the FATF are to set standards and promote effective implementation of legal, regulatory and operational measures for combating money laundering, terrorist financing and other related threats to the integrity of the international financial system ...'[28] To this end, the Task Force had developed a set of recommendations that are recognised as the international standard for combating money laundering, and for countering the financing of terrorism and the proliferation of weapons of mass destruction.

Following an evaluation in 2009, the FATF requested South Africa to remedy a number of deficiencies in existing legislation. This led to the FICA Amendment Bill, which Zuma appeared so reluctant to sign. Once enacted, the new law will oblige financial institutions to monitor the activities of politically exposed, prominent or influential people and their families and close associates, earning it the nickname of the 'Gupta clause'.

If proof of this concern was required, it appeared in October 2016, when Pravin Gordhan filed papers at the High Court in Pretoria that contained details of R6,8 billion of 'suspicious transactions' by the Gupta-owned companies. The data was obtained from the Financial Intelligence Centre and his papers were filed in response to efforts by the Gupta brothers to compel Gordhan to intervene in a dispute that had seen South Africa's largest banks all terminate their banking relationships with the Guptas and their companies.[29]

Following further amendments to clause 32, relating to the issue of warrantless searches, the Bill was again passed by the National Assembly and sent to Zuma in April 2017. The extent to which patronage had become the norm in certain circles was evident from the extraordinary submission by a director of the Progressive Professionals Forum and former Cabinet spokesman Mzwanele Manyi, who described the Bill as an attempt to bankrupt the ruling ANC before the next national elections in 2019. 'We are going to have a situation where everyone is tainted by this … We are also going to be embarrassed because of this, this is a dangerous piece of legislation,' said Manyi.[30] What Manyi is effectively saying is that the ANC is funded through means that would be considered to fall within the scope of money laundering, as defined by the FATF.

The FATF subsequently gave South Africa an extension to June 2017 to pass the amendment and to comply with its recommendations. If South Africa did not pass the Bill, it could be declared delinquent by the task force, creating difficulties for the country's banks in their relationship with foreign banks. Examples of the potential impact of non-compliance are the possible inability to invest money offshore, to pay for imported goods or to transfer funds to families staying overseas if international companies refuse to accept a money transfer from South African banks.[31]

After a dinner with big business, during which the implications of non-compliance were made clear to him, Zuma signed the Bill into law on 28 April 2017.[32] He had been cornered by an application from a civil-society advocacy group, the Council for the Advancement of the South African Constitution, who gave Zuma until 5 May to sign the Bill, failing which they threatened to take the matter to the Constitutional Court.

Late on 30 March 2017, Gordhan and his deputy, Mcebisi Jonas, were fired and replaced by former Minister of Home Affairs Malusi Gigaba and Sfiso Buthelezi, respectively. Although Zuma was dissuaded from installing his preferred candidate, disgraced former Eskom CEO Brian Molefe,[33] the SACP nevertheless noted that Gigaba was selected 'solely to do the Gupta family's bidding at the Treasury'.[34]

The Public Finance Management Act and the regulations that accompany it require the signature of the finance minister on a broad range of transactions. Gordhan had used that power to ensure that due process was followed in key decisions but, with his new appointment, Zuma had now unblocked resistance to key deals and processes.

A national howl of protest followed these events. Three of the top six members of the NEC, Deputy President Cyril Ramaphosa, Gwede Mantashe, and Treasurer General Zweli Mkhize, came out publicly to criticise the decision, but after an extended ANC National Working Committee meeting on 4 April (which included provincial chairpersons and secretaries, most of whom supported Zuma), the three accepted that they had made a 'mistake' in going public, although they did not back down on the lack of consultation on the reshuffle.

During the meeting, Zuma apologised for the way in which he had dealt with the reshuffle, but insisted that he was within his constitutional right to do so. Zuma had reminded members that he had, in November the previous year, indicated his desire to fire Gordhan, since their personal relationship had broken down.[35] The ANC now pulled out all stops to avoid further embarrassment to the president – even going as far as to withdraw a letter from its own integrity commission that had asked for Zuma to resign – but pressure mounted.[36]

In the wake of the removal of Gordhan and his deputy from the

Cabinet, the DA scheduled yet another vote of no-confidence, which was delayed after the United Democratic Movement and others approached the Constitutional Court for a ruling to allow a secret ballot. In its application to act as an *amicus curiae*, the ISS argued that the prevailing levels of intimidation prevented ANC Members of Parliament from exercising their constitutional mandate in Parliament. The court application and no-confidence debate followed some of the largest public displays of disaffection with Zuma yet seen, with marches in Pretoria, Johannesburg, Cape Town, Durban and elsewhere. Since the SACP was now also calling for Zuma to step down, much hope was pinned on the 50 or so SACP Members of Parliament, who were also members of the ANC, that they would vote with the opposition. In the meantime the NEC held yet another meeting at the end of May 2017, during which the opposing factions now came out in open battle. Still, Zuma survived.

With the economic writing now clearly on the wall, business had also found its voice. Full-page adverts expressed industry's disappointment with the March 2017 Cabinet reshuffle. In a strongly worded statement, Business Leadership South Africa, which represents most of the listed companies on the Johannesburg Stock Exchange, said that the youth-employment initiative, a joint project between business to create a million internships and a R1,5 billion fund for investment into small and medium-sized enterprises, was 'in danger of being undone by a simple act of a sitting president'.[37]

Neither business nor organised labour participated in the trip that Gigaba undertook to meet with investors and ratings agencies in the US in April in an effort to stall a downgrade by a third ratings agency. The CEO Initiative, which collectively represents companies worth more than R500 billion, and was set up to work with Gordhan to prevent the downgrade, refused to meet with Gigaba ahead of his trip to Washington.[38]

Such is the state of the ANC under Zuma.

Despite the efforts by many in the Tripartite Alliance to bring the voting process for a new ANC leader forward or get Zuma to step down, the defining moment will occur during the party's December 2017 national conference. The national elective conference meets at least once every five years to elect the 86-member NEC, including the 'top six': the president, deputy president, national chairperson, secretary-general, deputy secretary-general and treasurer-general.[39]

Although not stated in the ANC's constitution, there is general agreement that the ANC president should serve no more than two terms of office.[40] Mbeki's efforts to seek a third term as leader of the ANC was an important factor in the support that Zuma was able to muster against his predecessor – hence it would be difficult for Zuma to attempt the same.

Speaking during a radio interview in January 2017, Zuma said, in any case, he would not accept nomination for a third term. By his own admission, it would also be difficult for him to remain as South Africa's president beyond December 2017, when a new leader of the ANC has been elected, with the two existing in parallel, because, as Zuma said, 'if that's the case you are creating two centres of power that could in a sense compete'.[41]

Still, legally, Zuma may stay on as president of the country until the next general elections in 2019.

The South African Constitution states that the president of the country may serve a maximum of two terms, but 'when a person is elected to fill a vacancy in the office of the President, the period between that election and the next election of a President is not regarded as a term'.

The South African president is elected by majority vote in the National Assembly. That election can occur at any point when there is a vacancy and is therefore not bound by the schedule of national elections, which occur every five years. Since the ANC has more than 50 per cent of the 400 seats in Parliament, it determines who is president of the country.

This book went to print shortly before the June 2017 policy conference of the ANC, but I think it very unlikely that the ANC will convene a national conference to elect a new leader of the party before the scheduled date in December 2017. However, once a new president of the ANC has been elected I think it is unlikely that Zuma will survive for very long as president of South Africa. It is most likely that he will step down in December 2017 or be recalled in 2018.

It is possible that the ANC will lose its majority at some point in the future. But even if the ANC's support were to drop below 50 per cent around the time of the next elections, the next president of the ANC is still likely to become the president of South Africa, as it is unlikely that opposition parties will be able to form a governing coalition.

The Traditionalists and the Reformers

I have adopted the terms 'Traditionalists' and 'Reformers' as shorthand for the two dominant and competing ideological strands within the ANC. Although these labels oversimplify the complex machinations in the ANC's big tent, they serve as useful broad definitions when discussing the manifold divisions and factions in the party at national, provincial and local level.

These two groups have been involved in an increasingly public battle for control of key institutions, such as the Treasury and SARS, and state-owned companies, as well as for control over the levers of power when it comes to senior government appointments and tender processes. That battle was essentially won by the Traditionalists when Gigaba was appointed as finance minister, providing that faction with direct access to the public purse. But this is more than a struggle for power – it is also about contending visions of South Africa's future pathway.

The larger Traditionalist faction is broadly rural, black nationalist, socially conservative, largely loyal to Zuma and dominated by Zulus. This group shows a strong commitment to a centralised state and redistributive policies. Many in this group are uncomfortable with the liberal-democratic orientation of the Reformist camp and the focus on individual rights reflected in the South African Constitution.

They instinctively orientate themselves around a collectivist ideology and black-nationalist policies – and even a degree of populism, although not to the extent espoused by Malema and the EFF. The Traditionalist grouping would like to install a suitable successor to Zuma at the December 2017 national conference, who would probably take over in the following year.

The Traditionalists are keen to perpetuate the policies and practices that have benefited a large circle of family, friends and business associates around the president through state procurement and government appointments to senior positions.

Among the Traditionalists is a coterie of loyalists within the security cluster, many of whom have benefited from Zuma's policies, who seek to protect him from criminal prosecution, including the signs of the establishment of parallel security structures that intimidate others within the ANC, propagate alternative storylines and generally fight Zuma's corner.

These developments have seen large numbers of ANC supporters abstain from voting for the ANC – both unwilling to continue voting for the ANC under Zuma, and unwilling to vote for another party. This phenomenon I call the 'shift vote'.

The damage experienced by the party during the 2016 local government elections and the litany of embarrassments associated with him make it unlikely that Zuma would lead the ANC into the 2019 national elections, resulting in a concerted campaign around a Traditionalist successor.

Key among the Traditionalist group, as well as the president himself, are the leaders of the Free State, Mpumalanga and North West provinces – referred to as the Premier League – as well as a large faction from KwaZulu-Natal (the province where the Traditionalists gained ascendency in 2016 with the removal of Senzo Mchunu and his replacement by Willies Mchunu as premier), including Zuma loyalist Sihle Zikalala, the ANC chairperson, and the chairperson of the ANC Women's League, Bathabile Dlamini, the Minister of Social Development, and the Youth League.

The group also includes a number of potential presidential aspirants, such as the Speaker of the National Assembly, Baleka Mbete. But its most prominent presidential hopeful is the former chairperson of the African Union (AU) Commission and ex-wife of Zuma, Nkosazana Dlamini-Zuma. She had begun positioning herself for a shot at the presidency while still serving at the AU, a position she left in March 2017. In preparation, she started to spend more time in South Africa, campaigning particularly hard in her home province of KwaZulu-Natal.

Dlamini-Zuma is, however, an uncomfortable Traditionalist front-runner, and her campaign is sullied by her association with the likes of Bathabile Dlamini and the Premier League and, of course, her ex-husband. These associations link her with an element in the party who are directly associated with patronage and corruption – and who are insisting on key positions in exchange for their support.[42] In her election campaign her rhetoric has steadily became more populist and radical as she has positioned herself as successor to her former husband.

She also faces an uphill battle in an ANC that has yet to elect a woman even to the position of provincial leader, in addition to hailing from a region that is perhaps more stoutly patriarchal than any other.[43]

Nevertheless, she has considerable Cabinet experience and her previous tenures as Minister of Health, Foreign Affairs and Home Affairs were solid performances in which she proficiently executed her mandate. In the public mind, she perhaps also benefits from the fact that she has less public association with the Guptas, (other than uncomfortably accepting a R250 000 cheque from Atul Gupta when she 'won' the ANN7 2015 South African of the Year Award).[44] Her main drawbacks as president would be the fact that she has no private-sector experience and her lack of public charisma. But, under her, the ANC is likely to be able to cohere and pull in the same direction.

Given the near-certainty that Jacob Zuma will face criminal charges at some point in the future, he has a clear personal interest in securing a suitable successor. In terms of Article 84(2)(j) of the Constitution, the president of South Africa has the right to pardon or reprieve offenders, but a presidential pardon does not give one the chance to avoid criminal prosecution. No president can offer anyone impunity from the law. A future president could therefore only pardon Zuma after he has gone through a due legal process and has been found guilty.

So Zuma faces the real threat of several months of court hearings and a sentence before his chosen successor can even decide whether to pardon him or not. At first glance, the only way out of this mess is to ensure that the legal process itself is tainted or collapses. While he is in power, Zuma has considerable potential to influence events by, for example, appointing a suitably pliant head of the NPA, most recently Abrahams. Perhaps more likely is some type of legal finesse in which the former president pleads guilty to some of the minor charges and apologises for any misunderstandings, cites work pressure, and matters splutter to an undignified conclusion that keeps Zuma out of jail.

Either way, it is quite likely that a successor would need to make an upfront commitment to a subsequent pardon if Zuma is to agree to step down before his term as president ends in 2019.

The 'Reformers' is the term I use to describe the minority social-democratic-aligned faction within the ANC. This group, often better educated than the Traditionalists, and largely urban, younger and multi-ethnic, is increasingly dissatisfied with the current political and economic trajectory. The Reformers are concerned about their future in a party that is steadily declining. Some find themselves outside the current patronage circle and are motivated by the desire to shift the allocation of state resources closer to home, but, in general, this is a faction appalled by the extent of corruption and patronage under Zuma.

The Reformers generally believe in a mixed economy and the importance of inclusive economic growth. They are largely committed to a more enterprise-driven or opportunity-based economic model as the driver of future empowerment.

Key among the Reformers are the majority of the ANC politicians in Gauteng (who face the threat of losing their majority, positions and influence to the opposition in 2019), in the Eastern Cape (who lost out when the previous Xhosa power group in the ANC was replaced by a Zulu grouping) and minorities in a number of other provinces.

The Reformers are generally associated with Gordhan, and the current deputy president, Ramaphosa, still the most likely successor to Zuma. The group also includes many stalwarts of the party and those who left with Mbeki, including the group of veterans who, in November 2016 and in April 2017, came out publicly in support of a re-evaluation of Zuma's leadership, and some senior commanders and commissars of the former military wing of the ANC, who sent a memorandum to Mantashe in March 2017 demanding a special national conference of the ANC (to get rid of Zuma).

Besides his role during the negotiations from 1990 to 1994, and as Mandela's preferred protégé, Ramaphosa had a career as general secretary of the National Union of Mineworkers, served as secretary-general of the ANC, and is a successful businessman who has been able to build a large empire on the back of black economic empowerment deals and has served as deputy chair of the National Planning Commission (which drew up the National Development Plan). His career in labour, business and government would therefore indicate a comprehensive understanding of South Africa's challenges and opportunities.

However, Ramaphosa's public image has been sullied by revelations of an email that he sent to Lonmin's chief commercial officer, Albert Jamieson, shortly before the Marikana massacre in 2012, in which he wrote: 'The terrible events that have unfolded cannot be described as a labour dispute. They are plainly dastardly criminal and must be characterised as such. There needs to be concomitant action to address this situation.' During the subsequent violence just 24 hours later, the police used live ammunition, killing 34 mineworkers and injuring 78 others.[45] At the time, Ramaphosa was a board member of Lonmin.

Ramaphosa has also had to apologise for taking part in an auction in which he bid for a buffalo cow and calf worth around R18 million, earning him the nickname of 'Buffalo'.

He does not have an ANC exile pedigree, which has previously been a requirement for the top job, and there are concerns about his power base within the movement. As a result, he has had to sit by and be associated with one Zuma failure after the other – a passive spectator to corruption and looting on a grand scale – rather than challenge the president. That stance changed, however, in April 2017 as Ramaphosa began to speak out more forcefully, calling, among other things, for a judicial commission of inquiry into state capture, as reflected in Madonsela's report on state capture.

In terms of their ideology, the Reformers are closer to the thinking within the DA under the helm of Mmusi Maimane, if perhaps not sympathetic to it. The Reformers are concerned about the damage that Zuma is inflicting on the country and the party and they are intent on replacing Zuma as early as possible with their preferred candidate to lead a reinvigorated ANC into the 2019 elections.

In the intensifying political competition for the leadership of the ANC, alliances and support networks are constantly evolving, as are the political concepts used to describe them. For example, the SACP and COSATU, which were both actively in favour of ousting Mbeki and ushering in Zuma, now support Ramaphosa despite efforts to paint him as being in support of a neoliberal, pro-market agenda. This stance is seen as contrary to efforts towards the so-called national democratic revolution used by various factions within the ANC, which convey an intent to undertake 'radical economic transformation' – a fluid concept that conveys support for Zuma rather than any definable policy content. (Interestingly, the same phrase has also been used to refer to the implementation of the purportedly market-friendly National Development Plan).

The challenge of how to improve the livelihoods of the majority of black South Africans who make up the lower and unskilled classes remains an important focus of both groupings, although they differ starkly in their views on how to achieve this and who should benefit in the process. It is essentially a choice that can be captured in the phrases 'redistribution through growth' and 'growth through redistribution', the former associated with the Reformers and the latter with the Traditionalists. Few terms have evoked as much hot air as these two sides of the same coin.

The balance of forces between the Reformers and the Traditionalists will be influenced by the swing voters, a successively larger group of voters who stay away from the polls either because they are disillusioned with the ANC and politics in general or with Zuma. The swing voters will have a significant influence on future results should they decide to cast their votes for the ANC, the EFF, the DA – or a new party that could emerge if there is another split in the ANC.

Two other considerations are important. The first is developments within COSATU, which is steadily losing coherence and influence. In April 2017, disaffected COSATU unions and others launched the South African Federation of Trade Unions, the country's second-largest labour federation. COSATU's loss of power – it was originally the largest organised member of the Tripartite Alliance – provides a future ANC leadership with significant policy space that Mandela, Mbeki and Zuma did not have.

In line with a global trend, the labour movement in South Africa is fracturing. It is no longer coherent or united, but COSATU has cleverly hedged its bets by coming out in support of Ramaphosa, who, in theory, is the only presidential candidate who could be in favour of greater labour-market flexibility and therefore might well clip the wings of organised labour. As president, Ramaphosa would therefore be in debt to labour and his ability to move ahead with labour market flexibility may already have been neutralised.

The second consideration is the extent to which – and the manner in which – young voters (the so-called born-frees) will participate in the next elections. Based on recent trends and on this segment's current disaffection with the ANC leadership, the likelihood is a further decline in voter turnout. At the same time, however, none of the main opposition parties have yet been able to fully capitalise on this disgruntlement, and none are able to galvanise South Africans into voting for them in sufficiently large numbers – although things could well change, as we will explore.

CHAPTER 2

The Republic of No Consequences

... the ANC had made a disastrous choice in 2007 and ended up with a man who is not only unfit to head a modern government, because he cannot be bothered to read the bare minimum of documents needed to lead and chair a cabinet properly, but is also deviously corrupt.

– Richard Calland[1]

When the ANC came to power in 1994, it inherited a country in a deeply troubled situation. There were high expectations that radical change in the character of South Africa's politics would unlock a better life for all.

The first democratic election set in motion a comprehensive process of social, economic and political re-engineering. What had been a centralised, racially determined state with a franchise limited to whites adopted a universal franchise and a semi-federal model, and extended political, economic and social rights to all citizens through a progressive Bill of Rights.

Concerted efforts were made to alleviate extreme poverty and advance the interests of the majority black population, but these progressive objectives had to be balanced in ways that would retain investor confidence and economic stability. The ANC therefore introduced successive policy initiatives, such as the 1994 RDP, the 1996 GEAR plan, the 2005 Accelerated and Shared Growth Initiative for South Africa and, most recently, the 2012 National Development Plan.

Despite these initiatives, the extent of destitution, hunger and suffering that apartheid left in its wake is a legacy that will remain with the country for generations to come, and that will require ongoing efforts by successive future governments, irrespective of their political composition.

There are many publications on the successes and failures of states all over the world, but perhaps the most useful for the purposes of this discussion is the expansive study *Why Nations Fail*.[2] This account shows how states that manage to advance political inclusiveness do significantly better in economic and developmental terms over the long term than do states with exclusive systems.

Despite brief periods of rapid economic growth after World War II and shortly after becoming a republic outside the Commonwealth in 1961, apartheid South Africa epitomised extractive politics and economics. In other words, driven by a policy of extracting maximum benefit for the white minority population, education, healthcare and infrastructure development occurred to the detriment of the majority, who were systematically excluded from influence, land and commerce.

Extractive systems, like South Africa pre-1994, can be replaced by inclusive ones. But the process is neither automatic nor easy. And it takes time – lots of it. A confluence of factors, in particular a critical juncture coupled with a broad coalition of those pushing for reform or other propitious existing institutions, are often necessary for a nation to make strides towards more inclusive socio-economic systems. Also, some luck is key because history generally unfolds in a contingent way.[3]

South Africa has indeed been very lucky. The crisis that engulfed the apartheid extractive system during the 1980s coincided with the collapse of the Berlin Wall and the domestic leadership change from PW Botha to FW de Klerk. These events made the unthinkable possible.

The miracle birth of the Rainbow Nation changed the course of a country headed for civil war. After the political miracle, though, comes the hard work of running a sophisticated and diverse country, and trans- forming the economy. Many see the transition to democracy as a triumph of good over evil and believe in the inevitability of continued progress. But South Africa's dismal past and escape from disaster do not them- selves guarantee a bright future. 'Hyperbole and moral repugnance aside,' write Heribert Adam, Frederik van Zyl Slabbert and Kogila Moodley, 'it is not difficult to end up in a position of sanctimonious paralysis, of be- lieving that the future guarantees one a good deal because the past has given a bad one and to approach the complex problems of transition with an attitude of moral entitlement.'[4]

Creating an inclusive economic and political system is now indeed proving to be a hard task for a relatively small liberation party that was unbanned in 1990, assumed power in 1994, and now suffers from debilitating internal conflict, lack of capacity, poor leadership and factionalism.

In addition, it is important to remember that the outgoing National Party also made life as difficult as possible for the incoming adminis- tration, doing everything possible to make the ANC fail. There was no political handover. It is also no surprise that the ANC came into gov- ernment with a strong belief (not without justification) that everything associated with the previous administration had to be reconfigured. And, of course, no one was prepared to brief them or explain why things were done in a particular manner, for fear of being labelled as somehow in defence of apartheid.

New systems and new ways of doing things were required for everything, from how to provide education to the structure of the military. The new governing party was caught between a rock and a hard place. It needed to break the institutional hold of the previous bureaucracy over content and policy processes yet retain key skills while transitioning to a system that now served all South Africans. The result was eventually a wholesale restructuring of previous systems and processes during which much progress was made in modernising governance while much damage was done in reinventing things.

By 2017 it is evident that, as much as the country has made progress in several spheres, South Africa has made an incomplete transition to inclusive politics and inclusive economics. The challenge of moving towards a high-income economy (South Africa is currently classified as an upper-middle-income economy, with income levels about half those of high-income nations) and a knowledge society (the key to growth in the modern world) – while simultaneously making up for the apartheid legacy – constrains South Africa's growth prospects.

A cacophony of contradictory and confusing government policies has intensified these constraints. As academic and writer Adam Habib points out, 'the ANC is a divided party apparently seeking its collective economic *raison d'être*.'[5] In this respect, South Africa has largely only itself to blame for growing at a level that is below its potential and for the likelihood that it will, unfortunately, continue to grow more slowly than other upper-middle-income countries for several more years.

It is worth taking a look at why this policy paralysis has come about, and in particular how the ANC's various policy approaches over the years since the transition have been shaped by the party's requirements at certain key moments in its history.

The RDP and GEAR

The economic policy framework of the ANC at the time of the 1994 elections was the RDP. This started out as a five-page document developed by the National Union of Metalworkers of South Africa as· an electoral pact in return for which the organised-labour federation, COSATU, would support the ANC during elections.

The RDP went through an intensive consultation process until the alliance partners signed off on an expanded version well ahead of the 1994 election campaign.[6] The most important feature of the RDP was not its somewhat idealised content; it was the fact that the programme was the result of a concerted and deliberate consultation process among the Tripartite Alliance partners.

As mentioned, COSATU was the most powerful partner in the Tripartite Alliance and a very different organisation from what it is today. The ANC under Mandela and Mbeki was effectively beholden to COSATU because it had a national structure, a disciplined set of cadres and a number of key intellectuals within its fold. By contrast, despite its massive popular appeal, the core ANC of pre-1994 was not a big organisation, and many of its members had not set foot in South Africa for a very long time.

Consequently, the ANC was largely dependent upon COSATU for its ability to mobilise black voters when elections loomed in 1994. The ANC's reliance on organised labour entrenched the perspective of COSATU and placed the rights of workers at the core of economic policy, effectively framing the growth and development choices available to the ANC for successive decades. COSATU's policies on labour and the economy largely determined ANC, and therefore government, policy.

That lengthy consultative process provided the RDP with a legitimacy and buy-in that have not been equalled since – and as a result the programme was later mythologised, gaining near cult-like status among many. It is for this reason that Mbeki's decision to move on from the RDP created a political furore. COSATU felt deeply betrayed by him.

According to Jeremy Cronin, deputy general secretary of the SACP, the RDP sought to integrate 'growth, development, reconstruction and redistribution into a single programme'.[7] But, not surprisingly, the challenge proved too much for a new administration distrustful of its largely white bureaucracy and with no previous experience in government.

Instead of mainstreaming the RDP into government departments, the ANC established a separate RDP ministry without portfolio headed by Jay Naidoo, a former head of COSATU. But the efforts by the ANC to work around government departments that were often still staffed by white technocrats who had served the apartheid government soon came to naught. Policy failure was followed by implementation failure.

Apartheid had also left South Africa broke. In 1994, 25 per cent of government revenue was consumed by interest payments on debt. By way of comparison, by 2008 that ratio had fallen to 6 per cent. At the time of the April 2017 credit downgrade, to which we will return later, the figure had moderately deteriorated to 10 per cent. But even with one in every ten rands servicing interest payments, that figure is still significantly better than the miserable situation that FW de Klerk had bequeathed to Mandela.

The Mandela government soon faced the real prospect of having to enter into discussions for a rescue package from the IMF and the World Bank. The crux of the matter was that the ANC would not be able to redistribute enough wealth to satisfy its major constituencies without killing off private-sector confidence, investment and growth. It had to grow the economy. Enter the 1996 GEAR programme, which broke with the RDP by placing economic growth ahead of other considerations. Under the guidance of Trevor Manuel, finance minister from 1996, South Africa rapidly adopted positions accommodating the 'unavoidable realities of globalization'. Subsequent bilateral agreements, such as the 1998 free-trade agreement with the European Union, reinforced this approach.[8]

For the first time in decades, the South African economy grew, productivity improved, jobs followed and the country saw steady improvements in many indicators. South Africa has always had an extremely low rate of participation in the workforce, but between 1994 and 2008 employment expanded steadily.

The reason why GEAR worked and the RDP (and, for that matter, the later National Development Plan) did not, was that it had a specific, limited focus. Rather than requiring complex, interdepartmental coordination across numerous government ministries, GEAR focused on a small number of macroeconomic interventions that could be implemented by a small team in the central bank and the Treasury.[9]

The associated political costs of the new policy, however, would become apparent only much later, when GEAR triggered public tensions between the Treasury and other government departments. It would eventually also play an important role in the ousting of Mbeki some years later.

Essentially, GEAR was a macroeconomic stabilisation programme that sought to cut South Africa's alarming deficit in the wake of the sharp depreciation of the rand in early 1996. It was designed to ensure access to capital markets and rein in inflation, but at the cost of delaying public investment. Subsequent analysis would often point to a simultaneous increase in inequality and the effective deindustrialisation of South Africa due to the rapid opening of the economy to international competition, and the withdrawal of state support from agriculture and industry.

But the causality is complicated by the simultaneous failures of the education system, a rapid decline in state efficiency and a lack of microeconomic reform.[10] In the words of Jeremy Seekings and Nicoli Nattrass from the University of Cape Town, who have studied post-apartheid economic policy in considerable depth, 'GEAR seemed to embrace free markets far more than it promised to discipline them ...'[11]

But, most threatening to COSATU was the fact that GEAR sought, unsuccessfully, to introduce greater labour-market flexibility. Since 1994 South Africa has followed an approach that constrains the ability of the economy to create new jobs, as employers are not incentivised to hire more workers. This means that labour costs rise while improvements in productivity may lag behind. We therefore have a labour regime that continues to penalise smaller businesses, a situation that eventually led, among others, to the establishment of labour brokers to circumvent the onerous legislative labour provisions.

Under GEAR, the economy started generating a surplus, but fiscal responsibility had come at some cost, including delays in making up for the backlogs in infrastructure inherited from apartheid. The subsequent programme, the Accelerated and Shared Growth Initiative for South Africa, tried to compensate for the lean GEAR years with a greater focus on capital expenditure – but it was too late for Mbeki. Hostility towards GEAR and Mbeki's denialism on HIV/AIDS played a large role in the events at the December 2007 national conference of the ANC in Polokwane, when Zuma led a successful campaign to depose him. Zuma was able to do this in alliance with COSATU and the SACP, who both railed against the ideological underpinnings of GEAR.

In the latter years of the Mbeki administration and thereafter, a huge effort was made to caricature GEAR as the '1996 class project' – a neoliberal policy that was helping the capitalist system to perpetuate itself. Or, in the words of Cronin, it created 'an investor-friendly climate and macroeconomic conditions [that were] helping the established capitalist system to go back to its old ways – highly concentrated, dependent upon exports, with poor beneficiation, dominated by the mining houses and the big banks to the detriment of the manufacturing sector ...'[12]

Habib has written an entire book that traces all of South Africa's current travails to GEAR, *South Africa's Suspended Revolution: Hopes and Prospects*. There is truth to this critique, particularly in the extent to which the economy became more capital-intensive with a lower ratio of jobs being created for every unit of growth, and in the enthusiastic embracing of globalisation and the associated destruction of local industry.

However, the essential challenge is not that South Africa needs to restructure the economy – on this there is broad agreement – but how it should be achieved and what is realistically possible in the short and medium term.

Growth provides options. Without growth or with slow growth (South Africa's current outlook), the available options are limited and necessarily penalise one sector in favour of another. And rather than the broad-brush approach to restructuring favoured by proponents of the RDP, it is a complex task to manage a structural shift in a relatively sophisticated economy such as that of South Africa. It takes at least a generation to shift fundamentals – not one or two electoral cycles.

Global events, particularly the 2008/09 recession and its aftermath, marked by lacklustre recovery, have dealt progress in South Africa a cruel blow, as have uninspiring domestic leadership and an apparent loss of vision by the ruling party. Although an estimated 1,6 million jobs were created between 2003 and 2007, 800 000 were lost in 2008, when the global financial crisis started to make itself felt in South Africa.[13] In 2010/11 only an estimated 350 000 jobs were created when the economy sluggishly started to recover from the global shocks.[14]

The recession came shortly after a massive crisis in the ANC, when Mbeki relieved Zuma of his duties as deputy president after he was implicated in corruption at the Durban High Court trial of his former financial advisor, Schabir Shaik. This set in motion a train of events that would see Zuma wage a guerrilla-style fight-back campaign and eventually unseat Mbeki as leader of the ANC. Zuma and his 'coalition of the wounded' were not prepared to wait for Mbeki's term as president to conclude. On 20 September 2008, with about nine months left of his second term, Mbeki announced his resignation after being recalled as president of South Africa by the ANC.

His recall followed a conclusion by Judge CR Nicholson that there had been improper interference by the NPA in the prosecution of Zuma for corruption. In January 2009, the Supreme Court of Appeal unanimously overturned Judge Nicholson's judgment, but it was to no effect. Kgalema Motlanthe temporarily served as president, and after the elections in April 2009 Zuma assumed the presidency.

Always the astute observer, academic Richard Calland noted that Mbeki had been hoist by his own petard.[15] Since Mbeki had used the NPA to prosecute his political enemies, it should have come as no surprise that Zuma would do likewise.

Zuma's election as president intensified the polarised political legacy of Mbeki. The Anyone but Mbeki campaign, which ended in his undignified dethroning, was considered as much a victory for COSATU as for the SACP, and appeared to enhance their already considerable leverage in government.

South Africa entered the Zuma presidency effectively with a coalition government consisting of the three alliance partners that had brought Zuma to power – the ANC, COSATU and the SACP, plus others who had assisted Zuma's rise to power, such as the ANC Youth League, then led by Malema, who had famously intoned in June 2008 that 'we are prepared to take up arms and kill for Zuma'. Today it would come as no surprise if Malema shouted, 'We are prepared to kill Zuma', such have relations changed in the intervening years.

To accommodate this large and disparate coalition, Zuma required an exceptionally large Cabinet and a constant process of political bargains and trade-offs that did not always point in the same direction. Zuma's ascent also resulted in an exodus and purge of many of the ANC's intellectual and experienced top brass, whom Mbeki had managed to attract. This had long-term adverse consequences on the public, mining, industrial and information technology sectors, as well as on government and the management of state-owned enterprises.

The battle left deep scars on Africa's oldest liberation party, splitting the ANC in two. It provided fertile ground for the emergence of the division evident today, most prominent in the opposing factions of Reformers and Traditionalists.

Sadly, the breakaway faction forming a new party, led by ANC stalwarts Mosiuoa Lekota, Mbhazima Shilowa and Mluleki George, which eventually decided on the uninspiring name of Congress of the People (COPE), was so engrossed in infighting that it completely lost the plot and imploded. COPE managed to gain some 7,4 per cent support during the 2009 elections (that is more than the 6,4 per cent that the EFF garnered during their first participation in national elections in 2014). However, it was significantly lower than expected, and COPE has been on a downward trajectory ever since.[16]

A new broom ...

In the 2009 elections, with Zuma as president of the ANC, the party won with close to a 66 per cent majority (3 per cent down on 2004). Zuma now had his own mandate, directly from the electorate. Once ensconced

49

in the Union Buildings, he moved rapidly to stamp his authority on the executive. An important first step was to break up Mbeki's advisory unit, the Policy Coordination and Advisory Services (PCAS), which had been led by Joel Netshitenzhe. Under Mbeki the PCAS advised the Presidency on all aspects of policy coordination, implementation and monitoring, and assisted on special cross-cutting projects and programmes. It kept track of policy debates in different departments on issues such as poverty relief, restructuring of state assets and integrated rural development. Its core function was to facilitate an integrated approach to all policy development and implementation.

The PCAS was core to Mbeki's increasingly imperial style of presidency – an approach that many of his critics had come to dislike. Through the PCAS, Mbeki kept a tight central control over the functioning of the state and usurped the role of some ministries. The unit was accused of having effectively centralised state power. Under Mbeki, government policy, however, generally pulled in the same direction and ministers were mostly held to account, although his Cabinet also included a significant amount of dead wood.

Zuma was determined to sweep the Union Buildings clean of everything associated with his predecessor. It was no surprise, then, when he disbanded the PCAS in 2009, replacing it with two new wings that would provide for national planning. One was the National Planning Commission; the other was the Department of Performance, Monitoring and Evaluation (DPME), established to monitor government performance.

But without the leadership and vision to drive and coordinate development, the DPME, which was the larger of the two new entities, proved an uninspiring replacement for the PCAS. The minister in charge of the DPME was the relatively young Collins Chabane, who, together with the director general, Sean Phillips, eventually oversaw a number of DPME outcomes that were supposed to tie government together through a tightly managed system of performance and delivery agreements. The DPME had no authority over other departments, however, and, after the establishment of a separate Economic Development Department (which contested policy issues with the Treasury and the National Planning Commission), governing South Africa moved at the speed of a snail trapped in grease.

In subsequent years, the DPME became adept at measuring what progress South Africa was making over time, rooted in the view that the main challenge facing South Africa is often not policy but implementation and follow-up. Yet it provided no direction to an increasingly rudderless ship.

In theory, that firm hand on the tiller should have been provided by the president and Cabinet by implementing the National Development Plan. But the National Planning Commission was, by design, little more than an advisory body that reported to Cabinet. By shifting Trevor Manuel to the National Planning Commission, Zuma had found an innovative way to get rid of Mbeki's powerful Minister of Finance.

Thus, the National Planning Commission served two purposes: to remove Manuel from his power base and to present a plan to Cabinet that it could adopt, reject or ignore. In addition, the plan, in Zuma's mind, apparently obviated the need for constant decision making and oversight (the role of the former PCAS) by a president who hardly read documents ahead of Cabinet meetings and acted as a convenor rather than as a leader.

All of this politicking was not obvious at the time, however. Zuma appointed 25 part-time commissioners to the National Planning Commission in April 2010 and, at its launch a year later, noted: 'The mandate of the commission is to take a broad, cross-cutting, independent and critical view of South Africa, to help define the South Africa we seek to achieve in 20 years' time and to map out a path to achieve those objectives. The commission is expected to put forward solid research, sound evidence and clear recommendations for government.'[17]

Manuel's commission made the best of the situation by developing a very impressive diagnostic analysis of South Africa, thus setting the scene for the National Development Plan itself. In the optimistic words of Manuel during a media briefing on the implementation of the plan in January 2013, 'the National Development Plan offers a long-term perspective. It defines a desired destination and identifies the role different sectors of society need to play in reaching that goal.'[18]

In brief, the purpose of the National Development Plan was to eliminate poverty and reduce inequality by 2030. The plan notes three first-order priorities and lists them in appropriate sequence:

1 Raise employment through faster economic growth.
2 Improve the quality of education, skill development and innovation.
3 Build the capability of the state to play a developmental, transformative role.

Having found a way to move Manuel sideways, Zuma appointed Pravin Gordhan to take over as Minister of Finance in 2009. Gordhan had no discernible power base within the ANC or the SACP, of which he was a leading member, but had built an impressive track record as head of SARS.

In 2013 the ISS published its first forecast on South Africa, 'Highway or Byway? The National Development Plan 2030', which explored some of the plan's human-development targets. The report found that an economic growth rate of 5,4 per cent was 'very ambitious' and could be achieved only with

> a huge effort, clear leadership and painful adjustments … but it is hardly possible to overestimate the effort that will be required from … South Africa's diverse interest groups and affected communities. Clearly, the current capital-intensive nature of South Africa's

economic growth model will not succeed in delivering sufficient jobs without structural changes to the economy and to current policies.[19]

However, many of the plan's other targets, for example in education and infrastructure, the report found to be achievable, even with lower rates of economic growth.[20]

Perhaps the biggest failure was the failure to implement the National Development Plan, largely because of Zuma's need to include all his disparate alliance partners in government. (And, if the size of the Cabinet is anything to go by, Zuma has created a significant number of new jobs by constantly ushering in more government positions and Cabinet appointments.) At the start of his second term, the Cabinet included 35 ministerial positions. The size of the civil service exploded. For example, instead of simply reducing the obstacles facing small business – as recommended in the National Development Plan – government's response to calls to unshackle the small-business sector was to establish another ministry (led by Lindiwe Zulu) in what was an already bloated Cabinet. The result is significant overlap and intense competition between ministers and their fiefdoms, large expenditure on operating expenses and little output.

Although the Zuma administration reversed Mbeki's disastrous HIV/AIDS policies which, had cost thousands of South African their lives, his bad management and poor decision making have snowballed during his two terms.

Turning to China

Moving into the Union Buildings in the wake of a devastating global recession, Zuma was desperate to find a new source of growth. That was clearly not going to come from the West, where Mbeki had largely placed his trust (or Africa, through the New Partnership for Africa's Development, NEPAD). In Zuma's eyes, only China offered economic growth opportunities for a country that remained a large exporter of commodities and very dependent on global cycles at a time of Western recession.

For Zuma, a pivot to China had the added advantage of charting his own course, one that was different from Mbeki's. Becoming a member of the BRIC grouping of Brazil, Russia, India and China would cement that relationship. Zuma and his advisors eagerly pursued this opportunity.

In August 2010, Zuma undertook his first state visit to China and the two countries announced a comprehensive strategic partnership, signing the Beijing Declaration, which formally elevated bilateral ties from the previous strategic partnership.[21] The declaration underlined the extent to which South Africa and China shared views on international affairs, and committed to strengthening the countries' relations and interaction. Later in 2010 came the establishment of a joint inter-ministerial working group on China–South Africa cooperation, to which Zuma appointed five Cabinet ministers, although this initiative was ratified only in March 2013 when President Xi Jinping visited South Africa.[22]

It is unclear which developments led to the decision by the BRIC group to invite South Africa to attend their third summit meeting, in 2011, but South Africa's admission to the group followed a concerted campaign. China had previously lobbied hard to join the Mbeki-inspired IBSA (India, Brazil, South Africa) grouping, but neither India nor Brazil had been keen on bringing in a permanent member of the UN Security Council – a non-democracy at odds with India on a number of issues – especially at a time when Chinese–Brazilian relations were still limited.

Gaining membership of BRICS, on top of South Africa's existing membership of the Group of Twenty (G20) major economies, is the most important foreign-policy achievement of the Zuma administration. It cemented South Africa's position within the big BRICS league, where the country rubs shoulders with the purported alternative club of global leadership to the G7 developed countries. Under Mbeki, South Africa had often sought to serve as a bridge and facilitator between the developed world and Africa/the Global South. As a member of BRICS, South Africa chose sides. South Africa was now part of the next great global club, achieving wider scope than was the case with merely strong bilateral relations with these individual states. South Africa would increasingly look to China to meet its development aspirations.

For Zuma and the Department of International Relations and Cooperation (DIRCO), BRICS compensated for an otherwise uninspiring tenure, which included a number of spectacular blunders in South Africa's relations with the international community. These included South Africa's ill-fated involvement in the Central African Republic in 2013, which led to the death of 17 soldiers and efforts to push for a superfluous peacekeeping initiative at the AU, the African Capacity for Immediate Response to Crises.

Then there was the subterfuge that accompanied South Africa's questionable invitation to President Omar al-Bashir (charged with war crimes and crimes against humanity) to attend the 2016 summit of heads of state and government of the AU in Sandton. The fallout from this spurious decision, which involved subverting the country's constitutional obligations, led to South Africa announcing its decision to withdraw from the Rome Statute on the International Criminal Court, only to have the Constitutional Court reject the process as procedurally flawed in February 2017. Earlier, South Africa's Supreme Court of Appeal had ruled that, even though al-Bashir was attending an AU summit, the Diplomatic Immunities and Privileges Act '… did not confer immunity on President al-Bashir and its proclamation by the Minister of International Relations and Cooperation did not serve to confer any immunity on him'.[23]

A similar lack of follow-through would also undo many of the gains achieved when South Africa succeeded in getting Nkosazana Dlamini-Zuma elected as chair of the AU Commission in 2012. The country invested considerable resources to get her into the post but then she announced in 2016 that she would not pursue a second term at the AU and embarked on an all-out campaign to succeed Zuma as president.

Inspired by the 'big fast results' methodology adopted by Malaysia, Zuma later pursued a series of efforts under the brand name Operation Phakisa (Sesotho for 'hurry up'). The first Phakisa programme saw investments in the so-called blue (maritime) economy (which had not been mentioned in the National Development Plan), followed by efforts in education and healthcare. In February 2017, Zuma launched the Operation Phakisa for agriculture, land reform and rural development.[24] Phakisa is one of Zuma's many efforts at growth.

Meanwhile, under Zuma, trade with China expanded by leaps and bounds (see Chapter 9), but not always as envisioned: China has directly contributed to the de-industrialisation of South Africa and the loss of tens of thousands of jobs in its manufacturing sector. In addition, China and South Africa compete head-on in a number of African countries.

But the most important reason for the decline in South Africa's industrial base had little to do with the ANC, which had been set up for failure by organised labour and the outgoing apartheid regime. During the Uruguay Round of negotiations on the General Agreement on Tariffs and Trade, which was finalised in Marrakesh in January 1994, the FW de Klerk government made a 'single undertaking', according to which South Africa was accorded developed-country status. This bound the incoming ANC government to extensive trade liberalisation and, instead of challenging the agreements, which may have been possible under the exceptional domestic circumstances at the time, the ANC stood by the international commitments.

In fact, an influential train of thought within the SACP and COSATU was that inefficiencies and low productivity in South Africa's manufacturing sector (which had been built on the back of exploitation) could best be addressed by exposing the industry to the discipline of the international market. Therefore, when former National Union of Metalworkers of South Africa national executive Alec Erwin became Minister of Trade and Industry in 1996 he reduced tariffs even faster than required by GATT.[25]

The new South African team in Geneva, where the World Trade Organization is based, had to engage in the complex negotiating environment of the GATT talks, which required keeping many balls in the air. In these circumstances the more experienced US and European Union negotiators ran rings around the developing countries, gaining greater access for their global corporations and stripping away the ability of others to protect their infant industries.[26] This was summed up accurately by Trade and Industry Minister Rob Davies as a 'historical injustice that required us to cut industrial tariffs deeper and faster than many peer developing countries'.[27]

Grasping at straws

In 2017, South Africa is approaching the concluding phase of what can only be described as a lost decade. Although the seeds of these developments were planted during the Mbeki presidency, it is clear that the Zuma administration has compounded their impact, and that of the global recession, on South Africa.

Lack of policy coherence, poor implementation and little or no accountability have become hallmarks of the Republic of No Consequences. For example, shortly before he was appointed as the fourth finance minister in under two years in March 2017, Malusi Gigaba proudly announced that the Department of Home Affairs (which he previously headed) had not approved a single new business application between January and December of 2016.[28] Gigaba, something of a dandy, is now responsible for facilitating South Africa's future economic growth.

A few weeks after his appointment, on 25 May 2017, an in-depth report by nine heavyweight academics, representing institutes at the University of Cape Town, Wits University and Stellenbosch University, placed Gigaba at the centre of a systemic political project responsible for the establishment of a shadow state. The report followed hard on the heels of the Unburdening Panel Process of the South African Council of Churches, which expressed its alarm at a systemic design to create chaos and instability, 'pivoted around the President of the Republic'.

At the same time, Gigaba, was assuring investors and business that he was committed to protecting fiscal sustainability, the intention to stabilise government's debt and tightly control expenditure. He also reiterated government's commitment to the procurement of nuclear energy at a pace and scale that the country can afford. These goals, the pursuit of expansive populist policies and the need for fiscal sustainability, are essentially incompatible.

There are many examples of incompetence and lack of accountability in government under Zuma – as well as the establishment of a parallel state structure where decisions are increasingly made outside of mandated government processes. For example, after the late-night Cabinet reshuffle in March 2017, Mantashe said: 'We were given a list that was complete and my own view as the Secretary-General, I felt like this list has been developed somewhere else and it's given to us to legitimise it.'[29]

Under Zuma, economic policy is seemingly at odds with industrial policy and both are undercut by restrictions on skilled immigrants, to give one of many examples. Hence, the party speaks left, walks right and constantly trips over itself in its stop-start catalogue of changing policies, reflected in the composition of a Cabinet with overlapping mandates and lack of cohesion.

Ministers regularly contradict one another on the intent behind policies and decisions, and it is unclear which department is responsible for the coordination of which services, such as the stability and design of the electricity grid, or digital policies and standards, or the fight between the home affairs and finance ministries on the responsibility for customs and excise collection with the establishment of a border agency. Nor is it clear which of the latest multitude of Cabinet committees would oversee state-owned enterprises or social grants. Rather than long-term planning, the emphasis is on crisis management – a situation only likely to improve once Zuma steps down as president of the ANC and the country, and is replaced by a capable leader and a competent, smaller team.

The lack of coordination has debilitating consequences for domestic and international investor confidence, because at the heart of the executive sits a president unable to provide national leadership and a traditionalist faction that does not project a growth vision for the country.

In his 2015 state of the nation address, Zuma announced his latest economic rescue plan, a nine-point programme for accelerating economic growth and creating jobs. The plan could, he announced, boost the economy by an additional 0,8 percentage point in the short term and one percentage point in the medium to long term.[30] Eighteen months later, when questioned about progress with this plan in Parliament, the president appeared only able to recall that one of its nine points concerned agriculture.

In 2016, the economy hardly registered any growth, although prospects for 2017 were slightly better – at least until the March Cabinet reshuffle unsettled the markets, weakened investor confidence in South Africa and triggered three ratings downgrades. During the 2017 state of the nation address, Zuma forecast a growth rate of 1,3 per cent for the year, only to sink that forecast some weeks later with the reshuffle, which triggered the downgrades. By June, South Africa was in a recession.

By late 2016, public perception of the governance of many state-owned enterprises, such as South African Airways, Denel, Eskom, the South African Broadcasting Corporation and the Passenger Rail Agency of South Africa, was in tatters. And it was unclear where government policy stood on visas or immigration, how to proceed with the move to digital television, how to reconcile water scarcity with the intention to expand the agricultural sector, the future of renewable energy versus nuclear, and so on.

This policy confusion is also apparent in the Industrial Policy Action Plan of the Department of Trade and Industry, which is at odds with the New Growth Path of the Economic Development Department, and neither share the analysis set out in the National Development Plan, even though it was adopted by the National Executive Committee of the ANC, Cabinet and Parliament.

In January 2015, the then newly appointed finance minister, Nhlanhla Nene, delivered what *Business Day*'s Carol Paton termed 'a brutally honest message' to the ANC's internal planning meeting. According to Nene, 'in part, the government was responsible for eroding South Africa's economic growth potential ... Among reasons offered for the government's shortcomings were: weak regulatory institutions, poor service delivery, governance problems at state-owned companies, extended periods of regulatory uncertainty and contradictory policies.'[31]

The most important insight to appear from the leaked version of Nene's briefing was the view that South Africa is unlikely to achieve more than 2 per cent growth a year before electricity supply improved – at the time still considered an important cap on economic growth.

It will take several years, if not a decade or longer, for South Africa to recover from the tribal politics and incoherence of the Zuma regime. In addition, the country will soon be caught in an election cycle quite that is quite likely to be marred by violent infighting within the ruling party ahead of its December 2017 conference and between rival political parties in the run-up to the national elections in 2019.

CHAPTER 3

What do recent elections tell us?

When one with honeyed words but evil mind persuades the
mob, great woes befall the state.

– Euripides, *Orestes*

The political choices that the ANC will make in December 2017, and that South Africans will make during the elections in 2019, will determine the future of the country for many years to come. It is therefore useful to review past voting trends at elections, as well as the rules and procedures that will govern proceedings at the 2017 conference, before presenting election forecasts in Chapter 4.

The ANC went into the last national elections, in 2014, under particularly difficult internal conditions, with both its youth and women's leagues compromised, and suffering from a series of corruption and leadership scandals – not to mention the death of its iconic former leader, Nelson Mandela, a few months before. Various blunders, such as the introduction of the expensive e-tolling system in Gauteng, led to an unprecedented mobilisation of citizenry across the political spectrum. Nevertheless, the bulk of ballot support for the ANC held steady with an electoral majority of 62,2 per cent, although down from its 2009 level of 65,9 per cent.

The situation during the August 2016 local government elections was worse, with even more leadership incoherence and policy confusion. High levels of pre-election violence, including several killings (see Chapter 8), compounded the sense of a party struggling with factional battles that are becoming overtly violent. Although the dynamics of national and local elections are different, the final figures for the 2016 poll reflecting overall national support tell an interesting story. When the votes had been counted, ANC support had declined to 53,9 per cent (down from its 70 per cent peak in 2004), while support for the DA had increased to 26,9 per cent (from 9,6 per cent in 2004).

But, perhaps the starkest marker of the declining support for the ANC can be seen not so much in its share of the votes but in the falling numbers of those turning out to vote for the party.[1] This phenomenon is important because it indicates that the ANC could benefit from a resurgence in the prospects of the party under the right leadership and circumstances. It also presents an opportunity for other parties to capitalise on this voter discontent. The large portion of former ANC voters who are not voting, the so-called shift voters, could have a decisive impact on South Africa's future.

Support for the ANC has declined for a number of reasons, but mainly as a result of the failings of its president, and the inability to grow the economy and reduce unemployment. In addition, its youth and women's leagues have been weakened, and its most important ally in the Tripartite Alliance, COSATU, is a shadow of its former self. The general trend has been clear over several years – declining trade union membership has been compounded by the emergence of new unions, many of them outside the fold of the congress. In December 2013, the National Union of Metalworkers of South Africa made two crucial decisions: first, not to endorse the ANC in the 2014 elections and, second, to abandon the principle of one union per sector and recruit along the manufacturing value chain, for which it was subsequently expelled from COSATU. Later the Food and Allied Workers Union also left the federation. Subsequent events have hastened the decline of organised labour, and future trends see the splitting of the various union federations into smaller, competing unions and a rise in the number of non-unionised workers. The establishment of the South African Federation of Trade Unions in Johannesburg in April 2017 by disgruntled former members of COSATU reflects these trends.

Populist politics has become the order of the day among unions competing for membership, and relations between employers and labour have become ever more acrimonious as the economic situation in South Africa deteriorates.[2] Coming from a past where organised labour suffered from poverty wages, COSATU appears increasingly out of touch with sentiments in the broader pool of the unemployed and the poor, who are much worse off than their unionised counterparts. The influence of organised labour is declining following the fracturing between the unions and the inevitable challenge of agitating for benefits to a small membership amid a large pool of unemployed.

ANC membership – declining in favour of Zuma?

The outcome of the national conference (scheduled from 16 to 20 December 2017), during which a new ANC leadership will be elected, is hugely uncertain. According to the ANC's constitution, at least 90 per cent of the delegates at the conference must be from 'properly constituted branch general meetings' where the number of delegates per branch is in proportion to their paid-up membership.

The bigger a branch, the more members they can send. Similarly, the more ANC members there are in a province, the greater the influence that province can exert at the national conference.

Like the events that culminated in the ousting of Mbeki at the 2007 ANC conference, the preparatory work at branch level by the different slates vying for support will therefore prove decisive.[3] What is certain is that these preparations and the December elections will be heavily contested. Come voting at the conference, the number and composition of ANC members in the various branches will be crucial, as it is likely that voting for candidates will occur according to informal lists of candidates, which are negotiated within the various factions. These lists, or 'slates', were the defining feature of the ANC's Polokwane conference and have become a feature of subsequent elections despite efforts by the party's leaders to discourage the practice. Slate voting has proven to open up opportunities for systemic corruption within the party and significant amounts of money allegedly change hands to secure a position on a slate. The practice has also found its way into provincial elections and elections for the women's and youth leagues. Although many ANC leaders have spoken out against slate voting, the practice continues and is likely to be a determining feature in December.

All party members who were in good standing by 30 April 2017 were allowed to participate in the various branch general meetings. May and June 2017 saw a membership audit, followed by an opportunity for queries, objections and appeals. Although the June 2017 policy conference discussed amendments to the ANC's constitution, these will not affect the vote in December.

Since the local government elections in 2016, the Premier League has steadily become more powerful in determining electoral outcomes and they can again be expected to play an important role in December 2017. At least two leaders of this Premier League, David Mabuza of Mpumalanga and Ace Magashule of the Free State, have their sights set on the top six positions.[4] But there are equally important developments in the establishment of an anti-Dlamini-Zuma 'super slate' led by Cyril Ramaphosa, which apparently includes the likes of Mcebisi Jonas, Lindiwe Sisulu (Minister of Human Settlements), Zweli Mkhize (treasurer-general of the ANC) and possibly even Gwede Mantashe. That this alliance presents a credible threat to Zuma is evident in the death threats that its members receive.

ANC membership numbers have been declining since Polokwane. In his report to the party's National General Council in October 2015, Zuma revealed that the ANC's membership had dropped by 450 187 members to 789 870 – a decline of 37 per cent since the Mangaung conference in 2012. Membership numbers were down to the levels seen in 2010, with KwaZulu-Natal now accounting for 21 per cent of all members, up from 16 per cent in 2007.

Writing in the *Daily Maverick*, Ranjeni Munusamy described this situation as an ANC that 'is shrinking in Zuma's favour, with people who are disillusioned or in opposing factions becoming inactive or turning against the party. Those loyal to Zuma dominate party structures and are also the dominant voices speaking for the party.'[5]

Since 2010 KwaZulu-Natal has had the largest number of paid-up ANC members within the organisation (as shown in Figure 1), where it benefits from an ethnic factor (Zuma is a Zulu) and from the fact that the ANC government has done deals with traditional leaders in pursuit of their support.

Under Zuma's socially conservative leadership, the ANC is clearly strengthening its rural support base. Successive efforts to introduce and reintroduce the Traditional Courts Bill (in 2008, in 2012 and again in January 2017), which will bolster the authority of traditional leaders and provide for large salary increases for headmen across the country, are but one among a raft of measures. In mid-2015, in the run-up to the local government elections in 2016, the salaries of traditional leaders were increased by 28,4 per cent as the party prepared to challenge the Inkatha Freedom Party in its remaining stronghold in deep rural KwaZulu-Natal. Eventually this tactic failed when the ANC's proxy in the province, the National Freedom Party, failed to pay its registration fees and was barred from contesting the elections in August 2016. As a result, the Inkatha Freedom Party (from which the National Freedom Party had originally split) regained its position as the largest opposition party at local government level in the province.

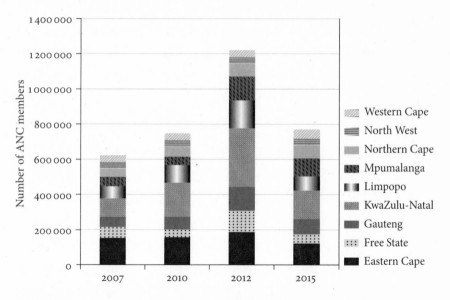

Figure 1: Paid-up ANC membership by province, 2007–2015
Source: Ranjeni Munusamy, ANC NGC: Zuma, Mantashe ring alarm bells as membership plunges by 37%, *Daily Maverick*, 9 October 2015

It was therefore no surprise that it was in KwaZulu-Natal that the first blood was drawn in preparing for the 2017 elective conference, when the province's premier, Senzo Mchunu (an opponent of President Zuma), was ousted by former KwaZulu-Natal secretary Sihle Zikalala in November 2015 but clung on as premier for several more months. Later that month

Sbu Ndebele, a close ally of the president, became ANC leader in the province.[6] Ramaphosa drew the next blood in the Northern Cape when Zamani Saul was elected as chairperson after challenger Sylvia Lucas, the former provincial treasurer and current premier, declined nomination.

Election trends

During the 2016 local elections, only 15,2 million out of 26 million registered voters went to the polls as the steady trend of low voter turnout continued. As mentioned, the ANC received a pummelling at these municipal elections. Voting patterns during national and local elections differ, however, when one compares the ANC with the official opposition, the DA.

The ANC tends to do slightly worse during local elections than in national elections, whereas for the DA the converse is true. This is probably because municipal service-delivery issues predominate during local government elections and the ANC is generally found wanting in this domain, while, on the other hand, its liberation credentials enable it to benefit during national elections. If that trend were to continue, the ANC may do slightly better in 2019 than the 53,9 per cent that it received in August 2016, and the DA may do slightly worse than the 26,9 per cent that it polled during the same elections.

That said, the DA has been on a generally sustained upward trajectory in its support levels since the national elections in 2004, when it received 12,4 per cent of the vote and the ANC received 69,7 per cent (its best result ever). In addition, an analysis of the local election results indicates a national shift away from the ANC towards opposition parties, except in KwaZulu-Natal where the ANC has been able to increase the number of votes that it attracts.

The DA has increased its support base nationally and in every province, doing particularly well in the Western Cape, Gauteng and the Northern Cape. Its prospects elsewhere are slim, however, as the ANC is expected to continue to command a large majority in more rural provinces for the foreseeable future.

Most embarrassing for the ANC during the 2016 local elections was that it lost Nelson Mandela Bay municipality (consisting of the city of Port Elizabeth and the industrial towns of Uitenhage and Despatch) in the Eastern Cape to the DA, although the latter was not able to achieve an outright majority, with 46,7 per cent of the votes.

The ANC also lost the capital, Tshwane, after the party imposed former minister Thoko Didiza as their candidate in a divided local party. As a result, the DA managed to squeeze past the ANC with slightly more support, at 43,1 per cent.

And, on 22 August, Herman Mashaba from the DA was elected mayor of South Africa's largest city, Johannesburg. The DA therefore became the leading party in the city that hosts the legislature, Cape Town, the seat of the executive, Tshwane, and the commercial capital, Johannesburg.

The upstart party, the EFF, also did well in August 2016 – obtaining 8,2 per cent of the overall vote, a solid increase on the 6,4 per cent that it gained in 2014, and looks set for a further increase in support during the 2019 national elections – but perhaps not as well as it had expected. During the 2016 local elections, the EFF became the largest opposition party in Limpopo and the North West, and saw its fortunes improve, although not to the levels that it had expected. Rather than joining the DA in a coalition of smaller parties after the local elections, the EFF chose to remain outside of the agreements that were brokered.

The future developments in Gauteng could well mirror what happened in the Western Cape, where the DA first wrested Cape Town from th

ANC, initially running the city in coalition with smaller parties, and eventually the province. Gauteng is now within the grasp of a DA-led alliance during the upcoming 2019 national/provincial elections.

Gauteng is South Africa's population and economic hub. The province has 24 per cent of the country's population and is responsible for 34 per cent of its GDP. In 2014, the gap between the ANC and the DA was a substantial 27 per cent. Two years later, in the 2016 local elections, that gap shrank to 7,5 per cent.

The 2016 local elections therefore reaffirmed and accentuated the trend at national level, with the DA and the EFF steadily eroding ANC support. Compared to the previous local elections in 2011, the ANC had lost 8,4 per cent total support and the DA had gained almost 3 per cent more support than in the 2014 national elections.

Despite these travails, the ANC remains a formidable party that still commands an absolute majority nationally (currently with 249 out of 400 seats in the National Assembly), and it governs all but one of South Africa's provinces. But it has become evident that the ANC would have to do more than simply get rid of Zuma if it were to turn its election trends around. It needs a complete reset, including a generational change in its leadership composition.

The trends in electoral support can be seen in Figure 2, which shows the results for both national and local elections. The broad trend lines tell a clear story as the gap between the support for the ANC and other parties narrows with each successive election, although it still remains significant.

Future election trends will be influenced by the increased number of ᵗʰ Africans, a pattern that will inevitably have a detrimen-
n the ANC, given that the older electorate associate
ole in South Africa's liberation.

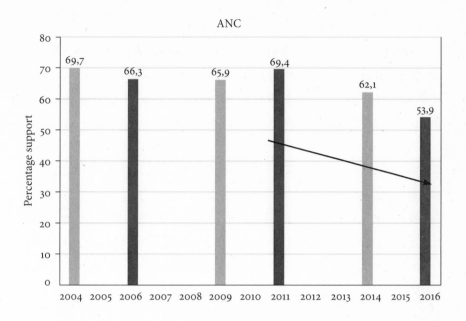

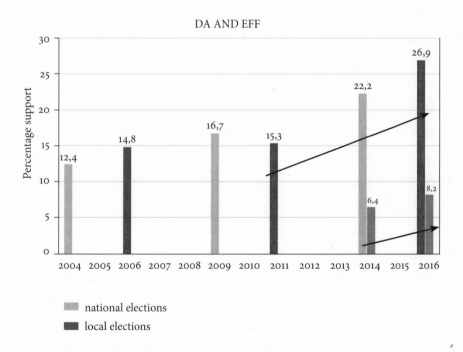

national elections

local elections

Figure 2: Trends in electoral support since 2004 for the ANC, DA and EFF
Source: Independent Electoral Commission of South Africa

Future voters

Table 1 shows the changing size of four age-group cohorts that will play an increasingly important role in future elections. It reveals the estimated size of South Africa's population age groups at the time of national elections from 2014 onwards.

Table 1: South Africa's population by voter age group during national election years

Election year	Population	Persons of voting age	Potential number of born-free voters	Born-free voters as proportion of total electorate
2014	54,0 m	34,9 m	3,3 m	9,5%
2019	57,0 m	38,0 m	8,5 m	22,4%
2024	59,8 m	40,8 m	13,6 m	33,3%
2029	62,3 m	43,3 m	18,4 m	42,4%

Source: Author's calculations based on IFs v 7.28 initialised from UN Population Division medium-fertility variant total population

The cohort of potential born-free voters (i.e. South Africans born from 1994 onwards) is an interesting demographic segment to watch because they are generally expected to exhibit different voting behaviour from that of their parents. In 2014, only 3,3 million born-frees were of voting age (equivalent to 9,5 per cent of those of voting age). However, by the time the 2019 elections come around, this number will have increased to 8,5 million (22,4 per cent of potential voters), and will grow to 33,3 per cent by 2024, and 42,4 per cent by 2029.

The impact of this large increase in the number of born-free voters will therefore already be felt in the forthcoming 2019 national elections and that impact will increase with each subsequent election. However, successive rounds of the Afrobarometer opinion surveys in a number of African countries, including South Africa, have found that political and civic engagement by African youth is declining, and that it is particularly weak among young women.[7] So, the crucial question is, will political parties be able to persuade the born-free voters to register and vote? And, if so, for which party will they cast their votes?

Pundits generally agree that the majority of South Africans vote for the ANC on the basis of its liberation credentials – in other words, theirs is a vote of solidarity in recognition of the party's legacy in having played a key role in unshackling South Africa from apartheid. As the number of born-free voters increases with each election, however, the memory and experience of apartheid, and the (somewhat exaggerated) role played by the ANC in South Africa's freedom struggle, will diminish. By contrast, for the born-frees, the demand for effective policies that deliver jobs, education and services is likely to increase. Born-free voters are also expected to be more willing than older voters to switch parties, increasing volatility in voting behaviour.

In addition to the expanding cohort of born-free voters, growing urbanisation and improvements in levels of education will also influence future voting patterns. The effect of apartheid policies, which sought to keep black South Africans hemmed into rural homelands, exerted downward pressure on the normal urbanisation process until the relaxation of influx-control measures in the 1980s, after which urbanisation rates increased. During the first democratic elections in 1994, slightly more than 50 per cent of South Africans were living in urban areas, a figure that had increased to 64 per cent by the 2014 elections. By 2029, up to 76 per cent of South Africans are expected to live in urban areas.

The result is that parties that appeal to a rural   espouse traditional values and emphasise social conserva ingly the case with the ANC under Zuma and Traditionalist successor to Zuma – may struggle increasingly urban-orientated, digitally connec

73

culture. However it pans out, the rural–urban divide will feature strongly in South Africa's future politics.

Current trends would also see the level of education steadily increasing – another factor that might work against parties that rely on family socialisation for continued voter support. Other things being equal, voters with higher levels of education should be expected to be more critical of a government that fails to improve the livelihoods of its citizens in accordance with its policy programmes and promises. The mean number of years of completed education among South Africans aged 15 and older will have increased from 8,7 years during the 2014 elections to 10,2 years at the time of the national elections in 2034.

It is possible that a reinvigorated ANC may sustain its currently high levels of popular support. But this is unlikely to be the case without a comprehensive leadership change, new policies and a break from the current trend towards state capture and patronage.

Data from research network Afrobarometer indicates that the level of public dissatisfaction with government performance, particularly in the executive, is at its highest since 2000. In 2015, only a third of South Africans said they trusted President Zuma 'somewhat' or 'a lot' – a sharp fall from the two-thirds positive response to the same question in 2011.[8]

And this dissatisfaction extends beyond Zuma to key governing institutions. The 2015 Victims of Violent Crime Survey, for example, suggests that 46 per cent of the population is dissatisfied with the performance of the courts. Afrobarometer data also shows that Indians, white people and, to a lesser degree, the Coloured community feel increasingly discriminated against by the government, while black South Africans are much more positive in their assessment – sentiments that reflect extent to which the ANC has moved away from its non-racial tradi-The ANC of 2017 no longer pretends or aspires to be a non-racial movement; it became increasingly black nationalist in orientation under Mbeki, and has become rural and traditionalist under Zuma. These negative sentiments have doubled on average since 2006.[9]

The increasingly vocal anti-Zuma protest movement is also indicative of growing impatience with the president and the ANC more generally. In addition, the party is led by someone who has been promoted significantly above his level of competence,[10] and the party is fracturing. It seems almost inevitable that the ANC will become increasingly populist in its orientation as it grasps for ways to extend its stay in power and succumbs to the allure of patronage, as opposed to investment in long-term growth.

Even twenty years ago, Adam, Slabbert and Moodley told the story of how 'post-apartheid South Africa has transformed itself into a liberal democracy and a conventional consumer society. American consumerism has always lurked under the surface of racial restrictions,' they write. '[A] new elite of black South Africans has now embraced money-making and conspicuous consumption with a zeal that few older capitalist states have experienced.'[11]

The result is white retreat and disaffection, and investor concern – given the financial muscle and business skills of this group. Although there is much evidence of positive change in the distribution patterns of power and wealth since South Africa became a democracy, patience seems to be running out with government policies intent on building a small elite of wealthy family and friends, rather than investing in the future – on education, job creation and economic growth.

On a comparative basis, the scope and depth of South Africa's transition to democracy remain unparalleled globally. Nevertheless, many young voters born shortly before or after the transition are increasingly disconnected from the past, and those who lived through these tumultuous years are often disillusioned. Against this background, the next chapter presents various political scenarios for the future.

CHAPTER 4

Three scenarios for the immediate future and beyond

'Would you tell me, please, which way I ought to go from here?' asked Alice. 'That depends a good deal on where you want to get to,' said the Cat. 'I don't much care where—' said Alice. 'Then it doesn't matter which way you go,' said the Cat.

– Lewis Carroll, *Alice's Adventures in Wonderland*

South Africa is at a critical turning point, perhaps the most significant since 1990, as momentum builds towards the ANC's national conference in December 2017. Who will lead the ANC in 2018? Will the party again split, as it has done three times before? Will the ANC be able to retain a majority in Parliament or will it have to depend on an alliance with another party to retain power? And, if so, which party might that be?

This chapter presents three political scenarios for the immediate future and beyond: Bafana Bafana, Nation Divided and Mandela Magic (as explained in the Introduction). There are also some variations on these three potential pathways. The intention is to map out a coherent set of storylines with which to frame South Africa's alternative futures and then to model the impact of each.

The chapter includes forecasts of the national election results scheduled for 2019, 2024 and 2029 for the three major parties – the ANC, the DA and the EFF. Subsequent chapters model the impact of these scenarios on economic growth, poverty, inequality and various other development indicators (see Chapters 5, 6 and 7), as well as on aspects such as levels of violence (Chapter 8) and South Africa's standing in the region and internationally (Chapter 9).

A key determinant of how the South African storyline will develop will be the struggle for dominance between the Traditionalist and Reformer factions within the ANC. In addition, the future of the ANC (and South Africa) in the short and medium term will largely be determined by the shift vote (those ANC supporters who are unhappy with the current trajectory of the party and have been withholding their vote, or voting for another party). Whether the shift voters decide to support a Reformist ANC or a less corrupt Traditionalist ANC, or are prepared to throw their weight behind a possible breakaway party, will play an important role in the future of the ANC and its ability to retain a majority at national level and in provincial government.

Following the 2014 national elections, the current allocation of seats in the National Assembly is as follows:

Party	Percentage support	Number of seats
ANC	62%	249
DA	22%	89
EFF	6%	25
Others	9%	37

Bafana Bafana

In the Bafana Bafana scenario, ANC members elect a mix of Traditionalists and Reformers at the December 2017 conference. An example of such a mixed ideological bag would be Ramaphosa as president and Dlamini-Zuma as deputy president, although there are various other contenders who could fulfil these roles. Such a mix may also result from the choice of a compromise candidate should the competition between Ramaphosa and Dlamini-Zuma end in stalemate or threaten the unity of the party.

Rather than waiting for Zuma's constitutional term as South African president to conclude in 2019, the new leadership is likely to recall him in 2018 to avoid a 'two centres of power' problem between Luthuli House and the Union Buildings. Zuma has become such an unbridled liability to the party that it is unlikely that a new leadership could countenance Zuma serving out his full term, although his recall may happen only towards the end of 2018.

Although this balancing act between opposing ideological spheres might keep the party together, it won't be good for the country, and South Africa will merely muddle along.

The ANC will therefore go into the 2019 elections with a new but conflicted team that talks left and walks right. As a consequence, the shift vote will remain uncommitted (see Figure 3), generally not coming out to vote in sufficient quantities to stop the ANC from suffering an unprecedented drubbing at the polls. ANC support dips to 53 per cent in 2019 (see Figure 4); it maintains an overall majority, but the party is weakened, and possibly still divided.

The Bafana Bafana scenario is largely a future of more of the same, although government policy is more coherent and government is more efficient than under Zuma, as there will be more competence in the

TRADITIONALISTS	REFORMERS
• Rural, black nationalist	• Social democrats
• Socially conservative	• Typically urban
• Loyal to Jacob Zuma	• Supported by born-free
• Dominated by Zulu speakers	voters with jobs
• Centralised state	• Multi-ethnic
• Redistributive policies and not	• Mixed economy and
constitutionalists	inclusive economic growth
➢ Premier League, ANCYL,	➢ Gauteng ANC and others
ANCWL and others	

• Unhappy
with Zuma
• Not voting or
protest vote
➢ Former supporters of
Mbeki and others

SHIFT VOTERS

Figure 3: Shift vote under Bafana Bafana scenario
Source: Author

Cabinet. Private and public disagreements between Cabinet ministers, state-owned companies and departments are muted, although the ANC remains divided on how to manage the country and the economy. Publicly, there is much reference to the need for radical economic transformation but, in practice, government remains committed to responsible macro-economic policies as it seeks to extract itself from the impact of the 2017 investment downgrade – which it manages to achieve by 2024.

Figure 4 shows the forecast for voter support for the three elections in this scenario, as well as the allocation of seats in the National Assembly in 2019. In Bafana Bafana, the ANC loses control of Gauteng in 2019 for a number of reasons – decades of mismanagement, the e-tolls saga, the impact of urbanisation, a better-educated electorate and ongoing deficiencies in service delivery. Gauteng falls to a DA-led coalition and, by 2024, the DA is able to obtain an outright majority in the province.

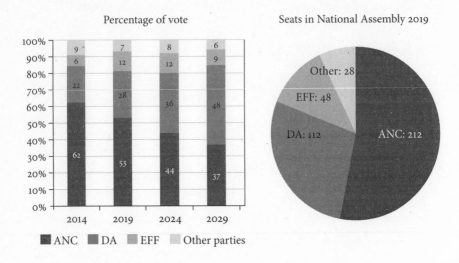

Figure 4: Bafana Bafana election forecast and party seats in the National Assembly in 2019
Source: Author

The loss of South Africa's economic heartland, on top of the Western Cape, would deal the ANC a fatal blow and accelerate its decline ahead of the 2024 elections, when it gets only 44 per cent of the national vote. Now essentially a party with its remaining power base in rural South Africa, the ANC struggles to provide meaningful direction in an increasingly urban South Africa.

Theoretically, the DA, the EFF and the smaller parties should, at this point (2024), be able to put a governing coalition together, but in practice such a combination would be very difficult to achieve given the wide ideological differences between them. A much more likely outcome is that the ANC enters into an alliance with the EFF or with smaller parties to form a governing coalition.

In the Bafana Bafana scenario, ANC support drops with every election as voter apathy, already at a high level, increases, as does the sense of drift and lack of direction. The shift vote of potential ANC supporters slowly drifts away, with some voting for the EFF, others for smaller parties; many simply don't vote.

Government's initiatives to convey a more positive message through efforts such as good-news reporting are drowned out by a cacophony of reporting on graft, corruption and poor service delivery – much of it involving senior party members. Irregular, wasteful and unauthorised government expenditure, at almost R47 billion in 2015/16, slowly falls, but many municipalities and state-owned enterprises, such as the South African National Roads Agency and the Passenger Rail Agency of South Africa, struggle to contain abuse and wastage as they try to execute their development mandate.[1]

In a practice established by Mbeki and perpetuated by Zuma, a large number of senior and sensitive appointments to key positions continue to be made on the basis of personal and party loyalty, and not on merit – although this is not a blanket approach. The integrity of a number of the institutions in the criminal-justice sector, such as the police, the National Prosecuting Authority and the Special Investigating Unit, continue to face leadership challenges, although they register some successes in dealing with violent crime, and in tackling corruption and malfeasance. The results are continued high levels of societal crime and service-delivery protests.

With poorer than expected returns on state investments in policing, middle- and upper-class South Africans increasingly rely on the private security industry to supplement the services provided by the police. In poorer areas, vigilantism increases.

Without a clear support plan for industry, South African manufacturing exports to the rest of Africa, the only region where the country runs a consistent trade surplus, steadily lose ground to other countries, such as China and India. On the other hand, South African telecommunications, banking, retail and hospitality industries that specialise in providing luxury and lifestyle goods and services to the emerging multiracial middle class retain their dominant positions.

The domestic manufacturing sector in other African countries benefits from government support, which potentially disadvantages South African exports. Meanwhile, South African government efforts to 'buy local' fizzle out with little impact. Because domestic investors do not invest, foreigners remain hesitant. As a result, South Africa continues to attract only modest levels of foreign direct investment at below USD2 billion annually.[2]

In the Bafana Bafana scenario, the country struggles to attract sufficient capital to fund a consistent trade deficit with much of the rest of the world – Asia and Europe in particular. Business leaders from elsewhere continue to invest in Africa, but largely bypass South Africa.

Although increasing in absolute size as the economy expands, the South African manufacturing sector continues its slow decline in terms of its percentage contribution to GDP. Meanwhile, the services sector and mineral commodities increase in terms of their relative contributions to the economy. Some of the remaining larger commercial farmers, unable to compete with subsidised agriculture in Europe and North America, emigrate northwards to benefit from more fertile soils, higher rainfall and more favourable government support. Like the manufacturing sector, the trend in agriculture is one of a continuing decline in the size of its contribution to GDP.

However, by comparative middle-income standards, South Africa continues to grow, although significantly below the average rate of its upper-middle-income peers, at around 2,3 per cent per annum to 2034. The country gains a reputation as a chronic underachiever: it should be dominating the region, but it isn't.

Policymaking is more consistent than under Zuma, but with a continued high turnover of senior government officials, to the detriment of follow-through on policy and the build-up of a suitable knowledge base. Since no single faction is in control, turbulence in the Tripartite Alliance and the upper ranks of the ANC continues to detract from investor confidence in the years immediately after 2019. Fearful of too quick a transition and the threat of even higher levels of social conflict, South Africa muddles along. Growth has limited impact on unemployment and inequality levels, which remain stubbornly high – although life for the middle- and higher-income groups is good.

The ANC remains nominally committed to the National Development Plan as the most important of its multitude of socio-economic programmes and strategies, but the new compromise leadership does not update the plan or determinedly implement it, and it is largely consigned to the bookshelf after the 2019 elections (ironically, as Ramaphosa was the deputy chair of the National Planning Commission). ANC policies continue to reflect a mixture of progressive and regressive measures that leave the economy stuck.

All is not doom and gloom, however. Over time, the investments made in education start to pay off, schooling improves and social grant programmes continue to alleviate the worst effects of dire poverty.

Beyond 2019, the impact of fracking in the Karoo and natural gas extraction in the deep waters off the country's west coast provide some stimulus to South Africa's economy, without which growth would be lower. These, together with substantial imports of natural gas from Mozambique, alleviate energy pressures and costs towards the end of the time horizon. Government proceeds with building two nuclear power stations instead of the original fleet of six, despite a deluge of evidence pointing to the importance of investing in renewables rather than nuclear.

Regionally, South Africa continues to engage in limited peacekeeping and peacebuilding efforts. The capacity crisis in the South African National Defence Force becomes acute as its bloated ranks continue to squeeze out expenditure for modernisation. South Africa's ability to back up its talk of African solutions with commensurate military capacity for stabilisation operations and peacekeeping continues its steady decline.

In its engagements with other African countries, South Africa cannot shake off the perception that it is acting more in the interests of its political elites and their business friends than in national, or continental, interests, partly because key contracts are awarded to well-connected individuals as part of black-empowerment deals. Perceived ruling-party patronage for business contracts, increasing division in the ANC and the country's influential role in the continent decline steadily.

South Africa remains a member of the G20 and BRICS, but loses its influence in these and other groupings, particularly after the BRICS Plus process sees other African countries also becoming members. In response to the impact of rapidly growing economies, such as that of Nigeria, South Africa opts for co-leadership in Africa.

Bafana Bafana is a pathway where most South Africans expect less from government, withdraw from participation and become less active in the political economy. Skilled South Africans continue to leave (or at least talk about leaving) for other destinations in Africa that appear to offer greater business opportunities, or for Europe, North America, Australia or New Zealand for reasons of safety and quality of life. On the other hand, the country remains a magnet for unskilled migrants from the rest of the continent.

The clock remains firmly stuck at five minutes before midnight in discussions around dinner tables in upper-class suburbs.

Nation Divided

A worst-case scenario for the country is one where Zuma continues as South Africa's president to 2019 (i.e. despite the election of a new leader of the ANC in December 2017), or where a Traditionalist slate, who are committed to a vision of fiscal populism, gain key positions at the December 2017 national conference, after which Zuma steps down and hands the reins over to a grouping that is intent on frustrating any prosecution of the former president and committed to fiscal populism.[3]

The promise of either an extended Zuma presidency to 2019 or a Traditionalist successor will inevitably impact negatively on voter support for the ANC. Although Dlamini-Zuma (the most likely presidential candidate in this scenario) is generally an able administrator (albeit a terrible communicator), she would be able to convince some of the stay-away voters to again vote for the ANC during the 2019 elections, even though support from rural communities for a female president is far from assured.

Still, Dlamini-Zuma is an uninspiring and tired choice for a party in need of reinvigoration and young blood, and, in the run-up to the 2019 elections, the ANC under her is likely to adopt a series of policy measures that restrict majority foreign ownership and impose minimum black ownership quotas on domestic business. Most prominent among these are additional measures to appropriate and redistribute land, with all its attendant emotional connotations.

In the former homelands, the Traditionalist cadres continue with their efforts to chip away at the liberties and rights enshrined in the Constitution. More powers are given to traditional leaders and, despite the fact the country may be led by a female president, the legal rights of women suffer, and the government proceeds to roll out what is essentially a segregated judicial system for rural communities.

A victory for the Traditionalists at the party's national conference is likely to lead to a split in the ANC in 2018, reducing support for the party to below 50 per cent during the 2019 national elections. Such a split would be led by the Gauteng province (the strongest Reformist faction within the ANC), who would effectively have been marginalised by the victory of the Traditionalists. In a sign of things that might come, the Gauteng ANC resolved to 'fight state capture in whichever way it manifests itself' – a clear reference to Zuma – within days of his March 2017 Cabinet reshuffle.[4]

The most likely intention of the new breakaway party, which I will call the New ANC, would be to enter into an alliance with the DA to govern Gauteng or, possibly, depending on the size of the split, to engineer a large enough breakaway to place the New ANC in a position to form a national governing coalition with either the DA or even the ANC. These events are likely to unfold only after the 2019 national elections. Given the short period within which the New ANC would have to organise itself ahead of the 2019 national/provincial elections, it would, however, be difficult to convert their frustrations into a well-functioning party machine.

The result, depicted in Figure 5, is that some of the shift vote would go to the ANC, but many die-hard potential ANC supporters would simply not vote. The result is that the Traditionalist faction would remain the dominant grouping within the ANC, but it would be a smaller party, potentially populist, black nationalist and ruralist in its orientation.

TRADITIONALISTS	REFORMERS
• Rural, black nationalist • Socially conservative • Dominated by Zulu speakers • Centralised state • Redistributive policies and not constitutionalists ➤ Premier League, ANCYL, ANCWL and others	• Social democrats • Typically urban • Supported by born-free voters with jobs • Multi-ethnic • Mixed economy and inclusive economic growth ➤ Gauteng ANC and others

SHIFT
VOTERS
TO ANC

SHIFT
VOTERS
TO NANC

Figure 5: Shift vote in Nation Divided scenario
Source: Author

In recent years, the ANC has split twice, first when the Congress of the People was formed and, more recently, when the EFF was born. (The party also split during the apartheid years when a group broke away to form the Pan Africanist Congress.) When the Congress of the People split off from the ANC, it managed to obtain slightly more than 7 per cent of the vote in the 2009 elections. It could have done much better had it been able to avoid the leadership infighting that effectively crippled the new party.

The consequence of a third split would be to reduce ANC support to below 50 per cent at national level. Depending on the size of the breakaway party and the level of national support and votes in Gauteng that the New ANC would be able to garner in 2019, the ANC would, after the elections, either be able to enter into an alliance with smaller parties at national level, or, in the case of a large split, have to look at the EFF as coalition partner. Such a development is not unforeseen. Julius Malema has already expressed his intention to engineer a merger with the ANC.[5] An agreement, possibly a merger, with the EFF would appeal to the dominant Traditionalist grouping in the ANC, but, irrespective of an agreement with the EFF (or not), the ANC will clearly adopt more populist and ruralist policies.

This is an outcome that could see a subsequent boost in support for the ANC in 2024 as the government prioritises creating jobs and alleviating poverty at the expense of investment in healthcare, education and infrastructure. Government effectiveness would continue to decline and foreign direct investment is unlikely to materialise under these circumstances.

The impact of these two options, a small or large split, is shown in Figure 6, with the New ANC standing as a separate party in 2019 ('Nation Divided One'), but entering into a coalition with the DA thereafter. The result is a surge in support for the DA in 2024 (to 39 per cent of the vote) to rival the ANC. At this point, either the ANC or the DA would most likely be within striking distance of a national majority; in the case of the ANC, this would be likely to entail an alliance with the EFF.

In Nation Divided Two, an ANC–EFF alliance is likely to implement a package of popular but unaffordable policies in urban areas while expanding the rights of traditional authorities in the former homelands. Examples might be restrictions on private-sector education in favour of further subsidies for tertiary education, rapid increases in a national minimum wage, even more aggressive policies of redistribution, stringent black economic empowerment requirements and a national health

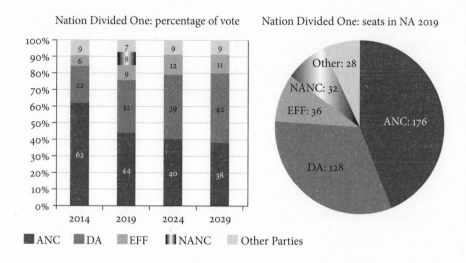

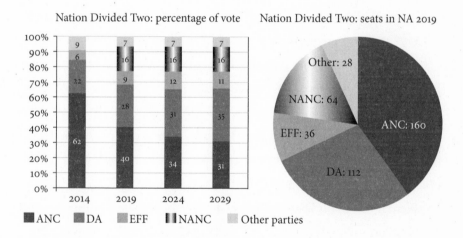

Figure 6: Nation Divided election forecasts
Source: Author

scheme, which, collectively, see South Africa unable to exit from its sub-investment status until around 2029 or later.

Above-inflation increases in remuneration and growth of the public sector are likely to crowd out other spending. These measures, including the ramping-up of social grants at the expense of investment in infra-structure and education, would allow the ANC to temporarily contain its decline (i.e. it will do better in 2024), but the long-term outcomes for the party, and for South Africa, are disastrous. In rural areas, the ANC will continue to woo traditional leaders as a valuable political resource, able to influence its rural constituency, but these trends put it at odds with a modern democracy.

The redistributive policies and the influence of tribal leaders subse-quently stem the haemorrhage of ANC support, and the party obtains between 34 and 40 per cent of the vote during the 2024 elections, while the EFF peaks at 12 per cent (see Figure 6). Thereafter, however, the ANC fares very badly on the back of slow growth, large increases in poverty and unemployment, and even greater inequality. Over time, the South African economy grows much more slowly than under the other two scenarios and the result is a smaller economy by 2034 compared to Bafana Bafana and Mandela Magic.

In the Nation Divided scenario, the DA is expected to eventually emerge as the largest beneficiary in 2029, doing better in the elections than in all other scenarios, but by then South Africa would be in a sig-nificantly worse condition. Nation Divided is a scenario where the new president – perhaps Dlamini-Zuma or Baleka Mbete – finds herself unable to provide a developmental pathway that attracts business and in-spires international confidence, as their vision of collectivism is at odds with the requirements of a modern economy. Competition for resources within the provinces among the various ANC factions and leaders could turn violent, particularly in Limpopo, North West and Gauteng. The result is that South Africa's economic and democratic momentum slows. Government borrows more to fund its current expenditure, and interest payments, already the fastest-growing item on the budget, balloon.

A study by the ANC-aligned Mapungubwe Institute for Strategic Reflection has warned of the extent to which patronage, poverty and inequality are linked to protests in communities, the extent to which poor people distrust local government, and the associated loss of legitimacy facing the state's democratic institutions. 'Structures and systems of accountability, such as ward committees and processes to develop integrated development plans, seem largely not to have delivered the initial promise,' the study reported.[6]

Levels of foreign direct investment decline in response to increasing political uncertainty, and domestic investment rates steadily drop. Deteriorating governance and competition for budget resources result in budgets for research, development and infrastructure being either cut or partially lost to inefficiency and poor management. Administration in the former homelands is particularly poor, a consequence of the large oversight role accorded to traditional authorities, which are unaccountable, systemically corrupt and largely self-serving.

A sense of doom and gloom becomes pervasive in the private sector as investors flock to other emerging markets, such as Nigeria and Angola, and steadily reduce their exposure in South Africa. Other investment destinations, including Mozambique, Tanzania and Kenya, overtake South Africa as we move off the investment radar.

Citizens become resigned to the decreasing quality of governance, expect less and less from the state, and look to themselves rather than government for their livelihood. Poverty in rural areas, the former homelands in particular, is deep and grinding. Meanwhile, those at the top of the economic pyramid continue to enjoy a comfortable life inside their gated communities.

Marginalised from a closed-shop, capital-intensive economy, poor South Africans take to the streets with greater frequency and in larger numbers as violent protests increase. In response, government is forced to increase defence and security expenditure, which further constrains spending on social services and infrastructure.

Unable to look forward with inspiration and confidence, the ANC increasingly looks backwards, emphasising its role in the liberation struggle and its shared history with other countries with a common disposition. The public discourse is peppered with references to race, anti-colonialism and anti-imperialism, much as these pronouncements serve increasingly to irritate the country's trading partners and other countries in Africa that have graduated from blame politics. There is much reference to the national democratic revolution as the next stage in the emancipation of (black) nationals. The use of race-based social analysis becomes the order of the day, dividing and polarising South Africans. South Africa experiences a loss in the quality of its democratic system as constraints on the executive branch weaken and political participation suffers. It remains a democracy, but one less confident in the viability and fairness of its system.

South Africa also becomes more isolated internationally, even from key partners such as China and Russia. It loses its moral legitimacy, and its voice, although less influential globally, becomes increasingly strident. Other countries on the continent become the partners of choice for fast-growing and larger established economies. Over time, as its global influence wanes, South Africa becomes more inward-looking, focusing on domestic policies in an attempt to contain its increasingly critical and restless population.

In 2012 former energy minister Dipuo Peters called South Africa's reserves of shale gas (the eighth largest in the world) a 'blessing from God'; others who support its exploitation as a fuel called it a potential game-changer for the coal-dependent country.[7] However, the publication of regulations that allow the South African government a dominant free carried interest plus additional black economic empowerment requirements effectively halt the proposed exploitation of the country's abundant potential, as investors are hesitant to sign deals in a sector that faces nationalisation.

Finally, a Traditionalist government decides to invest about R1 trillion in six new nuclear power stations, as proposed in its updated 2016 Integrated Resource Plan, awarding the entire contract to Russia's Rosatom State Nuclear Energy Corporation. Most of the subcontract includes either significant shareholding from the ANC's in-house investment firm, Chancellor House, and Gupta-linked companies.[8] Shortly after stepping down, Zuma takes up residence in a luxurious *dacha* in Russia for ever-longer periods, fuelling suspicions that the Rosatom deal was influenced by considerations other than the demand for clean electricity.

The nuclear plan is given the green light despite the fact that South Africa's energy requirements under this lower-growth scenario are significantly less than in the other two. Growth rates, already negligible in 2016, average just 1,5 per cent a year over the time horizon to 2034.

Mandela Magic

Given the burden he has become to the ANC, the early departure of Jacob Zuma as president of both the ANC and South Africa could point the country towards the Mandela Magic scenario, if it is accompanied by a rapid transition to a new leadership dominated by a Reformist grouping.

This is an ANC that adopts a modernist policy agenda that seeks to reverse the decline in its urban support base. Part of such an agenda would entail the party turning its back on the extension of powers to traditional

TRADITIONALISTS	REFORMERS
• Rural, black nationalist • Socially conservative • Loyal to Jacob Zuma • Dominated by Zulu speakers • Centralised state • Redistributive policies and not constitutionalists ➤ Premier League, ANCYL, ANCWL and others	• Social democrats • Typically urban • Supported by born-free voters with jobs • Multi-ethnic • Mixed economy and inclusive economic growth ➤ Gauteng ANC and others **SHIFT VOTE TO A REFORMED ANC**

Figure 7: Shift vote in the Mandela Magic scenario
Source: Author

authorities, such as those contained in the Traditional Courts Bill (among others), which would go against the grain of the Traditionalist elite within the party, as well as segments of its large support base in KwaZulu-Natal.

As the name suggests, the Mandela Magic scenario has the greatest potential economic and developmental benefits for the country. It also sees the most positive election results for the ANC out of the three scenarios. Under Mandela Magic, support for the EFF eventually declines on the understanding that many EFF supporters' votes were actually a protest vote against the current leadership of the ANC.

In addition, ANC voters considering voting for the DA (particularly in Gauteng) may be persuaded to give the ANC the benefit of the doubt under a Reformist and revived commitment to leadership that echoes Mandela's vision of a rainbow nation. In fact, the ANC may even be able to retain a majority in Gauteng in 2019 under the Mandela Magic scenario. The crucial shift vote therefore moves back to the ANC (see Figure 7). This will bolster the support and influence of the Reformist grouping and the leadership of the ANC.

This scenario gains its impetus from the governing party's poor results in the August 2016 local government elections – a performance that emboldens the Reformers and takes the wind out of the sails of the Traditionalists, who are accused of being responsible for the poor election results. It is also driven by the distaste with which Zuma is viewed by many in the party. This scenario is based on the assumption that the ANC steadily moves away from its current rural support base, particularly in KwaZulu-Natal, and that the party modernises. But it will not be easy.

Implicit in the Mandela Magic scenario is the fact that a newly elected Reformist president of the ANC (likely to be Ramaphosa and with someone like Paul Mashatile as deputy – or the Reformist slate referred to in Chapter 3) becomes the president of South Africa shortly after the party's December 2017 conference, or earlier, and does not wait until the 2019 elections. Change will be meaningful only if it is substantive, however, implying that the Reformist grouping in the ANC is successful in wresting control of the organisation from the Traditionalists and implementing policies that break with the past, setting South Africa on a sustainable growth trajectory.

Key among the required measures is agreement among labour, business and government on a range of confidence-building measures and clear leadership. It requires the steady reversal of the powers, and separate legal system, that have been developing in rural areas and an end to much of South Africa's system of communal land tenure in favour of individual title.

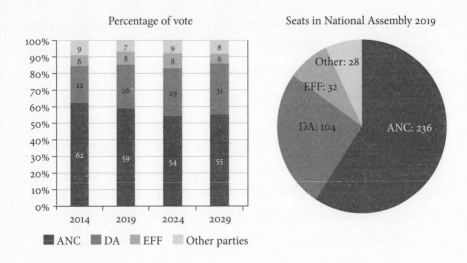

Figure 8: Mandela Magic election forecast
Source: Author

Under this scenario, South Africa does not invest in additional nuclear power, despite the much higher associated electricity demand from a more rapidly growing economy. South Africa instead imports large quantities of natural gas from neighbouring Mozambique and embarks on the aggressive exploitation of shale gas in the Karoo. It levies an excise tax on local gas production, which is invested in renewable-energy production (wind and solar), and invests heavily in developing a smart electricity grid.[9]

Gas imports, fracking and renewables collectively relieve the energy constraints on growth, although coal still remains by far the largest source of electricity generation for the growing South African economy, with all its attendant challenges.

Improved government effectiveness helps in various sectors, and by 2034 the average life expectancy of South Africans in Mandela Magic is more than a year higher than is the case in the other two scenarios. The opportunities for change in rural South Africa are most dramatic of all, since communal land tenure is steadily replaced by individual freehold title and the country moves from a pre-industrial system of tribal authority in the former homelands to a democratic system of elected local government and respect for the Constitution and Bill of Rights.

Growth in savings further boosts investment and fuels economic growth. The larger economy that ensues in the Mandela Magic scenario allows the government to collect R4 175 billion more in tax in the period 2017 to 2034 than is the case with Bafana Bafana, and R6 131 billion more than in the Nation Divided scenario.

With its largest economy firing on all cylinders, the Southern African Development Community (SADC) grows even faster as the good neighbourhood effect has a positive impact on the region. South Africa retains its position as the major gateway into southern Africa, an attractive investment destination that is open for business, and a safe and attractive tourist hub.

The dynamic, growing South African economy supports the development of a coherent and strategic foreign policy that is aligned to domestic interests. The South African Development Partnership Agency, South Africa's vehicle through which it provides development assistance to other African countries, employs trade specialists to open up opportunities for South African businesses and strengthen South Africa's imprint in terms of peacebuilding on the continent.

As a successful growth economy, South Africa leads in Africa on global governance reforms, and is able to push for an Africa-friendly agenda. It capitalises on its unique vantage point of access, becoming a facilitator for partnerships on the continent, and between Africa, the BRICS nations and the G20.

Mandela Magic will not be smooth sailing all the way, however. The

ANC will face internal resistance from those who lose their power and ability to access resources. Factions within the SACP and COSATU will rebel against the party's more social democratic policies.

The most dogged resistance, however, will come from traditional authorities, chiefs and royalty, who keep millions of South Africans in the former homelands hostage to their collectivist authority. Under Zuma, the government has steadily given more powers to such leaders, undermined the legal rights of women in rural communities and created a segregated judicial system that often falls foul of the Constitution and Bill of Rights. Funds given to these authorities have regularly increased ahead of elections.

All of this will have to change if the Reformers wish to place the ANC on a different trajectory.

The impact of the downgrade

In March 2017, the government scored a spectacular own goal when, after a dramatic late-night Cabinet reshuffle that saw Finance Minister Pravin Gordhan and his deputy's being fired, two agencies downgraded the country to sub-investment status. South Africa now joins countries like Russia, Brazil and Nigeria, which have all suffered a similar fate. With this decision, which was the sole prerogative of the President of South Africa, Zuma brought his efforts at state capture and the undermining of responsible fiscal management to its miserable conclusion.

The ability of the country to regain investment grade after a downgrade depends on the quality of leadership that is at the national helm. For example, when South Africa defaulted on its debt in 1985 after PW Botha's 'crossing the Rubicon' speech, it managed to recover only after seven years. The subsequent financial pressure played a large role in forcing the historic settlement between the National Party and the ANC.

The impact this time around is likely to be less serious, since South Africa has limited foreign debt. The world is also flush with liquidity, sentiments towards emerging markets are positive, commodity prices have rebounded and, domestically, the current-account deficit has shrunk in recent months. Other potential sources of finance, such as the New Development Bank (the BRICS bank), could help offset the impact of borrowing from the IMF and others.

In the months leading up to the April announcements of the downgrade, markets had already factored in much of the impact of a foreign-debt downgrade, but not yet that of the impact on the downgrade of South Africa's domestic debt which is only expected later in 2017. In fact, 'South African government bond yields have been priced similarly to the likes of Brazil and Russia for the best part of a year', notes Adrian Saville from the Gordon Institute of Business Leadership.[10]

All three scenarios include the impact of a loss of South Africa's investor-grade ratings in 2017 but the time spent in junk status differs. The downgrade has the following impact on the size of the economy by 2034:

❏ Bafana Bafana – in this scenario South Africa regains its investment grading in 2024, i.e. after seven years, and the result is an economy that is R1 375 billion smaller in 2034 than it otherwise would have been;

❏ Nation Divided – in this scenario South Africa regains its investment grading only in 2029 (i.e. after 12 years) and the result is an economy that is R327 billion smaller in 2034 than it otherwise would have been. The smaller amount compared to Bafana Bafana is because the economy generally grows more slowly over the entire forecast horizon. The longer time period in the Nation Divided scenario is a function of the continued efforts by a populist-inclined government to live beyond its means.

❑ Mandela Magic – in this scenario South Africa regains its investment grading in 2020 (i.e. the year after the election of a reformist slate in the ANC in 2019). The result is an economy that is R63 billion smaller in 2034 than it otherwise would have been.[11]

Although more than 90 per cent of South Africa's government debt – roughly R1,3 trillion – is denominated in rands, foreigners own 38 per cent of that debt. Of this, about a quarter tracks the Citibank World Investment Grade Bond Index (WGBI). When local debt is downgraded, the South African Government Bond Index is removed from the WGBI, which, in turn, triggers the forced selling of South African bonds – estimated at about R120 billion. Removal from the WGBI signifies that professional investors, such as hedge funds, pension funds and asset managers, are prevented (by policy) from investing in the country. The results raise borrowing costs, weaken the rand and increase inflation.[12]

In the February 2017 budget review (before the downgrade), South Africa planned to issue R220 billion of debt in the financial year starting 1 April 2017. Of that, R167 billion would be to fund the deficit and the remaining R54 billion would be to roll over debt that matures in the current financial year. These amounts now have to be increased substantially and the new finance minister, Malusi Gigaba, will have to cut expenditure elsewhere to do this and probably also raise taxes. In economic-speak, 'to stick to the original budget deficit and debt sustainability targets [set by Gordhan], the fiscal consolidation measures already in place will have to become even more aggressive'.[13]

This has the effect of closing off a large source of cheaper financing and makes the country more reliant on international financial institutions and hedge funds for support – each coming with its own set of risks. The international financial institutions will lend to South Africa only on stringent conditions (known in the past as structural adjust-ment programmes), while hedge funds are at the mercy of volatile global markets and associated machinations.

Accessing capital at a reasonable cost is indispensable for South Africa, a country with an exceptionally low national savings rate. Relegation to sub-investment status on the international markets would both increase borrowing costs and dampen growth. Increased borrowing costs would put pressure on government funding for its large welfare commitments and its bloated public service, thereby reducing funds available for investment in infrastructure, healthcare, education and other factors that drive long-term growth, such as electricity and water provision. These factors combine to reduce growth.

Given the country's low levels of savings, respected economist Iraj Abedian is of the view that South Africa cannot grow its economy beyond 1,5 per cent on a sustainable basis without access to global capital markets.[14]

Despite having done poorly during the 2016 local elections and with the ongoing negative impact of President Zuma on his party's prospects, it is unlikely (but not impossible) that the ANC would drop below 50 per cent during the national elections in 2019 without a split in the party – the Nation Divided scenario.

The more likely outcome is that the ANC holds together, resulting in a combined Reformist–Traditionalist slate that is elected in December 2017 and is able to maintain party cohesion (the Bafana Bafana mud-dling along scenario) during the 2019 elections and thereafter.

Once the ANC loses South Africa's economic heartland of Gauteng, it will find itself essentially a rural party, and its future support could slip quite dramatically, particularly if the relatively higher decline in

ANC turnout in rural provinces (as opposed to more urban provinces) continues.[15] Regaining momentum in urban areas, such as Gauteng, will require a Reformist-led ANC.

For its part, if the DA does not win Gauteng during the 2024 elections with an outright majority, the party will most likely have plateaued in terms of its electorate support at that point and will have to accept a future as a desirable coalition party, but not as a government-in-waiting. This is, however, only likely to become clear during the 2021 local elections and would probably mean the end of the leadership of Mmusi Maimane, a politician who has repositioned the DA as a substantively non-racial party.

Concerns about party cohesion are not limited to the ANC. Of the three main parties, the EFF is most at risk from a collapse in support because it is young party that lacks structures and systems, and because of the extent to which its fortunes depend on its charismatic leader, Julius Malema. The EFF did poorly during the 2016 local elections compared to its own (and expert) predictions, and it may well be closer to its ceiling than many believe.

Populists seldom present an alternative policy agenda that maps out their vision of the future, and the EFF is no different. Most important for the EFF is the clear desire by its leader to return to the ANC fold, either in a senior position, in an alliance or through a full merger.

There are, of course, many variants on these prospects as South Africa heads into uncharted 'big alliance' politics. Future prospects of alliances will also test the cohesion of the DA, with potentially far-reaching results. These prospects will depend largely on whether the DA is able to deliver on its promise of cleaner, more efficient government in those metros where it took charge in 2016. The party did better than expected during these local elections but its hold on those metros is tenuously based on alliances with a number of smaller parties. It also depends on the outcome of the disciplinary process instituted against former leader Helen Zille (and Western Cape premier) because of a number of contentious tweets on colonialism that she made during a trip to Singapore earlier in the year.

Despite the potential disruptions within the DA and the EFF, it is the developments within the ruling party that will be key to the outlook for South Africa through to 2024, and that will be likely to continue to influence developments to 2034. It is the dynamics between the Reformists and the Traditionalists within the ANC that will determine whether the country can be characterised as business as usual (Bafana Bafana), worse off (Nation Divided) or markedly improved (Mandela Magic).

The next chapter reviews the long-term impact of each of these three scenarios in terms of human and development outcomes.

CHAPTER 5

Economic and human-development impacts of the scenarios

Now, here, you see, it takes all the running you can do, to keep
in the same place. If you want to get somewhere else, you must
run at least twice as fast as that!

– Lewis Carroll, *Alice's Adventures in Wonderland*

This chapter compares the impact of the three political scenarios, Bafana Bafana, Nation Divided and Mandela Magic, in terms of economics, levels of income, changes in poverty levels and other indicators. The forecasting system used for the scenarios (International Futures, or IFs) is known, in the jargon of the modelling world, as an integrated assessment model.

Its 12 submodules (demographics, economics, education, health, environment, energy, infrastructure, technology, agriculture, governance, government finance and international politics) are dynamically connected. This means that a change in one variable, such as improving primary school intake rates, leads to changes across all other systems over time, such as positive adjustments in levels of national income and reductions in fertility rates.

Originally developed for educational purposes, the IFs model is probably the most sophisticated and comprehensive forecasting tool available in the public domain. Working with our partners in Denver, the African Futures and Innovation programme at the ISS has used IFs for various forecasts, including the potential for African countries to meet many of the UN's 17 Sustainable Development Goals to 2030, including the global poverty target, and targets relating to healthcare and the provision of water and sanitation. After a recent visit by a delegation to Denver, the Parliament of South Africa announced that it was working on a partnership agreement with the Pardee Center aimed at enhancing its long-range strategic planning.[1]

The IFs forecasting system is large. It contains 3 618 data series covering a huge number of variables, from primary school intake rates to the amount of tarred roads per country. It covers historical data for 186 countries, generally going back to 1960.[2] The forecasts are initialised from the historical data in the model (which is constantly being updated) and then dynamically extended into the future based on relationships drawn from academic literature, algebraic formulations derived from historical precedent and comparisons with the situation in other countries at similar levels of development.

For example, the population forecast within IFs initialises from the 2014 medium-term population figures of the UNDP, but the forecast is endogenously determined by the impact of births and deaths, and migration rates (so-called primary drivers). Births, deaths and migration are, in turn, determined by a number of secondary drivers, such as contraception use, levels of female education, smoking, conflict and income.[3]

No software can predict the future. The tools used in forecasting are, at best, aids to understanding likely future developments. Models are, by definition, simplified representations of reality, and the forecasts here are a best effort at framing that future. Nevertheless, thinking systematically about the future, with the assistance of quantitative models, allows one to explore the likely impact of particular policies or decisions, making it possible to compare and evaluate, in this instance, the potential implications of the political choices that South Africans will make in the next few years.

The general point of departure in most forecasts, including in the National Development Plan, is first to get the population forecast right, as many other aspects (such as income levels) are closely connected with population.

The impact of a larger population

It is already evident that the population forecasts that were done for South Africa's National Development Plan are likely to have been underestimates. For example, its forecast was that South Africa would have a population of 58,5 million by 2030, but South Africa will probably have a larger number of people than that by 2022.

In hindsight, the most realistic population forecast in the National Development Plan is what Trevor Manuel and his colleagues refer to as the 'migration shock' scenario, which forecasts the population to be 61,5 million by 2030.[4] A more realistic expectation would be a 2030 population of 62,7 million people, growing to around 67 million by 2040. More people would need access to education and other services, but, at the same time, a larger population also means a larger economy.

The larger population is a function of an expected continued modest rate of inward migration (i.e. people migrating to South Africa, mostly from other countries in the region) because South Africa's total fertility rates (the average number of children per childbearing female) are expected to drop to below replacement level in 2024. It is, of course, always possible that rising xenophobia could dampen inward migration, which is the largest driver of the larger population size forecast in this book.

Using IFs, it would appear that South Africa will have a population of 64,5 million by 2034. Inward migration is likely to continue, driven by the large gap between income levels in South Africa and those of its neighbours. Figure 9 shows a history and forecast of the South African population by age cohort from 1990 to 2034.

The composition of South Africa's population tells an important story about growth and stability. For example, South Africa's working-age population (people between the ages of 15 and 64) currently forms 66 per cent of the total population; this segment will slowly increase, to eventually peak in 2042 at 69 per cent and then decline after that. In 2016, for example, the working-age population of South Africa increased by 489 000 from the previous year and it will continue to grow annually for many years to come.[5]

The average size of the rest of Africa's working-age population is much lower, at only 55 per cent, meaning that South Africa has a significantly larger worker population compared to the number of dependants. That means that South Africa will remain in this sweet spot for some years to come, although, when comparing the size of South Africa's working-age population with the average for upper-middle-income countries, we are about 4 per cent below the average.

There is a strong correlation between the size of the working-age population (as opposed to rest of the population, i.e. dependants, consisting of children and the elderly) and economic growth. The larger the proportion of the working-age population, the more rapid a country's economic growth. A 2015 report published by the McKinsey Global Institute reveals that increases in the labour force have accounted for more than half of global growth over the past 50 years.[6] Therefore, the fact that South Africa is growing more slowly than other upper-middle-income countries may partly be due to our slightly smaller worker age, but it does not explain why we are growing so much more slowly than the rest of Africa – actually quite the contrary.

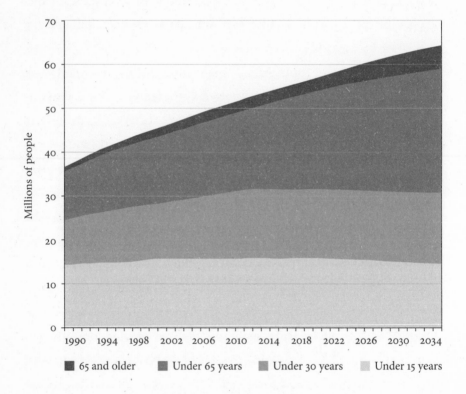

Figure 9: South Africa's population by age cohorts, history and forecast
Source: IFs v 7.28, forecast initialised from UNPD medium-fertility variant

The problem, however, is that a large proportion of the South African working-age population is unemployed. The International Labour Organization estimates that youth unemployment (i.e. those who are unemployed and aged between 15 and 24) in South Africa is 52 per cent – more than four times the rate for the rest of sub-Saharan Africa.[7] Recent publications by Statistics South Africa (Stats SA) confirm these alarming findings.[8] This grouping has not benefited sufficiently from economic growth. As a result, the absolute number of unemployed is growing – although it is important to recognise that employment is also growing in absolute numbers.[9]

A larger population translates into a larger economy, although not necessarily into higher levels of average income per person, because the larger cake has to be shared among more people. A larger working-age population should also raise total economic productivity. An increase in the pool of workers relative to dependants tends to increase specialisation, and provides thicker markets and greater potential for knowledge spillovers. South Africa is therefore fortunate as regards the optimal size of its working population compared with much of the rest of Africa.

That said, it is well known that many of South Africa's workforce lack key skills needed for a relatively sophisticated economy, owing to poor education; they are also comparatively in poor health, largely as a result of the double disease burden of HIV/AIDS and tuberculosis.

However, compared to a country such as Tanzania (a low-income country), which has a much younger but less educated population, South Africa (an upper-middle-income country) does very well. In 2017, 83 per cent of adult South Africans had completed primary education compared to 70 per cent in Tanzania. By 2034 the figures would be 90 per cent and 80 per cent. However, whereas 28 per cent of adult South Africans have completed secondary education, in 2016, the figure for Tanzania is only 4 per cent. By 2034 the figures will be 41 per cent in South Africa and 13 per cent in Tanzania. South Africa is in a much better position for the future.

A second consideration relates to the size of South Africa's youth bulge (ages 15 to 29) – a group that has been continually in the news because of the #FeesMustFall campaign. The size of South Africa's youth bulge as a proportion of the total population peaked in 2010/11 and is steadily declining.[10] A large youth bulge, evident in much of the rest of sub-Saharan Africa, is generally associated with higher levels of social turbulence, including violence. Or, to put this a different way, the higher the median age of a population (South Africa is currently at 26 years), the more stable a country tends to be. The median age is the point at which half the population is older and half younger. Statistically, once the median age is more than 26,3 years, countries tend to have a higher annual probability of maintaining their democratic status.[11]

Low-income countries in Africa have a median age of around 18. Based on population structure, it would be safe to forecast, therefore, that many African countries will continue to face significant levels of social turbulence in the years that lie ahead, whereas this should diminish in South Africa. Older people (and older societies) tend to be less violent.

Economic growth and size of the economy

Economic growth does not in itself lead to inclusive development outcomes, because growth generally increases inequality, but, without economic growth, development can occur only at the expense of one group or class over another. With a growing population in South Africa, much more rapid economic growth is a necessary, if insufficient, condition for improving human well-being and a good starting point for comparing the impact of the three scenarios.

The average growth rate from 2017 to 2034 under the most optimistic scenario, Mandela Magic, is 3,3 per cent; in the Bafana Bafana scenario it is 2,3 per cent; and in Nation Divided 1,5 per cent. These are all significantly below the 5,4 per cent average growth rate target to 2030 contained in the National Development Plan.

Even in the most positive scenario, South Africa grows around two percentage points below the average forecast for the 51 upper-middle-income countries globally. In the Mandela Magic scenario, South Africa catches up with the average growth rate for these countries by 2031 and then grows faster than the average forecast. This reflects the potential for more rapid growth in South Africa, in part due to investments made in healthcare, education and other areas since 1994.

Collectively, the improvements modelled under Mandela Magic would not see South Africa graduate from its current upper-middle-income status to high-income status in the next few decades. For that to happen, the country needs to grow much more rapidly.

The initial low-growth results are in line with the expectation by others that South Africa will achieve only modest GDP growth for several years to come. After zero growth in 2016, the IMF January 2017 forecast, for example, was for 0,8 per cent growth in 2017; 1,6 per cent in 2018; and an average of 2,2 per cent for the three years 2019 to 2021.[12] These forecasts will all be revised downward when the IMF releases its next forecast to factor in the impact of the March 2017 Cabinet reshuffle.

The size of the South African economy differs greatly when comparing the three scenarios (see Table 2). Compared to its size in 2016, by 2034 the economy could be 81 percentage points larger (in Mandela Magic), 49 percentage points larger (Bafana Bafana) or just 31 percentage points larger (Nation Divided). None of these figures are particularly impressive, however, with average incomes increasing by just R40 900, R22 200 or R10 500 per person over the intervening 18 years. The average income increase for upper-middle-income countries globally over the same period would be R81 250 – double the improvements under South Africa's best-case Mandela Magic scenario.

When compared with other upper-middle-income countries, South Africa will lose ground in all scenarios, even in Mandela Magic. In the Bafana Bafana and Nation Divided scenarios, South Africa falls from being the eighth-largest upper-middle-income economy globally to the eleventh largest, and to the ninth-largest in the Mandela Magic scenario. Whereas, in 2016, the South African economy is 29th in size globally, by 2034 (in the Bafana Bafana mediocre-growth scenario), it will be ranked 33rd in the world, having been overtaken by United Arab Emirates, Thailand, Colombia and Malaysia.

It is important to underline that things get better for South Africans under all three scenarios, but that we progress more slowly than our peers, generally dropping behind progress elsewhere.

Table 2: Scenario comparisons

	Nation Divided	Bafana Bafana	Mandela Magic
Average growth rate 2017–2034	1,5%	2,3%	3,3%
2034 size of economy in market exchange rates (MER)	R5 505 billion	R6 280 billion	R7 593 billion
Increase in size of economy, 2016 to 2034	31%	49%	81%
Average income levels by 2034 (in purchasing power parity)	R125 230	R136 930	R155 650
Increase in income since 2016	9%	19%	36%

Source: IFs v 7.28, forecast initialised from IMF World Economic Outlook 2016 and UNPD 2016 medium-fertility variant

South Africa runs a regular negative trade balance, in that the value of imports exceeds that of exports when the economy expands, and it will experience a ballooning from this trade deficit, requiring reliance on foreign investments and borrowing to offset the difference. In line with its counter-cyclical approach to fiscal management, the South African Reserve Bank inevitably increases interest rates to cool the economy, and the result is a cycle of boom and bust. This pattern is unlikely to change under the three scenarios unless we are able to save much more and to consistently attract foreign direct investment.

Gauteng and the Western Cape have historically posted the highest average rates of economic growth, while rural provinces, such as the Northern Cape and North West, grow much more slowly. These trends are also likely to continue, although government has more leeway in the Mandela Magic scenario to shift resources from urban to more rural provinces.

Human development

The UN Development Programme's Human Development Index (HDI) is a composite index of life expectancy, education and income. The index is used to categorise countries into four tiers of human development – very high, high, medium and low.

South Africa is globally ranked 87th in terms of average levels of income; but it is ranked much lower, at 116th, on the HDI (placing the country in the medium level of human development).[13] This is because of South Africa's high levels of inequality and poor life expectancy due to HIV/AIDS compared with other countries at similar average income levels.

South Africa registers some improvements in the composite HDI under all three scenarios, although most rapidly under the Mandela Magic scenario. By 2034 South Africa could improve its HDI rating by 8 percentage points in the Mandela Magic scenario – slightly more rapidly than the expected increase in the global average. The large mismatch between average levels of income and human development reflects the duality of South African society, politics and the economy.

The infant mortality rate (defined as the number of deaths per 1 000 live births) is considered such a good proxy for the general state of governance in society that it is often used in models to forecast political instability.[14] In 2015, South Africa experienced around 34 infant deaths for every 1 000 live births, the same as Yemen, Uzbekistan and Eritrea, and slightly worse than Namibia and the Republic of Congo. We find ourselves in the bottom third globally, and, although rates of infant mortality are significantly better than in the Democratic Republic of Congo (DRC), at 75 per 1 000, Central African Republic (92) and Angola (96), we are not doing very well nevertheless.

In fact, 11 African countries do better than South Africa in this measurement, including Madagascar, Botswana, Namibia, Mauritius and the Seychelles. From a 1992 figure of 50,5 deaths per 1 000 live births, the previous steady downward trend was interrupted by the onset of the HIV/ AIDS pandemic, which has lasted for more than a decade (and which was exacerbated by Thabo Mbeki's denialist stance on AIDS), before resuming its downward trend.

The reason for South Africa's high infant mortality rate (as well as the high rate of mortality among children under five) is because of a high prevalence of communicable disease early in life. Young children in South Africa die from communicable diseases, such as respiratory infections, AIDS and diarrhoeal disease, flu, measles and others. Deaths from respiratory infections are often the result of the widespread use of traditional cooking stoves and poor indoor ventilation, and deaths from diarrhoea are the result of poor provision of clean water and healthful sanitation. These are all the legacies of apartheid, during which little investment was made in the provision of basic services for a large portion of South Africans. It will take time to reverse – despite the substantial progress that has already been made since 1994.

By 2034 South Africa could record an infant mortality rate of either 24 deaths per 1 000 live births (in Mandela Magic) or 28 (in Nation Divided). In the best of worlds, we would then have infant mortality rates comparable to those of Morocco today, which is a remarkably poor situation for a country that has much higher levels of income and education than its North African counterpart.

Poverty and inequality

In the poorest 20 per cent of households (which, combined, total 16,3 million people), only one in three households has a household member with a job. The average monthly income in this group is only R1 671, or R323 per person.[15]

The picture is only slightly better for the 12,9 million people in the 20 to 40 per cent range of households defined by income, where average household income is R3 125 per month, or R773 per person, and one-third of all households have no employed household members.

The story of household income is also one of massive income inequality. While 16,3 million people live in the poorest 20 per cent, 6,5 million people live in the richest 80 to 100 per cent. People in the poorest households survive on R323 per month, while in the richest households people earn R12 509.

Since 1994 the response of the South African government to underdevelopment, poverty and inequality among the majority poor black population occurred in two broad and overlapping phases. In the early 1990s, the state provided housing, potable water, electricity and immunisation coverage to most households, with some free services.

Improvements in these areas were rapid and demonstrable, although accompanied by significant wastage, and many challenges remain. For example, from 1994 to 2015 the government provided an estimated 3,7 million houses and serviced sites – but the housing backlog has increased in absolute numbers, and the number of informal settlements has gone up significantly.[16] We have to run very hard just to remain in the same spot.

The second phase began in the late 1990s with the provision of various cash grants, such as the Child Support Grant. Whereas, in 1994 4 million South Africans received a social grant, the number is now more than 17 million, and this is expected to increase to 18,1 million by 2020. In its 2017/18 budget year, the government allocated R151,6 billion to social grants – a huge amount by any standard. Social grants of some form or other are paid to a very large proportion – 45,5 per cent – of South African households.[17]

The Treasury has indicated that the current grant programme will be sustainable only if there is economic growth of 3 per cent per annum or more – which is only achievable in the Mandela Magic scenario. Below that rate of growth, South Africa could run out of the fiscal space to continue with its current efforts at poverty alleviation.[18]

During 2017 social-grant payments were repeatedly in the news as government became embroiled in a scandal that was set to bungle this important poverty-alleviation intervention. Fraud has been such a big problem in the payment of grants that the South African Social Security Agency (SASSA), which is responsible for this function, requires every grant recipient to be validated through a biometric system to prove that he or she is alive. In 2012, SASSA signed a contract with Cash Paymaster Services (CPS), which included in its service terms such a biometric identification system. After a long court battle brought by the losing bidder, AllPay, the Constitutional Court ruled in 2013 that the CPS contract was irregular and had to be set aside, although this finding was suspended so that the social grants could be paid until March 2017. In 2014, the court had ruled that CPS had no right to benefit from an unlawful contract, although it could cover costs, and ordered the company to file audited statements of expenses incurred, income received and net profit earned under the contract. Various calculations have subsequently surfaced regarding the profit that CPS makes, as well as its business model, which includes selling financial services to grant recipients, such as micro loans, life insurance and electricity.

Meanwhile, a December 2014 report from the Ministerial Advisory Committee recommended that SASSA should build its own payment system. Instead of allowing SASSA to proceed, Minister Bathabile Dlamini promptly set up an own process (at a cost of R45 million) that bypassed SASSA's own implementation processes. The result was to effectively sabotage any solution developed by SASSA and to empower CPS. By March 2017, SASSA had made no progress, admitting in April 2016, a year before the contract ran out, that it would not be able to take over the payment of social grants. During subsequent Constitutional Court hearings, minister Dlamini claimed to have been informed of this only six months later.

In October 2016, Chief Justice Mogoeng Mogoeng asked how this level of incompetence had been reached, and in March 2017 the Constitutional Court ruled that it had no choice but to extend the contract with CPS for 12 months while a new tender process unfolded. The court also ruled that the minister bore the primary responsibility for ensuring that SASSA indeed paid out social grants. In successive appearances before Parliament, Dlamini first indicated that SASSA would need R6 billion and five years to take over the grant-payment system and then that it could do it by November 2017.[19]

Since Dlamini is the head of the ANC Women's League and, in that capacity, a major supporter of Nkosazana Dlamini-Zuma in her quest to become president, she remained in her position when Zuma announced his March 2017 Cabinet reshuffle. In the current factionalised ANC, politics and loyalty trump competence – even when it comes to the livelihoods of millions of poor South Africans.

The social-grants debacle, including the relationship between Dlamini and CPS, has now been referred to the Public Protector, Busisiwe Mkhwebane.

One of the areas where the three scenarios most noticeably shift circumstances in South Africa is in their effect on access to the provision of services. In Bafana Bafana, South Africa manages to steadily improve rural access to electricity, in spite of population growth, from 69 per cent in 2016 to 77 per cent by 2034. Under Mandela Magic, the figure goes up to 86 per cent. The governance difficulties of Nation Divided persist, and South Africa achieves just 75 per cent rural access to electricity by 2034 in that scenario.

Differences in forecasted effects on other services are more modest, with access to safe sanitation improving from 66 per cent in 2016 to 73 per cent by 2035 in Nation Divided, and to 75 per cent in Mandela Magic. Access to piped water improves from 73 per cent in 2016 to 80 per cent (Mandela Magic), 79 per cent (Bafana Bafana) and 78 per cent (Nation Divided). Therefore, things get better under all scenarios but at different rates.

Under the most positive scenario, where a reformist ANC is able to rescue the party, and eventually the country, from its current malaise, South Africa makes steady progress, but it is clear that, even under Mandela Magic, ending poverty and reducing inequality will take several generations and a concerted effort in which resources are allocated to efforts that can advantage poorer communities. Although a regenerated ANC is the most direct pathway to the Mandela Magic scenario, it is also the most unlikely scenario of the three. Much more likely is the Bafana Bafana 'more-of-the-same'.

If the economy is unable to grow, it will increase competition for a slice of the South African cake, which has to be shared among many competing priorities, as well as the inevitable urge to opt for redistributive policies – taking from those who have, and redistributing wealth to the poor and needy. Unfortunately, the poor and needy in South Africa are likely to be frustrated by the ability of well-connected individuals to leverage political influence, particularly in the sphere of public tenders – all in the purported interests of black economic empowerment.

Since coming to power in 1994, the ANC-led government has made a large dent in the terrible legacy of apartheid. Progress can be seen in numerous areas, although it has been inconsistent. South Africa has experienced marked declines in multidimensional poverty and significant improvements in ownership of, or access to, private assets, such as a stove, a fridge, a television, a vehicle, and so on.[20] Many of these gains have been thanks to the ANC's commitment to roll out various services and, at least until 2008, steady, if unspectacular, economic growth.

However, there are many obvious things that the ANC is getting wrong, such as insufficient support for business, the burden of black economic empowerment, the appalling wastage and corruption in state-owned enterprises – not to mention keeping in power a president who is prepared to help his friends, family and loyalists, but unable to provide the leadership the country needs.

Our future is wholly dependent on how we will address four interlinked challenges: inequality, education, unemployment and poor governance. This is the theme of the next chapter.

CHAPTER 6

Our four greatest challenges

*From an analyst's perspective, it seems foolish for the ANC
government not to appreciate that its political mandate rested
in large part on its economic performance.*

– Frans Cronje[1]

Zuma assumed office as president during a global recession, when the
tailwind of economic growth that had bolstered South Africa's economy
under Mandela and Mbeki turned into an unrelenting headwind. The
South African economy shed 1,1 million jobs in the two years after the
recession hit in the fourth quarter of 2008. It took the economy nearly
five years to regain those lost jobs and get back to pre-recession employment levels.

And then South Africa experienced one of the worst droughts in
several decades in 2016, attributed to the global climatic phenomenon El
Niño. As a result, the entire agricultural sector contracted, exports plum-
meted and food imports rose sharply. The drought shaved off at least
0,2 per cent of growth compared to the previous year. The World Bank
estimated that about 50 000 more South Africans slipped into poverty
as a result of the drought, with households that depend on agriculture

carrying most of the burden, particularly in Mpumalanga, Limpopo, the Eastern Cape, the Northern Cape and North West.

Despite these external challenges, most analysis, such as works by Adriaan Basson[2] and Richard Calland,[3] emphasises that South Africa's poor growth, lack of employment creation, continued levels of poverty and poor governance are largely of its own making: the poor leadership, incompetence and corruption that have become the hallmarks of the Zuma administration. This sentiment is also shared by Susan Booysen in her 2015 study, *Dominance and Decline: The ANC in the Time of Zuma*, and by the government's own social-science body, the Human Sciences Research Council, which subtitled its 2016 annual report with the question 'who is in charge?'[4]

All these works warn of the challenges evident in the current ANC, which, in the words of Adam Habib, has become 'a grubby instrument of enrichment that speaks the language of empowerment and democracy, while its leadership and cadres plunder the nation's resources and undermine both the judiciary and the media – the former because it may be used to hold various actors to account, and the latter for having the temerity to broadcast the drama.'[5]

In his 2014 study of the reason for these developments, *What's Gone Wrong? On the Brink of a Failed State*, Alex Boraine argues cogently, in my view, that the underlying reason for these developments is that the ANC has transplanted its exile culture into the new South Africa.[6] All the negative aspects of an organisation that had existed in the shadows during the exile years are apparent, he writes – the stifling bureaucracy, poor administration, incorrect choices, deployment that places loyalty above competence, political incoherence and the high life enjoyed by some senior leaders. The ANC, he argues, is more concerned with the party than with the country.

That this is germane is evident from even a cursory reading of books from inside the ANC administration, such as that by Frank Chikane, *The Things that Could Not be Said*,[7] which lays bare the paranoia that permeated the Mbeki administration. My own experiences in engaging with the exile leadership, for whom I have endless admiration, confirm this interpretation; despite the fact that the vast majority are urbane, compassionate and thinking people, they cannot escape a worldview determined by conspiracy and shadows.

Under Mandela, Mbeki and Zuma, South African social policy has primarily focused on pulling poor citizens out of absolute poverty rather than on seeking to increase employment or pursuing growth. Employment and growth have been secondary concerns because the constraints of the Tripartite Alliance limited the ability of the ANC to pursue policies that would harm the interests of unionised workers or the egalitarianism that lies at the heart of the SACP's ideology. And South Africa's first democratic government cannot escape the fact that the poorest four income deciles (i.e. the bottom 40 per cent of income earners) for whom it had sought emancipation are predominantly black, unemployed and poor, often living in informal settlements and in the most terrible conditions.[8]

Poverty

Economic growth, I have argued, is a prerequisite for South Africa to progress, but it will not solve our problems. The ability to benefit from economic growth is significantly complicated by the fact that economic growth does not translate into reductions in poverty in countries with high inequality. In fact, as countries go up the income curve inequality generally increases. And the more free-market their policies and practices, the more rapidly inequality increases.

In fact, it is only government intervention that can constrain rising inequality. Trickle-down economics (the belief that the market should be left to its own devices and that income will automatically trickle down to the rest of us) only works in highly exceptional cases. Higher levels of income tend to accrue to those who already have some income and does not trickle down to poor people, even if the country manages to grow at much more rapid rates, such as those originally foreseen in the National Development Plan. It is for this reason that South Africa requires a capable interventionist state instead of a large, incapable, corrupt state.

The picture is very different when one looks at the progress that poor countries with low levels of inequality are able to make in reducing poverty, as is the current case with Ethiopia. My colleagues and I recently completed a large study on the future of Ethiopia to 2030 for the United States Agency for International Development. It is a country that I must have visited more than 50 times as part of work with the Organisation of African Unity, today the African Union.[9] Despite its manifold challenges, the development progress that Ethiopia has made over the past 20 years is astounding, such as reducing poverty by roughly 45 percentage points.

In Ethiopia (and it has also been the case in China), progress in poverty reduction was hugely facilitated by its low levels of inequality (and by the focused leadership of former prime minister Meles Zenawi). This is where trickle-down economics works – but only in these circumstances, for as incomes in Ethiopia (and China) have increased, inequality has also increased, which means that much greater government activism and intervention is required to maintain past rates of poverty reduction. South Africa therefore needs additional measures besides just economic growth to help alleviate the conditions for its large burden of poor people. If we leave it to market forces, the absolute number of very poor people in South Africa will increase.

Social grants were examined in the previous chapter, where I showed the extent to which state capture has come to play an important part in the allocation and management of tenders and the way in which government is bungling the process. Social grants play an important role as the source of income for low-income households, allowing otherwise destitute families to prioritise spending on the things that are most important for them – food, education, travel or medical costs. In fact, there is no other short- to medium-term measure that can deliver the same positive development impact on poverty reduction and improvements in livelihoods.

But, although social grants have been very successful in alleviating extreme poverty, they do little to shift inequality, since the amounts that poor people receive are often quite limited. Being in formal employment, on the other hand, allows for annual cost-of-living adjustments and the associated benefits that normally accompany such situations, but the obvious problem is that comparatively few people, particularly those in the lower-income categories, rely on wages as their main source of income. As explained in government's *Twenty-Year Review*, 'More than half of all households in the former homelands depend mostly on remittances or grants, compared with under a quarter in the rest of the country.'[10]

Also, the probability of being poor is linked to the age of the head of the household: households headed by younger people and children are significantly poorer. South Africa has a particularly large proportion of female- and child-headed households as a result of the impact of the HIV/AIDS pandemic. Female-headed households in South Africa are, on average, 4 per cent more likely to be poor than male-headed households. This is because more males than females are employed in the formal sector, and also because the median wage for females is only about 77 per cent of the male wage.[11] More females also tend to be employed in the informal sector, where levels of income are extremely low. As a result, poor females carry an extraordinary burden in South Africa.

Using the international income benchmark of USD1,90 per person per day in constant 2011 USD (roughly R17,80 today), 8,9 million South Africans were living in extreme poverty in 2016. Since South Africa is currently not growing, poverty rates are set to increase in 2018 and level off thereafter. The dire situation in which we find ourselves is evident in that the absolute number of people in extreme poverty will increase in all three of the scenarios analysed in this book – this despite the fact that both Mandela Magic and Nation Divided envisage a moderate increase in cash grants on top of the current expenditure. Although the proportion of extremely poor people comes down in the Mandela Magic scenario, as shown in Figure 10, by 2034 the numbers of extremely poor people will have increased to 11,2 million (Nation Divided), 10,8 million (Bafana Bafana) and 10,2 million (Mandela Magic) – out of a total population of 64,5 million.

The increased social-grant spend in the Nation Divided scenario is initially larger as a percentage of total government consumption (in line with the expectation that a more populist ANC will be prepared to spend more even without the means to do so), and this manages to contain further increases in levels of absolute poverty. Nevertheless, from 2024, the portion of poor people in South Africa again starts to increase and does so quite rapidly, as the economy grows more slowly in this scenario.

That said, even under the Mandela Magic scenario, the portion of extremely poor South Africans hardly shifts from the current rate of around 16 per cent – decreasing by less than one percentage point over 16 years. In the Nation Divided scenario, poverty initially declines but by 2034 the proportion of extremely poor people increases to around 17,4 per cent.

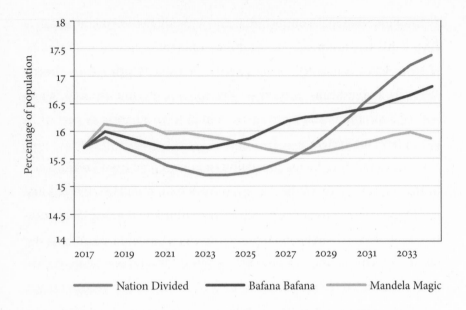

Figure 10: Extreme poverty in South Africa, percentage of population
Source: IFs v 7.78, data initialised from World Development Indicators

All of these figures should serve to underline the fact that South Africa's extremely high levels of inequality serve as a huge barrier to any effort to reduce poverty. One of the principal objectives of the National Development Plan was to reduce inequality by nine percentage points by 2030, as measured on the Gini index. (The Gini index represents the income distribution of a nation's population, ranging from theoretical complete equality, a score of 0, where everyone earns the same income, to complete inequality, a score of 100, where the entire national income goes to one person.)

None of the scenarios modelled for this book succeed in reducing inequality; in fact, inequality increases marginally under all three scenarios, in line with the global trend – between 2 and 3 percentage points. According to these forecasts, South Africa is likely to retain its position as the most unequal country globally, with all the attendant negative effects this has upon stability and development, followed by Namibia, Haiti and Botswana. This is despite the fact that South Africa already channels a significant portion of government revenue from richer to poorer households and from metropolitan to rural areas as part of its progressive tax system.

Gains made in reducing inequality can only come from creating jobs in the formal sector where wages are reviewed, annually adjusted and minimum conditions apply, paired with appropriate training and education as well as stringent efforts at the transfer of wealth (aka progressive tax and other policies). This requires a strong, developmental state, clear leadership and a determined effort to combat corruption and patronage, which are inevitably associated with such high levels of inequality.

One of the more recent debates concerning inequality is that of the minimum wage. Two days before his January 2017 state of the nation address, Zuma was able to deliver on a pledge made the previous year for a national minimum wage agreement of R20 per hour (or R3 500 a month for a 40-hour week) to be implemented from 1 May 2018.

The idea that minimum wages could be used as a stepping stone for enhanced productivity was first articulated by organised labour in 1994/95 as a means to force lower-wage, labour-intensive firms to move towards higher-wage, higher-productivity activities. The approach is informed by the view espoused by renowned Cambridge scholar Ha-Joon Chang and others that 'downward income redistribution can help growth, if done in the right way at the right time. For example, in an economic downturn … the best way to boost the economy is to redistribute wealth downward, as poor people tend to spend a higher proportion of their incomes.'[12]

There is, however, a huge difference between efforts at counter-cyclical policy and long-term approaches that can boost growth in productivity.

The intention to force firms to move into more capital- and skill-intensive activities through national minimum wage levels assumes that skills are commensurate, which is not the case in South Africa.

Much as I have deep empathy with poverty wages, the view that minimum wage levels will reduce unemployment in the South African context does not make sense. As noted left-wing labour expert Eddie Webster argues, 'It is time to confront the dilemma that for many a bad job is better than no job'.[13]

Education

One of the main factors driving structural poverty and inequality is the strong relationship between education levels and income. As a result of the priority given to the education of white children over many generations in South Africa, the earning potential of whites will continue to outstrip that of their black counterparts for many years unless much greater efforts are made, and even then improved education is a multi-generational challenge. There are no short cuts.

Efforts to transform economic ownership patterns without the new owners' having appropriate education and experience are punishing South Africa's government and private-sector effectiveness. There are measures to fast-track the speed of the transfer of ownership, but they should be steady and long term, rather than the current emphasis on creating a class of wealthy black industrialists overnight.

Thomas Piketty, the award-winning French economist who has looked at historical patterns of global inequality (as recounted in his 2014 best-seller, *Capital in the Twenty-First Century*), tells us that inequality largely arises from inherited wealth, and not from innovative and disruptive technology. Piketty punts a wealth tax (now also under examination in

South Africa), but acknowledges that education is the great leveller.

The relationship between income levels and education is strong. People with better education earn more money, but at the aggregated national level that relationship is contested by Chang, who argues that 'what really distinguishes the rich countries from the poorer ones is much less how well educated their individual citizens are than how well their citizens are organised into collective entities with high productivity – be that giant firms such Boeing ... or the smaller world-class firms of Switzerland. ... Development of such firms needs to be supported by a range of institutions that encourage investment and risk-taking – a trade regime that protects and nurtures ... a financial system that provides "patient capital" ... institutions that provide second chances ... public subsidies and regulation regarding R&D [research and development] and training ... '[14]

What Chang's analysis suggests is that even the narrow focus on comparing the education levels between racial groups (and hence the efforts to provide equality of opportunity) may be misplaced. Much more important is the ability of government and the private sector to create structured opportunities within which to harness productive enterprises and institutions.[15] And this requires agreement between labour, business and government about a desired developmental pathway. In my view, this approach is not possible amid the acrimonious labour relations that characterise South Africa. Without a clear agreement on where we are headed, business will not invest, labour will protest and government cannot regulate.

Clearly, if one takes a long-term perspective, improved levels of education lead to increased worker productivity, and hence to higher wages (better education also lowers fertility rates and increases life expectancy). However, those development benefits take a long time to materialise – at least two or three generations – and the relationship is more complex than it first appears.

The ANC post-apartheid administrations have been aware of the importance of education. It is envisaged in the Freedom Charter of 1955, the National Development Plan and virtually every other policy menu that has been offered by Mandela, Mbeki and Zuma to South Africans. And there has been good progress. The proportion of the black workforce with higher education almost doubled between 1995 and 2011, and the number of black people graduating from higher-education institutions every year now exceeds that of white people.[16] Similarly, over the same period, the numbers who completed secondary education more than tripled and there was a fourfold increase in the number who completed a bachelor's degree. Many of these graduates, however, cannot get a job. We should have made much more progress.

The problem is that the education sector has suffered from poor management, continual changes in policy and curricula, policy experimentation and political interference for two decades. These have had the combined effect of delaying improvements that should have been associated with the impressive budgets allocated to this sector.[17] We should be doing very well in class, but we are not. For example, the 2016 matric pass rate for government schools increased slightly to 72 per cent from the previous year, but, at the same time, 18 schools recorded a zero per cent pass rate. By comparison, the much smaller private schooling system, run by the Independent Examination Board, could not be more different, with a 98,7 per cent pass rate and more than 87 per cent university acceptance.[18]

What is going wrong in the state sector? A ministerial report published in May 2016 found 'widespread practices of improper and unfair influence affecting the outcomes of the appointment of educators', and that the 'current process for selecting candidates for appointment in the education sector is riddled with inconsistencies'. It concluded that 'where authority is weak, inefficient and dilatory, teacher unions [the South

African Democratic Teachers' Union, SADTU] move into the available spaces and determine policies, priorities and appointments, achieving undue influence over matters which primarily should be the responsibility of the Department [of Basic Education]'.[19]

The report followed widespread coverage of corruption and abuse of learners, including teachers paying union officials to appoint them to senior positions, and demands for sex in return for jobs. A January 2017 article in *The Economist* ('South Africa has one of the world's worst education systems') found that: 'A shocking 27% of pupils who have attended school for six years cannot read, compared with 4% in Tanzania and 19% in Zimbabwe. After five years of school about half cannot work out that 24 divided by three is eight. Only 37% of children starting school go on to pass the matriculation exam; just 4% earn a degree.'[20]

An education system can best be conceptualised as a pipeline. Children start at the beginning (pre-school, then primary school) and make it through each successive level in order to progress through the system and emerge, at the other end, with appropriate levels and types of education suited to the economic needs of the country.

The 2016 Community Survey results from Stats SA notes that 'significant progress has been made in the lower ages (5 to 9 years) with enrolment rates for five-year-olds having quadrupled'.[21] Furthermore, the number of people who indicated that they had no schooling declined from 3,7 million in 1996 to 2,3 million in 2016.

The problem is that the focus of government has been on quantity, not quality. Hence, the grade 12 pass rate has steadily improved year on year (it reached 78,2 per cent in 2013), but this has been on the back of a lowering of standards – to the extent that a grade 12 qualification has been diminished, with universities complaining about the need to lower standards and to provide bridging courses.[22]

Today, the primary-school completion rate for age-appropriate children in South Africa is 98 per cent (although only 83 per cent of South Africa's adult population have completed primary education). Under all three scenarios, South Africa achieves 100 per cent primary-school completion for age-appropriate children by 2021. However, by 2034 there is a 6 per cent difference in grade 12 completion rates for age appropriate learners when comparing the Nation Divided scenario with Mandela Magic, although progress in all scenarios from the current rate of 54 per cent (see Table 3).

Table 3: Education completion rates, by 2034

	Nation Divided	Bafana Bafana	Mandela Magic
Primary school completion rates by age-appropriate learners	100%	100%	100%
Lower secondary school completion rates by age-appropriate learners	76%	78%	81%
Grade 12 completion rates by age-appropriate learners	66%	69%	72%
Tertiary graduation rates of age-appropriate population	14%	16%	17%

Source: IFs v 7.28, historical data initialised from UNESCO

These forecasts do not take the quality of education into account, however – a problem that has been raised a number of times with regard to South Africa's education system.

Among its efforts to extract the maximum benefit for its members (i.e. teachers) at the inevitable cost of learners, SADTU has successfully lobbied for the cancellation of standardised tests, ensured that inspectors must give schools a year's notice before showing up, resisted efforts to set competency standards for teachers, is against merit-based pay and is opposed to a vetting process for teachers who mark grade 12 papers.

Six of the senior civil servants running education are SADTU members, a conflict of interest that has proven debilitating. Yet because SADTU is a powerful member of the ANC's alliance partner COSATU, nothing is done. We allow this abuse of political relations to the long-term peril of the education system.

The challenges in South Africa's education system stretch far beyond just schooling, however. They are also seen in the desire to pursue academic qualifications and the poor regard in which vocational training is held. If South Africa is to prosper, it needs a much greater focus on vocational education and training, as opposed to academic qualifications, with that parallel vocational stream beginning in secondary school. Vocational options need to be actively promoted in schools as a desirable and rewarding alternative career path.

Some progress has been made here. For example, in 2014 the Department of Higher Education and Training produced a White Paper for post-school education and training, outlining strategies that aim to achieve an integrated approach to post-secondary education, including vocational education training, within the next two decades. The White Paper envisions increasing enrolments at colleges from the current 710 500 to 2,5 million by 2030 to ease pressure on universities.

Yet, while spending on higher education and training is to grow at an average annual rate of 5,5 per cent to 2020, the allocation for Technical and Vocational Education and Training (TVET) colleges would grow at less than 2 per cent.[23] As with the Department of Defence following the 2015 Defence Review, the Cabinet apparently took decisions in education with huge financial implications without determining the costs. In a recent presentation to Parliament, the TVETC Governors' Council (which represents all 50 TVET colleges) was quite blunt in noting that colleges were so underfunded that 'it is a miracle that none have closed doors'.[24]

The department has belatedly recognised that the system that was in place – including the TVET institutions and the Sector Education and Training Authorities – was 'inadequate in quantity, diversity and … quality'.[25] In that process, technikons were replaced by universities of technology, but these all appear to shift towards the provision of degrees and diplomas, trying to move up the academic ladder, instead of focusing on their core vocational mandate. The TVET colleges are also struggling with a complex system where more than 20 separate Sector Education and Training Authorities are responsible for training in different sectors.[26]

According to *Business Day*, 'the average throughput rate in NCV [National Certificate Vocational] courses in 2013 ranged from a dismal 0,6% in civil engineering to 5,9% in tourism; the national certification rate was just 32,5% for first-year students and the dropout rate was 28,2% … 33 of every 100 students who enrolled for these courses passed their first year, 15 passed their second year and six graduated on schedule.'[27]

A key problem here is the lack of employer involvement in the vocational education system. This leads to a mismatch between skills that are in high demand in the workplace and those among the available workers, and there has also been poor progress in re-establishing a system of apprenticeships and traineeships. Thus, 'the government's most recent scarce-skills list, which the Department of Home Affairs uses to determine who gets work visas, includes carpenters, joiners, boiler makers and electricians – exactly the kind of skills expected from students attending vocational colleges'.[28]

Partly as a result of the country's poor education outcomes in terms of quality and skills acquisition, labour productivity has long been a source of concern to domestic and foreign investors. Although South Africa's per-unit labour productivity has steadily improved over the last decade (largely as a result of automation in production processes), nominal labour unit costs have risen at a faster rate and the value of productivity gains has not kept pace with the rising cost of the workforce.[29] Therefore, while employees have benefited from real improvements in wages, this has come at a cost to 'broader growth, investment and job creation'.[30] The result is a vicious cycle in which young people leave school without adequate numeracy and literacy skills, and employers reject high-potential youngsters because the school-leaving certificate is not an accurate indicator of ability or potential.

The importance of having a job

Appropriate education, as we have seen, is a prerequisite for a decent job, unless we are able to organise ourselves differently, as proposed by Ha-Joon Chang. Appropriate education does not necessarily mean academic education; it means education relevant to the job requirements – no more, no less.

Earlier, I made the point that only jobs in the formal sector can lift people out of poverty and reduce inequality. Decent work gives employees access to benefits such as annual salary increases and progress up the income ladder, allowing them to provide for their families, gain valuable professional experience and generally progress in society.

The problem is that the current South African economy does not allow this to happen. To generate more jobs, the economy needs to grow much more rapidly than is currently the case, particularly by encouraging the development of small and medium-sized businesses, which is where employment growth typically occurs.

But, instead of creating employment in small and medium-sized businesses in the formal sector, job creation has shifted to the informal sector. Year on year, from 2015 to 2016, the formal sector lost 113 000 jobs and the informal sector (non-agriculture) created 52 000 jobs where the compensation levels are typically survivalist.[31] Low or zero growth leads to people working in the less productive informal sector, as job-seekers struggle to survive and try to make ends meet. And the longer a person is without a job, the less chance that person will have of finding work, as the economy creates too few jobs.

The unemployment rate, currently at around 28 per cent, is defined as the percentage of the labour force that is unemployed but willing and able to work, and actively seeking employment. Unemployment has grown every year since 2008, when the global financial recession hit South Africa, a trend that, as we have seen, has been intensified by government policy. More than one in four people in the South African labour force in 2016 were willing and able to work but could not find employment.

The prognosis for South Africa's employment rate is not good, partly because of the uneven distribution of skills in the labour force, poor outcomes from an education system that is not delivering what the economy needs and poor labour relations. Government policies have steadily reduced employment intensity in the private sector. For example, mining companies prefer to mechanise operations rather than employ additional workers; there are too few small and medium-sized enterprises; and innovation is stifled. As a result, many people are excluded from the labour market. Most of South Africa's larger companies see their expansion potential outside of the national borders and remain hesitant to invest domestically while sitting on a mountain of more than R1,3 trillion of cash.[32]

The rigidity in the South African labour market is a recurring theme in mainstream analysis of the constraints on growth. Adversarial labour relations and restrictive employment policies have had the effect of reducing labour absorption rates. Without a comprehensive review of labour relations, government and the private sector will have to maintain and improve the current efforts at short-term employment creation, such as the Expanded Public Works Programme and the Comprehensive Rural Development Programme. Community work programmes, low-paid public-work projects and the like will also have to be rolled out.

So what do future job prospects look like under the three scenarios? According to the National Planning Commission, the number of jobs in the South African economy during the period 1995 to 2008 grew at 0,6 to 0,7 per cent a year for every 1 per cent of economic growth, although the exact rate fluctuates widely from quarter to quarter and year to year.[33]

Using the rough indication of 0,6 per cent growth in employment for each percentage of growth in GDP, it is possible to do a rough estimate of likely future rates of employment. This rough calculation indicates that South Africa is likely to have 17,7 million employed people out of a labour force of 26,3 million people by 2034. Around 2 million more South Africans will be employed in the Mandela Magic scenario than in Nation Divided (18,8 million compared with 16,9 million).

In summary, the absolute number of unemployed is forecast to slowly increase or, at best, remain stable to 2034. On the other hand, the proportion of employed people compared to the proportion of unemployed people steadily increases over time. This could be a good news story, for an increase in the number of employed versus unemployed contributes to taxes, stability and social cohesion.

Governing the governors: state capture, corruption and incoherence
In the years before defending the president became government's main preoccupation, the Tripartite Alliance was strongly in favour of a developmental state based on the example of the Asian Tiger economies and China. In those states, capable government – albeit invariably

authoritarian and undemocratic – played a central role in economic development. In that context, there has been much reference to one of my favourite authors, the South Korean scholar Ha-Joon Chang (who is cited earlier in this chapter).

Chang's three best-known books *Kicking Away the Ladder: Development Strategy in Historical Perspective*, *Bad Samaritans: The Myth of Free Trade and the Secret History of Capitalism* and *23 Things They Don't Tell You About Capitalism*, argue that all the major developed countries used interventionist economic policies to get wealthy and then tried to forestall other countries from doing the same – hence the notion of kicking away the ladder.[34] His books effectively debunk the fairy tale of the free market, the illusion of market objectivity, the idea that developing countries can largely skip industrialisation and enter the post-industrial phase directly, and the myth that governments are bad at development. The role of government has been particularly important in the rapid growth of the Asian Tigers and China, and currently in Africa's most rapidly growing countries, Ethiopia and Rwanda, Chang argues. I concur. It is also what the Afrikaners did in South Africa.

South Africa, Chang says, needs to emulate the example of others that have gone before, particularly in the establishment of a strong, developmental state. However, instead of a capable state, the ANC has expanded the public sector as its primary means of creating employment – not as a means for development. Successive above-inflation-level wage agreements have bloated the public-sector wage bill, which is squeezing out potential investment in other areas, such as healthcare, infrastructure and education. Successive ministers of public service and administration, the ministry that is in charge of the civil service, have buckled under threats from public-sector union members, which now form the powerful majority of COSATU.[35]

After the excessive trade liberalisation of Alec Erwin and Trevor Manuel during the 1990s, policy on trade and industry has belatedly been moving in the direction advocated by Chang, but only after the government's wooing of China has wrought additional devastation. Speaking in response to the 2017 debate on the state of the nation address, Minister of Trade and Industry Rob Davies presented a cogent argument for South Africa to nurture, support and protect emerging industries, pointing to a history where governments elsewhere have denied trade liberalisation to protect their vulnerable sectors.

Besides the ballooning public-sector wage bill, an excess of red tape stifles job creation in South Africa. State-owned enterprises have been assigned a 'development mandate' and use state procurement as the means to build a black industrial elite – a process that has contributed little to employment. Rather than creating additional value, efforts at black economic empowerment have come to derail value-for-money competition, deter investment and stifle the economy in all sectors, but particularly for small and medium-sized enterprises. Critics of these policies, such as political economist Moeletsi Mbeki, point out that, instead of empowering ordinary people, black economic empowerment ends up benefiting a small group of politically connected families, distorts the market and allocates contracts to certain people.[36] In this form, black economic empowerment is contributing to inequality and poverty in South Africa.

Among many other subsequent afflictions, these developments have set the stage for local-level patronage and for so-called tenderpreneurs. These individuals are skilled at obtaining government contracts through political contacts, and manage to get round the procurement processes and the law to access lucrative deals.[37] The tendencies have become rife at every level within the ANC but are most pronounced in local government, where the competition for tenders has become a major driver of violence.

It is no surprise that the proportion of South Africans who think that corruption is getting worse and that the government is not combating it effectively is among the highest globally.[38] While bribery and petty corruption are prevalent in much of South Africa, the big corruption issue, in the mind of the public, is the rapid accumulation of wealth by politically connected elites.[39] This is epitomised by the debate about state capture, which a study for the IMF defines as 'the efforts of firms to shape the laws, policies, and regulations of the state to their own advantage by providing illicit private gains to public officials'.[40]

State capture, such as that seen in the relationship between the Gupta family, the presidency and state-owned corporations, such as the SABC and Eskom (as two of many examples), is a deeper and more worrying type of corruption, because it does not involve how existing laws, rules or regulations are *implemented*, but how they are *written* in the first place. In South Africa, firms (and the people who control them) have been able to shape laws, rules and regulations to their own advantage, and this comes at a significant social cost. The authors of the IMF study contend that

> because such firms use their influence to block any policy reforms that might eliminate these advantages, state capture has become not merely a symptom but also a fundamental cause of poor governance. In this view, the capture economy is trapped in a vicious circle in which the policy and institutional reforms necessary to improve governance are undermined by collusion between powerful firms and state officials who reap substantial private gains from the continuation of weak governance.[41]

It has become apparent that a large number of government officials and ruling-party politicians have effectively been 'bought' to shape law, policy and appointments in a manner that is not in the broader interests of the country in a number of areas. Sometimes the real reasons for decisions are hidden from sight but the results can be deadly. In 2015, for example, the Gauteng health department decided to transfer some 2000 mentally ill patients to non-government institutions. Despite advice to the contrary from various quarters, the then Gauteng Health MEC, Qedani Mahlangu, insisted on the transfer. There ensued more than 100 deaths as efforts to cover up the tragedy unravelled. It would subsequently transpire that politically connected individuals had been informed (or perhaps had motivated for) government plans to outsource care for the mentally handicapped and hurriedly registered private facilities so that they would benefit from the contracts. As the *Sowetan* put it, 'Every rule relating to the care of patients was broken by people who should know better. The psychiatric patients were simply dumped in facilities that were unsuitable and ill-equipped to look after them.'[42] Some were moved without their medical records and a large number died.

Unsurprisingly, state capture is occurring at the same time that government's own anti-corruption agencies are being hollowed out from the inside, largely by ill-suited political appointments and attacks on institutions, including on the previous Public Protector, Advocate Thuli Madonsela. Madonsela had the temerity to find against the president and many of his political partners, following which a series of events culminated in a stinging rebuke from the chief justice of the Constitutional Court to the effect that Zuma had violated his oath of office.

There is a plethora of other examples of poor governance in the Zuma administration, such as the role of renewables in the electricity mix and plans by the industry regulator to auction broadband spectrum, later opposed by telecommunications minister Siyabonga Cwele. Thus the national Strategic Fuel Fund was able to bid for Chevron Corporation's assets in the country, including an oil refinery, without permission, but is apparently not held to account. In each incident, deeper analysis would indicate that business interests appear to lie behind each opposing position, facilitated by willing politicians, and that a shadow state is emerging.

And yet, ironically, South Africa has one of the most transparent budget processes in the world; in fact, we have been in the top three on the Open Budget Index since 2008.[43] However, with greater transparency comes greater public-sector financial malfeasance. Take, for example, the amount recorded by Auditor General Kimi Makwetu as 'irregular expenditure' by national and provincial government departments. That figure increased from R5 billion in 2007 to R25,7 billion in 2014/15, and to a whopping R46 billion in 2015/16.[44] After a five-fold increase in the previous seven years, the last year saw an 80 per cent year-on-year increase. The worst offenders were the Passenger Rail Agency of South Africa – which alone contributed R13,9 billion to the 2015/16 figure, the health departments of KwaZulu-Natal and Mpumalanga, the Department of Water and Sanitation, and Gauteng's road and transport and human settlements departments. No wonder the DA was able to trounce the ANC in Johannesburg and Tshwane during the 2016 local elections.

The analysis of state capture and government incoherence can also be approached from a different perspective, namely, the view that poor social capital currently serves as the most severe drag on economic growth in South Africa.

Traditional theories of economic growth contend that economic output is a function of the interaction between three factors – labour, capital and what is generally termed 'multifactor' (or 'total factor') productivity. The contribution of labour and capital are measurable and can be quantified. Multifactor productivity is the residual contributor to economic growth once the contributions from labour and capital are accounted for. Multifactor productivity can be thought of as being composed of four elements: human-, social-, physical- and knowledge-capital productivity. Each of these components can impart a positive or negative value depending on whether it contributes positively or negatively to economic growth.[45]

Compared with other countries at similar levels of development, social capital – in the form of government ineffectiveness and corruption – serves as the largest drag on South Africa's growth. This analysis concurs with a recurring theme in this book: inchoate governance and black economic empowerment (in its current crony-capitalist form) have a deeply negative impact on South Africa's economic performance and prospects.[46]

Most South Africans can personally attest to the declining efficiency of government (although there are some exceptions) and an increase in corruption.[47] Numerous projects, such as the introduction of e-tolls, mismanagement of key parastatals and poorly executed efforts to introduce smart electricity metering in Tshwane or to purchase new locomotives for the Passenger Rail Agency of South Africa, have shown breathtaking levels of corruption, incompetence, inefficiency and wastage.

Since South Africa has a relatively narrow tax base, questions need to be asked about the sustainability of these levels of wastage and fruitless expenditure. The annual Tax Statistics Bulletin, jointly released by the Treasury and SARS, revealed in November 2016 exactly how narrow that tax base is, noting that 60 per cent of South Africa's corporate tax comes from just 325 large companies. The contribution of corporate tax has, in turn, steadily declined to 18,1 per cent of total tax revenue, down from a peak of 26,7 per cent before the financial crisis in 2008/09.[48] The tax base associated with the private sector is shrinking.

The same sorry state is evident in personal tax. In the 2017 budget, the finance minister announced a 45 per cent marginal tax rate for individuals earning above R1,5 million per annum, a rate that would apply to a mere 105 668 people out of a total population of some 55 million.[49]

Where to from here?

The South African economy is growing below its potential, and significantly below the growth rate required by the National Development Plan to reduce unemployment and poverty. None of the scenarios set out in this book achieve the rates of growth envisioned in the plan. The damage that has been done by bad governance, cronyism and poor planning during the Zuma administration – on top of a hostile global growth environment – will not be easily reversed.

Although the country has significant growth potential, given the investments in education and healthcare, and other drivers of long-term prosperity since 1994, the forecasts are not looking good. When the ANC's subcommittee on economic transformation briefed the media days after the March 2017 Cabinet reshuffle that precipitated the downgraded to junk status by two ratings agencies, it admitted that a recession was now a distinct possibility.[50] It happened two months later.

The Cabinet reshuffle and subsequent downgrade will effectively cap growth because the effect will be to increase borrowing costs and crowd out the ability to invest in key areas. This comes on top of underinvestment in, and poor management of, energy, water and education, among others, further constraining the growth potential of South Africa, despite its diversified economy and good infrastructure, as it struggles with high levels of inequality, crime, unemployment and poverty.

The current outlook for South Africa – envisioned in the middle-of-the-road Bafana Bafana scenario or, perhaps increasingly, the Nation Divided downturn – is for continued sluggish growth and elevated current-account deficits, reflecting global developments and domestic factors that are largely of our own creation. Without structural reforms, growth will be insufficient to reduce exceptionally high unemployment rates. Risks are tilted firmly to the downside, unless new leadership and different policies emerge that are able to take us forward.

With its economic and various other policies up in the air, as well as its highly publicised leadership crisis, South Africa is at a critical juncture as the ruling party prepares for its December 2017 conference and elections for a new leadership.

CHAPTER 7

Why is our economy not growing?

We have allowed a situation to develop where a handful of individuals appear to be able to dictate, to some extent, where this country goes in terms of the use of its economic resources. We've allowed greed to become a factor in the way people behave ...

– Former Minister of Finance Pravin Gordhan[1]

Since the end of World War II, South Africa has averaged 3,4 per cent growth in GDP per annum. This includes periods of rapid growth after the war and again in the mid-1960s. After that, South Africa became a global laggard, its economy growing below the average rate of other countries in the same upper-middle-income category.

As the apartheid crisis deepened in the two decades from 1973, South Africa generally experienced negative per capita economic growth. By 1993, the average income was equivalent to the level it was at in 1970.[2] Capital investment also decreased and ever-larger portions of the national budget had to fund recurrent expenditure, including the escalating cost of state security. Infrastructure was not maintained and efficiencies declined.

In addition, the outgoing National Party had South Africa classified as a developed economy in 1994 as part of the negotiations on the General Agreement on Tariffs and Trade. This decision, which is also discussed in Chapter 2, required substantive reductions in protective tariffs. The ANC did not overturn this disastrous decision – seeing it as an opportunity for the market to discipline large unproductive sectors – and consequently large segments of the South African economy were rapidly opened to international competition.

The ANC had inherited a country with empty coffers and one that was buffeted by the impact of globalisation. It also faced high expectations from its majority black support base, who believed political change would rapidly redress the injustice and neglect they had suffered over generations.

Their expectations did not go wholly unmet. South Africa's economic fortunes changed with the end of financial sanctions and the country's readmission into the global community. Improved foreign perceptions of the attractiveness of doing business in South Africa translated into large foreign financial inflows – large at least by South African standards.[3] Labour productivity also began to increase from 1995.[4] Then, for the next 13 years or so, until 2008, the country grew and income levels improved, albeit slowly, as the country had lost out on a decade of the global commodities supercycle. Government policies had (necessarily) focused on redressing the socio-economic imbalance rather than planning for global economic success.

The opening up of the South African economy following its classification as a developed economy occurred at a time when the explosive export-driven growth of China and other countries was beginning to reach African shores. Without support from government, with limited investment to overcome major bottlenecks in transport, and without an enabling business environment, South African companies found themselves unable to compete with the deluge of cheap imports, often produced by state-subsidised competitors in China. South Africa consequently experienced unexpected de-industrialisation and significant job losses. The manufacturing sector shrank from 20 per cent of GDP in 1983 to 12 per cent in 2015.

At the same time, the country was not able to take full advantage of the growing African markets for its manufactured goods despite the positive hype around a potential African economic renaissance. Historically, few countries have been able to develop without a sizeable manufacturing sector, and the decline in South Africa's industrial base had a knock-on effect in other sectors, including mining, agriculture and services.

But, at the heart of South Africa's economic failures is the inability of government, labour and business to cohere around a common growth vision for the country, despite the establishment of the National Economic Development and Labour Council (NEDLAC) precisely for this purpose. This inability was largely driven by the increasingly divisive racial policies first espoused by President Thabo Mbeki, increasingly adopted by his successor and now promulgated by the Traditionalist grouping within the ANC, as well as by Julius Malema and the EFF.

But it is also a function of a business community that, until recently, had stepped away from engagement in the future of the country. Whereas, in the transition period, business had been an active partner in the settlement process, cajoling all groups towards a new political dispensation, once that political transition had been achieved the private sector stepped back into a profit-seeking mode.

Even when South Africa was growing rapidly under GEAR during the Mandela and Mbeki years, the country was still growing more sluggishly than the global average for other upper-middle-income countries. Figure 11 shows this historical trend, showing the annual changes in income level under each of the presidencies since 1994. It also includes a forecast for each of the three scenarios to 2034, indicating that the Mandela Magic scenario would eventually see South Africa achieve growth rates comparable to those of other upper-middle-income countries.

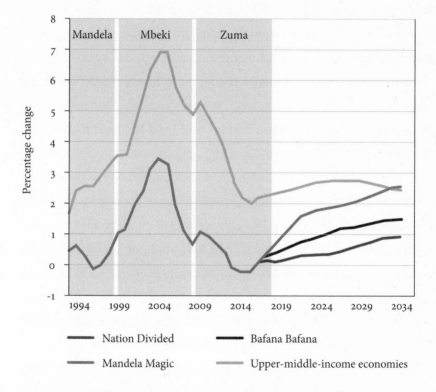

Figure 11: Rate of change in income levels – history and forecasts
Source: World Development Indicators data in IFs v 7.28
Note: this graph uses a five-year moving average

As Figure 11 shows, income growth in South Africa has been behind the average for upper-middle-income countries for several decades. After the 2007/08 global recession, the additional burden of poor planning, bad management and the high levels of social expenditure needed to alleviate the consequences of apartheid have successively reduced the breathing space of the Rainbow Nation. Future prospects are similarly unpromising.

Like many other emerging markets, South Africa has little influence over external global developments, such as a drop in the oil price or issues arising from something like the UK's Brexit decision. Nevertheless, the reasons why South Africa continues to grow much more slowly than comparable middle-income countries are largely self-inflicted.

For example, South Africa's export tariffs for non-beneficiated mining products are well below the world average, while its port charges are among the highest globally. Writing in *Business Day*, Mark Allix illustrates it thus: 'This means SA's export manufacturers are in effect subsidising existing Transnet port operations, while subsidies are passed on to exporters of primary mineral commodities and importers of manufactured goods.'[5]

South Africa has a lot going for it. According to the World Economic Forum's 2016/2017 Global Competitiveness Index, South Africa was the second most globally competitive country in Africa in 2015 (the year for which the rating is done), ranking 47th out of the 138 countries included in the report, which puts it just behind Portugal and Mauritius (the most competitive country in Africa).

Competitiveness, according to the World Economic Forum, is defined as 'the set of institutions, policies, and factors that determine the level of productivity of an economy, which in turn sets the level of prosperity that the country can achieve'.[6] The index scores countries on the basis of 12 pillars of competitiveness and the summary on South Africa reads as follows:[7]

> Most significant areas of progress include enhanced competition,
> both locally (up 13 places) and internationally (up 16 places); better

use of talent in terms of how pay reflects productivity (98th, up 29 places); and a small but important upgrade in the quality of education (up five places), with primary school enrollment also now passing 97 percent. However, a number of shortcomings may limit South African competitiveness going forward. Infrastructure development has stalled, both in transport and electricity, with power shortages experienced this year. Institutional quality has diminished, with increased political uncertainty, less transparency, some security concerns, and business leaders having less trust in politicians.

In 2017, the World Bank's Doing Business Index placed South Africa at 74th out of 190 economies (having fallen two places from the previous year). It fared particularly badly in the sub-index of the ease of trading across borders, starting a business, enforcing contracts, getting electricity and registering property. The country did best in protecting minority investors, resolving insolvency, paying taxes and getting credit. Compared to the previous year, South Africa did worse in nine of the ten sub-indexes, improving its ranking only in the sub-index of resolving insolvency.[8]

These indices provide a useful picture of areas where labour, business and government should make a collective effort to improve the country's ability to attract foreign investment and to position South Africa as an attractive business destination. Cabinet should be scrutinising the results regularly and setting clear targets for improvements in each of the sub-indices for each minister, while measuring progress.

Zuma's response to the country's low ranking in these reports over the past few years was to establish (yet another) inter-ministerial committee on investment, comprising 18 Cabinet ministers to promote, in the committee's words, 'a friendly and hassle-free investment climate in the country'. In 2015, government announced its decision to establish the

One Stop Shop InvestSA scheme. One Stop Shop offices would be established to serve as a focal point for various government departments that are involved in regulation, registration, permits and licensing for business. InvestSA would also coordinate with the World Bank on a reform memo over a period of three to five years to improve South Africa's ease-of-doing-business rankings.[9] However, it took two years for the first provincial One Stop Shops to be launched in March 2017.

One cannot but get the impression that these limp efforts are intended as window dressing. Without significant political will for economic reform and a truly momentous common effort, South Africa will not graduate from its middle-income trap to high-income status in the foreseeable future.

One of the problems is that the country has a hybrid economic structure, with both a 'rising middle-income economy and a low-income one'.[10] As an ISS study points out, this hybrid nature is typical of a middle-income economy with a heavy reliance on services, a struggling manufacturing sector, and an increasingly mechanised and consolidated agricultural sector. It is also the legacy of apartheid. South Africa simultaneously suffers from a high rate of unemployment, and an underskilled workforce, while government has legislated for barriers that inhibit business and entrepreneurship in the private sector, both major drivers of employment.[11] Furthermore, South Africa has a small informal sector by comparative standards, meaning that instead of finding work in either the formal or informal sector, a large portion of South African potential workers are economically inactive.

In short, apart from a brief period under the GEAR programme, the post-apartheid South African economy has been growing just as slowly as it did during apartheid. The level of human, social and capital investment needed by South Africa to ameliorate the human devastation of apartheid limits the investments available to unlock higher rates of growth. And the outlook does not offer positive prospects.

The most likely future scenario, Bafana Bafana, forecasts an average growth rate of only 2,3 per cent for South Africa from 2017 to 2034. This is some 2 per cent below the average rate projected in the IFs business-as-usual forecast for upper-middle-income countries glob-ally. Generally, a weaker-than-expected global economic recovery – particularly in Europe, an important trading partner for South Africa – combined with the impact of China's economic rebalancing, which has reduced its appetite for commodities from Africa, points to a low-growth environment for several years, although there are increased signs of more robust growth in the US and Europe, which would offset the tapering-off of growth in China.

The average growth forecast in Nation Divided is 1,5 per cent, which would mean South Africa would have one of the continent's lowest growth rates. By comparison, average growth rates for the rest of SADC are estimated at a robust 5 per cent, and slightly less for the rest of sub-Saharan Africa.

The more positive Mandela Magic forecast allows South Africa to close the gap with the average growth rate forecast for other upper-middle-income countries by 2031. Among the drivers informing that scenario are reduced corruption, greater government efficiencies, more economic freedom and investment in research and development.

Until mid-2015 the most widely publicised barrier to growth was the shortage of electricity – an issue that the National Development Plan skimped on. More recently, however, government's proposed investment in nuclear energy and the prospects for an acute water shortage will also add to future constraints on South Africa's economic-development pathway.

Energy supply as a constraint on growth and the nuclear build

Rolling electricity blackouts started in November 2007 (presciently, just ahead of the ANC's Polokwane conference, where Jacob Zuma unseated Thabo Mbeki). Large electricity price increases followed (prices have increased fourfold) and balance was restored in the system only when the economy contracted, causing electricity demand to decline, and after Eskom finally completed construction of the Medupi and Kusile power stations, hugely over budget and several years behind schedule.

To compound matters, the then energy minister, Dipuo Peters, ran South Africa's electricity production into the ground in the run-up to and during the 2010 FIFA World Cup in South Africa, allowing the bare minimum of maintenance and upkeep. Without enough electricity, the economy stalled and, without maintenance, the reliability of generation suffered.

The decision to delay investment in new electricity-generating capacity came despite repeated and consistent warnings to Mandela and Mbeki by Eskom since 1996. The Department of Energy's White Paper on the Energy Policy of South Africa, published in 1998, accurately fore- cast the dire situation that would occur exactly nine years later. 'Eskom's present generation capacity surplus will be fully utilized by 2007,' the paper warned.

In the intervening years, the government first did nothing and then tried, for several years, to get the private sector to invest in electricity generation. Unsurprisingly, business was not prepared to enter a market where government set the price of electricity and Eskom controlled both production and distribution. As the years passed, options became more limited but still nothing was done.

When the blackouts started, Mbeki apologised, but it was too late. The management of the electricity sector then rapidly spiralled further out of control, and by 2014 Eskom's credit rating was downgraded to junk status. This was particularly ironic as, in 2001, Eskom had won the *Financial Times* Global Energy Award for Power Company of the Year.

In his revealing book *Blackout: the ESKOM crisis*,[12] James-Brent Styan details the endless changes of bosses in the two departments most closely responsible for electricity – the Department of Energy and the Department of Public Enterprises – after Zuma became leader of the ANC, as well as the revolving door at Eskom management. By June 2015, Styan points out, no fewer than 21 people had been in charge of the four most important roles in the management of energy over a period of just seven years.[13]

The hard reality is, had it not been for the mismanagement of the electricity supply chain, the South African economy could have been 10 per cent bigger by the end of 2014 – or around R300 billion – and that deficit equates to more than 1 million lost job opportunities.[14] By July 2016, peak electricity demand was 5,4 per cent lower than ten years ago.[15] The Eskom crisis is a textbook case of bad planning and poor governance by successive administrations, resulting in dire economic consequences for the entire South African population.

It took several years before the Zuma administration settled on a solution that could boost South Africa's base-load electricity supply: a large new nuclear programme (the 'new nuclear build', as it has become known).

Hindsight is a perfect science, so it is important to remind ourselves of the very dramatic shifts taking place in the global energy mix at the time. When more nuclear power stations were first touted as a solution for South Africa's electricity shortfall, the average spot price of a barrel of Brent Crude oil was USD111,26 and no one was taking shale gas seriously or thinking that Saudi Arabia and the Organization of Petroleum Exporting Countries could try to flood the market with oil in an effort to force US shale-gas producers out of business. Since then, however, oil prices have come down dramatically. In 2016 oil prices averaged around USD43 a barrel and the average 2017 price forecast from the US Energy Information Administration is around USD55 a barrel and USD57 for 2018.[16]

The first Integrated Resource Plan (IRP) of the Department of Energy for the period 2010 to 2030 was gazetted in May 2011 and called for the construction of 9,6 GW of new nuclear capacity, intended to supply 12,7 per cent of the country's electricity by 2030. The first reactor was projected to come online by 2023 and the full six-plant project completed by 2029.

Heavy criticism followed this announcement because of the enormous associated cost, environmental concerns regarding radioactive waste, the potential for grand corruption and the apparent disregard for introducing an energy mix where renewables would provide the bulk of South Africa's electricity needs.

However, the IRP also found that 'the future capacity requirement could, in theory, be met without nuclear'.[17] The question then was, so why go down the nuclear path? The argument given by the Department of Energy was that nuclear would provide 'security of supply in the event of a peak oil-type increase in fuel prices and ensure that sufficient dispatchable base-load capacity is constructed to meet demand in peak hours each year'.[18] In other words, nuclear could produce electricity irrespective of changes in fossil-fuel prices or lack of wind and sunshine, etc.

Proponents of renewable energy have responded to this concern by pointing out that were South Africa to invest in sufficient renewable-energy production capacity, there would always be enough electricity in reserve, irrespective of cloudy days, lack of wind or other constraints, as well as pointing to the progress that is being made in electricity storage technology. And then there are obvious solutions, such as adopting day-light saving for portions of the country, which would flatten the peak demand for electricity over an additional hour or two.

Improvements in renewable-energy technologies and lower electricity demand changed the assumptions that informed the IRP 2010–2030. Forecasts of the demand for electricity have also changed, for two reasons. First, the economy is expected to grow more slowly, so we will need less electricity, and, second, in line with global trends, the South African economy is becoming more energy-efficient. It therefore requires less energy per unit of additional growth than in the past.[19]

Perhaps most importantly, however, South Africa's financial position has deteriorated significantly. Cost estimates for the nuclear programme vary from R600 billion to R1 trillion – roughly equal to the annual South African tax revenue, and the industry is notorious for significant cost overruns. Nuclear is not cheap to build, although once the initial outlay is paid off it provides reliable and clean energy for several decades.

The IRP was to be updated every two years, but Cabinet did not approve the 2013 update of the plan when it questioned the suitability of nuclear. That revision argued that, because electricity demand was growing more slowly than anticipated, the new nuclear build could be delayed. The Department of Energy would later reveal that Cabinet had taken the decision to proceed with developing the new nuclear programme in June 2015, 'subject to more work being done on the proposed funding model; the risks and mitigation strategies; and the contributions by countries as contained in the inter-governmental agreements'.[20]

On 21 December 2015, shortly after finance minister Nhlanhla Nene was fired, a notice in the *Government Gazette* confirmed Cabinet's decision to move ahead with the 9 600 MW nuclear procurement programme.[21] That initiative, taken by the Minister of Energy and the National Energy

Regulator of South Africa (NERSA), was, however, dated two years earlier, in late 2013, adding fuel to the speculation that Zuma had confirmed a deal with Russia in 2013 and that the government was trying to legitimise that arrangement.[22] Publishing a notice in the *Government Gazette* means that the department can call for quotes for the tendering process to begin. Up to that point there had been no public statements indicating that Cabinet had approved the nuclear build at the end of 2013, or that the required public consultation process had been initiated.

In November 2016, the then Minister of Energy, Tina Joemat-Pettersson, belatedly released an updated IRP for public comment and engagement, which included the new nuclear build in all of its scenarios – although on a smaller scale and to be rolled out at a slower pace. According to this plan, the first plant would be 'brought online after 2030 in a well-spaced-out manner. However, given the long lead times associated with construction of nuclear plants, planning with regard to the New Nuclear Build should progress and a decision on a vendor/country partnership should be expedited.'[23]

According to the IRP's base case, 1,36 GW of new nuclear capacity would be available by 2037 and 20,38 GW by 2050. Hence, instead of the planned 9,6 GW capacity to come online by 2030, the Department of Energy was planning a slower programme but one that would eventually deliver much greater nuclear capacity. Government simultaneously included additional wind and solar power capacity in its planning to 2030 and came out in support of the exploration of shale gas in the Karoo.

Eskom subsequently put out a 'no obligation' request for information on 23 December 2016 in an effort to validate its own assumptions and planning.[24] Responses were expected in April 2017, followed by a request for proposals two or three months later. Once the proposal process had been completed and a final funding model developed by the Department of Energy and the Treasury, it would be submitted to the energy security cabinet subcommittee before being considered by Cabinet (i.e. during the second half of 2017).[25] The intention was to appoint a successful bidder by March 2018, shortly before Zuma's second and final term as president comes to an end.[26]

Then, in a major setback to the nuclear plans at the end of April 2017, the Western Cape High Court set aside the determination signed by former minister Joemat-Pettersson[27] and found that Eskom's request for information, as well as the cooperation agreements with the US, Russia and South Korea, were unconstitutional and unlawful because the energy regulator, NERSA, had not followed the legal prescripts with regard to public participation.[28] The court's finding means that much of the progress achieved thus far has to be set aside, and that Parliament, in particular, needs to be involved. Effectively, the process needs to start again.

Despite this ruling, however, the Zuma administration has not abandoned its plans for a nuclear build and the question must be asked why South Africa is swimming so determinedly against the current.

The nuclear industry is struggling worldwide as countries move towards renewables.[29] Nuclear plants are simply too expensive in this day and age for South Africa's budget, particularly at a time when the price for renewables is coming down year on year. A considerable body of research has also pointed to the potential of moving away from industrial scale and central production of energy to a more decentralised and less capital-intensive model, particularly well-suited to large countries with dispersed rural populations, such as South Africa.

According to the International Atomic Energy Agency, construction on just three reactors started in 2016 worldwide; this is in stark contrast to the 1960s and 1970s when between 20 and 30 new plants were being constructed each year. Costs have spiralled out of control, leaving only three major players in global nuclear power plant construction: South Korea, China and Russia.[30]

It is almost impossible to see how South Africa would be able to benefit from nuclear or from investing in an industry that is globally in decline. It would be investing in the wrong technology, and doing so at great risk; there is also the potential for disastrously large cost overruns and delays. In fact, various submissions on the draft updated IRP, such as that drawn up by the Council for Scientific and Industrial Research (CSIR), comprehensively reject the calculations and assumptions that underpin the IRP. For example, the CSIR believes that the optimal energy solution is a blend of solar photovoltaic, wind and flexible power based on gas, concentrated solar power, hydro and biogas – with no nuclear power at all in the mix.[31]

As well as the notorious arms procurement deal, there have been a number of other mega-projects in post-apartheid South Africa that have been tainted by large-scale corruption, including the building of stadiums for the 2010 FIFA World Cup, the construction of toll roads, replacement of rolling stock for the railways, and others. Initially, these programmes simply illustrated the state's inability to manage large-scale projects and the extent to which large private-sector firms could run rings around government. In recent years, however, the situation has changed.

Today, it is evident that a number of powerful individuals and groups who have the president's ear, and with vested interests in black economic empowerment as a lucrative business model in itself, have very significant interests in the nuclear matter. These include the Guptas, whose Oakbay Resources & Energy group (of which the president's son Duduzane Zuma was then a director) acquired the hitherto unprofitable Shiva uranium mine in 2010. This mine can only become profitable if it were to become the uranium supplier to the proposed nuclear power stations.[32] The extent to which the Guptas, now among the richest people in South Africa, consistently have insider knowledge of decisions that can only come from the Presidency or Zuma's associates has long been a source of concern.

Since a number of countries and companies had indicated an interest in bidding for the nuclear build, the 2014 announcement by the Russian nuclear agency, Rosatom, that it had secured the contract for the entire build was an indication that something was afoot. Following a visit to South Africa in 2013, Russian president Vladimir Putin had made it clear that Russia wanted exclusive rights to South Africa's nuclear programme, going so far as offering to run the country's entire nuclear industry.

According to newspaper reports, Zuma and Putin had personally negotiated the nuclear deal on the sidelines of the 2014 BRICS summit and finalised the details during a highly secretive visit to Moscow shortly afterwards.[33] It was at this point that the plans ran into resistance from the Treasury on the basis of affordability and due process. This resistance apparently played an important role in the decision to move Pravin Gordhan from the key portfolio of Finance to that of Cooperative Governance and Traditional Affairs in 2014, and for Nene to be appointed in his place. When Nene also repeatedly advised against the nuclear procurement, Zuma also removed him, leading to the short-lived appointment of David van Rooyen as finance minister in December 2015 before market fallout forced Zuma to reappoint Gordhan, later fired in March 2017.

Only time will tell what the attitude of the new finance minister, Malusi Gigaba, will be in respect of the proposed nuclear deal, but the signs are ominous, as he was Zuma's second choice as Minister of Finance after Brian Molefe, ex-head of Eskom, close friend of the Guptas and hard-line proponent of the nuclear build.[34] Despite Joemat-Pettersson's best efforts to clinch nuclear, she had not managed to conclude the deal and was dumped by Zuma in March 2017.

Carbon emissions as motivation for nuclear energy

Another line of argument used by government in support of the nuclear build is that it would allow South Africa to meet its global carbon-emission target. However, the modelling done for this book indicates that this argument is fallacious.

In 2005, the Mbeki Cabinet initiated a consultative process to determine how best South Africa could contribute to mitigating greenhouse-gas emissions and moderate the impact of global climate change. The process survived Mbeki's defeat as ANC president in December 2007, and in July 2008 Cabinet endorsed South Africa's long-term mitigation scenarios.

Calculated from a base year in 2003 with a long-term horizon to review carbon emissions under different scenarios to 2050, Cabinet approved a mitigation strategy that would require an aggressive departure from the country's historical emissions-heavy growth pathway. Until 2008, South Africa had the cheapest electricity prices in the world (at an average of R0,25 per kilowatt hour) – almost all of it generated by dirty coal.[35]

In terms of the mitigation strategy, carbon emissions would initially continue to grow, peak between 2020 and 2025 at 550 million tons CO_2 equivalent, remain flat for a decade, then decline in absolute terms from 2030 to 2035 onwards. At the Copenhagen climate-change conference in 2009, Zuma internationalised this pledge. He committed South Africa to taking mitigation action that will reduce emissions by 34 per cent below the business-as-usual trajectory by 2020 and 44 per cent by 2025. This pledge was repeated in December 2015 at the UN COP21 climate talks in Paris. The commitment now forms part of what is referred to as South Africa's intended national determined contribution.[36]

South Africa cannot honour that pledge if it remains dependent on coal to produce electricity. The amount of carbon dioxide that a fuel emits is a function of its carbon content. Since nuclear generates electricity from fission rather than by burning fuel, it produces virtually no greenhouse gases or emissions associated with global warming (although there is considerable carbon release associated with the initial construction of nuclear plants).

Gas is generally considered a transition fuel when moving from a carbon-intensive economy (i.e. away from coal) to one that relies on renewables, such as solar and wind. The issue here is that South Africa's neighbour Mozambique has one of the world's largest concentrations of natural gas, estimated at around 3 trillion cubic metres, equivalent to 19 billion barrels of oil, in total recoverable reserves to date.[37]

Renewable energy is the cleanest and most desirable source of energy, but currently only coal, gas and nuclear can reliably increase the base-load production of electricity, since wind and solar are dependent upon the vagaries of Mother Nature. Hence, the only way that an energy system can depend on renewables for its base load is to build significant surplus renewable capacity or to find ways in which to store energy, as is the case with the Drakensberg and Tugela pumped-storage schemes. This kind of technology requires considerable investment in a smart grid, however, in which electricity can be drawn from various sources and can flow in different directions.

All three scenarios modelled in this book envision a transition away from coal towards cleaner energy, namely, gas, nuclear and renewables. The Bafana Bafana scenario provides for two of the originally envisioned six nuclear plants (operational in the period 2027 to 2030) in line with the slower scale of nuclear construction now reflected in the updated 2016 IRP. This is accompanied by greater reliance on shale gas from the Karoo and the import of natural gas.

In the Mandela Magic scenario, all of South Africa's future electricity requirements come from renewables and gas (as proposed by the CSIR and other bodies), and there is no further nuclear build. Government relies on gas as a transition fuel to graduate the country away from coal towards renewables.

The Nation Divided scenario simulates a much larger nuclear-build programme, with a full fleet of six nuclear stations, all completed by 2034. Fracking does not occur in this scenario, on the grounds that multinationals will most likely be deterred from investing by the uncertain policy environment and stringent requirements surrounding black economic empowerment.

Figure 12 shows the forecast for emissions (in billions of tonnes of carbon dioxide) under each scenario. In all three, emissions peak around 2024 or 2025 in accordance with South Africa's COP21 pledge, although the Mandela Magic scenario records the highest peak – because the transition to renewables and converting to gas-based energy is a slow process, and because the economy grows more rapidly.

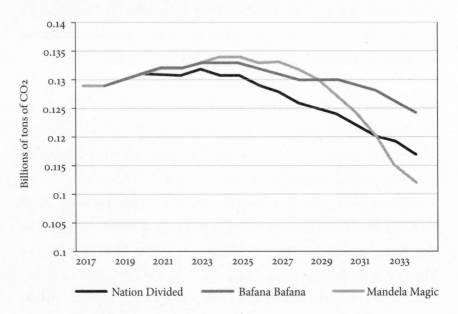

Figure 12: Forecasts of carbon emissions
Source: IFs v 7.28, forecast initialised from the Carbon Dioxide Information Analysis Center

The short- and medium-term transition towards a less carbon-intensive economy is most rapid in the Nation Divided scenario, as the economy grows slowly and depends on nuclear, which does not contribute carbon dioxide once the plants are built. A smaller economy consumes less electricity, and for many years the Nation Divided scenario fares best, in that South Africa releases lower carbon emissions than in any other scenario. Short-term gains are, however, offset in the longer term.

From 2030 the positive long-term impact of a shift to renewables is evident in the Mandela Magic scenario despite the fact that this would be a much larger economy than with Bafana Bafana or Nation Divided. In fact, after 2030 in the Mandela Magic scenario South Africa would release less carbon into the atmosphere than it did in 2016 and annual emissions would rapidly decrease thereafter. By 2034 South Africa, in this high-growth scenario, would be emitting 13 per cent less carbon dioxide than it did in 2016. This would be a remarkable turnaround for a country that currently is 14th in the rankings of highest emissions of carbon dioxide globally.

These scenarios show that the seemingly benign argument that the proposed nuclear build is motivated by commitments to reduce South Africa's carbon emissions does not pass muster. One can only come to the conclusion that the proposed nuclear programme is not based on science or cost but is driven by other considerations.

Besides the technology, and whether or not it is appropriate for South Africa's needs, the huge capital investment needed for the new nuclear programme will increase the capital intensity of the economy – at a time when the most important challenge is to create employment by stimulating small business, achieving a more flexible economy and thereby generating greater opportunity.

In addition, the Zuma administration has made it clear that a large component of all contracts will be subject to stringent black-economic-empowerment considerations. As in the past, this may well open the door for Chancellor House and other ANC-aligned front companies that represent a small, politically well-connected elite to cream profit for themselves off taxpayers' money, in exchange for probable delays in implementation and substantial cost overruns.

In the end, the biggest issue with the proposed new nuclear build is people's lack of trust in the president and the motivations that inform his decisions. However, following the ruling of the Western Cape High Court, it appears that a decision on nuclear procurement could now be delayed to a time when Zuma is no longer president of the country.[38]

Water supply as a constraint on growth

Perhaps even more serious than energy supply is the real potential for serious water restrictions in the years that lie ahead and the impact these could have on South Africa's growth prospects.

Research carried out by the ISS indicates that water-supply challenges will start to impinge on economic growth should current trends in demand and supply continue.[39] South Africa is a water-scarce country, and the 403-millimetre average rainfall that that the country received in 2015 was the lowest on record in the 112 years for which records are available, and significantly below the 608-millimetre average over that period. Moreover, the 2015 drought came on the back of three consecutive years of lower-than-average rainfall, making it the most severe and prolonged drought in South Africa since the 1940s.

The ISS research indicates that water consumption exceeds renewable supply and that this situation will repeat itself annually beyond 2034. Until recently, large parts of the country were experiencing water stress, and this condition is likely to be exacerbated by longer and less predictable droughts caused by the effects of climate change.

Moreover, a growing population will place further strain on renewable water supplies, while it is likely that increases in temperature will lower agricultural yields and reduce grazing capacity. The brunt of this impact will undoubtedly be felt by poor South Africans, who are already struggling to achieve food security and pay for essential services, such as schooling and transport.

Our most recent forecasts, based on data released by AQUASTAT (the Food and Agriculture Organization's information system on water and agriculture) suggest that national water withdrawals for South Africa in 2015 were 15,7 cubic kilometres. In 2015 reliable water supply was estimated to be only about 15,4 cubic kilometres. Comparing total water demand to total reliable supply, it is therefore clear that South Africa is overexploiting its water resources – although some regions may still experience a water surplus. Overexploitation of water resources leaves the entire water system vulnerable. When there is less precipitation than normal – as has been the case with the recent drought – we have no buffer or reserve, leading to municipal restrictions and crop failure.

The ISS study found that government's planned interventions for increasing water supply and reducing demand are not enough to close the gap between the two. The situation requires urgent and sustained attention. And it will also require lots of money, which, of course, may not be available if the nuclear programme proceeds.[40]

Figure 13 is a projection of the difference between South Africa's water supply and demand to 2034 for each of the three scenarios. Currently, South Africa has a water supply/demand gap of around 0,6 cubic kilometres and this will increase with each year. Because the South African economy grows most rapidly under the Mandela Magic scenario, which consumes more water per person, the water gap grows most rapidly in this scenario until, by 2034, it has reached almost 3 cubic kilometres. This is despite the fact that more water is recycled in the Mandela Magic scenario.

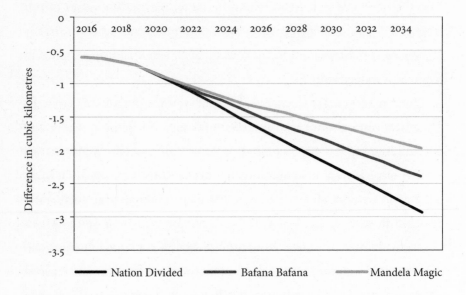

Figure 13: Gap between water supply and demand
Source: IFs v 7.27 initialised from AQUASTAT data

The National Development Plan states: 'The 1.5 million hectares under irrigation (which produce virtually all South Africa's horticultural harvest and some field crops) can be expanded by at least 500 000 hectares through the better use of existing water resources and developing new water schemes.'[41] This potential is unrealistic and the figure is likely to be much closer to 140 000 hectares. In time, water shortages may well echo the situation with the previous electricity shortages, and become a direct constraint on South Africa's growth prospects. Some 40 per cent of Gauteng's water comes from the 30-year-old first phase of the Lesotho

Highlands Water Project. The completion of the crucial second phase of this project was put back from 2017 to 2020, and more recently to 2025. These delays endanger the Vaal River system supply and put South Africa's economic heartland at risk. Since the ISS forecasts were premised on the timely completion of the projects currently planned by government, the potential water deficit could be significantly larger still.[42]

At some belated point in the future, the penny will drop and, just like during the electricity crisis, a very large amount of money will be urgently needed to respond to the crisis. Although there are some signs that government is starting to wake up to this problem, much better management of the country's water resources is needed at a senior level. Measures include substantial annual investment in water infrastructure, building and fixing sewage-recycling plants, curbing demand, a move to more efficient use of water (water must be priced at appropriate levels) and increasing water supply by greater exploitation of underground water sources. In the short to medium term more boreholes, a substantial increase in the use of treated wastewater and importing water from neighbouring countries will be the only ways to increase supply, along with expensive and energy-intensive desalination plants for coastal cities such as Cape Town and Durban.

To add to this concerning picture, all does not appear to be well with the Department of Water and Sanitation. In a press article under the front-page headline 'Nomvula Mokonyane's water department is bankrupt', dated 17 February 2017, it was reported that the Department of Water and Sanitation was R4,3 billion in the red, unable to pay hundreds of contractors, and under investigation by the Public Protector and the Special Investigating Unit in connection with fraud linked to infrastructure projects. According to sources quoted in the report, 'internal controls, project management and contract management have collapsed'.[43]

On the same day, the *Sunday Times* published a report that implicated the Minister of Water and Sanitation in what it described as an 'assault on the Treasury', seen as part of the factional struggles within the ANC in which key ministries, including the department headed by Minister of Social Development Bathabile Dlamini, were trying to get their hands on resources from the Treasury to bail them out for their lack of foresight and bad management.[44] Time will tell if finance minister Malusi Gigaba will be able to allocate more resources to the departments responsible for water and social grants, but it is unlikely.

Meanwhile, four years after the Department of Water and Sanitation had hired a credit-control firm, New Integrated Credit Solutions, to re-cover the R4 billion owing to it by municipalities, its outstanding debt had more than doubled, to R9,2 billion. Yet New Integrated Credit Solutions had been paid R322 million. The result of bad management and wastage is that the department could not go ahead with a number of water-infrastructure projects, including the Giewap Distribution Mopani emergency work and the Nandoni Nsami water pipeline and others.[45]

Like the electricity challenge that developed over several decades, the water issue is now a ticking time bomb. It can be managed only up to a certain point until, suddenly, it becomes a major crisis. And the water challenge is coming to the fore at a time when the ANC doesn't have its eye on the ball, distracted as it is by factional infighting and the struggle over its leadership before the December 2017 conference. It is likely that government will only get round to focusing on the crisis some years into the future, probably after a post-2019 Cabinet has settled in, replaced the previous senior government officials that had been appointed by Zuma, reviewed the evidence (as it is unlikely that it will trust anything that comes from the previous administration) and developed new policies. This is a process that will take several years. At that point, it may be too late to avoid punitive restrictions on water usage, which will serve to constrain economic growth.

The prospects for averting the next big crisis do not look good. It is doubly ironic that UNESCO hosted World Water Day in South Africa in 2017 under the theme 'Wastewater – the untapped resource' and that Zuma serves as a member of the UN High Level Panel on Water.

Some efforts are being made to address some of the country's economic challenges. But others, such as the establishment of a central procurement office under the Treasury, could actually empower the patronage network established by Gigaba and Zuma. South Africa's low-growth trap is essentially political and ideological. It is political, in that the president, his family and his business connections are often associated or implicated in many of the travails, and ideological in the sense that two of the three alliance partners (the SACP and COSATU) effectively frame discussions on economic choices within a narrow lexicon of statism and socialism, which precludes the consideration of practical policies – looking at what works elsewhere and adopting best practices. It is ideological in the extent to which current ANC leaders envision a traditionalist, tribal state, where customary law, as opposed to the Constitution, serves as the lodestar and where the state is the provider but it does not empower.

The low growth that South Africa is currently mired in is the inevitable result of a large, incoherent Cabinet, without leadership or direction, fighting and disagreeing with one another rather than focusing on the tasks at hand. It is a situation where too many senior government officials, heads of state-owned enterprises and ministers are appointed purely on the basis of their relationship to the president, and not on their skills or ability to contribute to economic growth and development.

CHAPTER 8

Crime, violence and instability

Effectively, South Africa is a society with a hidden civil war.
– Moeletsi Mbeki and Nobantu Mbeki[1]

Four decades ago, a combination of frustration with local government, the state's enforcement of an Afrikaans language policy, trade union activism and the impact of the Black Consciousness movement culminated in the Soweto uprising of 16 June 1976. In the weeks and months that followed, tens of thousands of South Africans from townships across the country took to the streets in violent confrontations with the apartheid state.[2]

Although the National Party government was eventually able to restore a semblance of order by force of arms, several thousand young South Africans fled the country, many to join the Pan Africanist Congress to fight apartheid. The PAC had a very limited presence in neighbouring states and the vast majority of those who left the country eventually joined the ANC, boosting the party in size. These events – combined with the impact of international activism, the fall of the Berlin Wall and internal revolt in the National Party – would eventually force a historical compromise when Nelson Mandela was released from prison in 1990 and, in 1994, elected president of South Africa.

Although there had been previous isolated events, such as the Sharpeville massacre of 1960, South Africa experienced sustained and ongoing high levels of public violence only from 1976 following the uprising in Soweto and its aftermath. After a brief respite, violent resistance to apartheid gained momentum again in 1979, culminating in a state of emergency in 1985/86.[3]

Mandela's release set in motion a prolonged and often bloody process of negotiation, which lasted until the first democratic elections. But the nature of violence also changed during this period. There was extensive black-on-black violence (facilitated by the National Party government) combined with the brutal actions of the Inkatha Freedom Party, the ANC's insurgency and resistance from some of the homeland leaders, such as Brigadier Oupa Gqozo in the former Ciskei and Lucas Mangope in Bophuthatswana. Violence spiked during the 1994 transition negotiations, with particularly high levels occurring between the ANC and the Inkatha Freedom Party in KwaZulu-Natal and Gauteng. Umkhonto we Sizwe, the ANC's armed wing, played an important symbolic but relatively minor practical role in these events.

Apartheid was a form of state-sponsored structural violence and the legacy of this system lives on in the high levels of violence still seen in post-apartheid South African society. The inhumanity of this evil system and the response to it has left South Africa a deeply traumatised and particularly violent society.

South Africa is also a patriarchal society where forms of socialisation have historically been exceptionally violent. For example, the system of movement control enforced through the apartheid pass system, as Rachel Jewkes and Robert Morrell explain, 'increased the likelihood of finding masculine affirmation in homosocial (sometimes criminal) settings and in [black men's] relations with black women.'[4] The former system of compulsory military service for white males and the country's general isolation from world developments had similar negative impacts on the white community.[5]

Successive generations of poor South Africans have never had a job, suffer from poor education and have little prospect of escaping from these debilitating circumstances. Structural unemployment condemns hundreds of thousands of households to poverty, leaving them frustrated with limited alternatives to generate income and maintain personal security, while a small multiracial elite often indulge in conspicuous consumption. High youth unemployment, coupled with social inequality and corruption, are significantly correlated with an increase in social instability and insecurity.[6]

Unemployment, inequality, poverty and poor governance impact on social stability in South Africa in complex ways. At the individual level, living in conditions of poverty significantly increases the likelihood that a person will engage in violence from increased exposure to violent subcultures, from substance abuse and from using crime as a means of control to 'redress the exclusion felt through not having material goods that define social inclusion'.[7]

That said, being poor does not in itself increase an individual's likelihood of being violent. Rather, the degree of inequality between segments of society, the degree of relative deprivation and the gap between the richest and poorest are the factors that are more likely to fuel violence and social unrest – particularly if this is accompanied by the opportunity for violence: people turn violent when they believe they can get away with it because state agencies are weak, corrupt or inefficient.[8]

High levels of violence lead to social instability. This, in turn, drives away foreign and domestic investment, polarises the voting public, reduces social cohesion and paves the way for populist policies. Violence also affects economic growth. Lack of growth makes a society that has a large component of young people without job prospects even more vulnerable to social instability.[9]

For these reasons, it is important to be aware of current trends in crime and violence when thinking about South Africa's future, and to factor levels of violence into the scenarios developed in this book.

Crime trends

Generally, in post-apartheid South Africa rates of violent crime (measured as incidents per 100 000 of the population) peaked in 2003/04, declined thereafter but have been on the increase again since 2011/12. In terms of crime, today there is less to celebrate than a decade ago.

More than 2,1 million crimes are recorded by the SAPS every year. The police service collects and releases crime data according to four broad categories: contact crimes (including murder and sexual offences, robbery, etc), contact-related crimes (such as arson), property-related crimes (burglary, theft, etc) and other serious crimes (including commercial crime).

Overall, serious crimes – including sexual offences, assault, murder, commercial crime, stock theft and theft of motor vehicles – constitute 80 per cent of the crimes recorded by the police. Ours is a violent society but, contrary to the general belief, things have generally improved since 1994/95. This can be seen in Figure 14, which shows the number of crime incidents on the left-hand axis and population size on the right. While South Africa's population has steadily increased from around 40,5 million people in 1994/95 to 54,6 million people in 2015/16, total incidents of crime first peaked in 2002/03 and then declined to around 2,3 million incidents. With a bigger population, one would expect more crime. Therefore, the risk of being a victim of crime has generally decreased since 1994. The fear of crime, however, has increased.

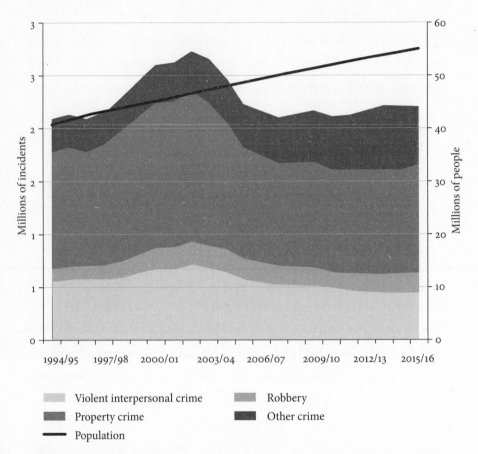

Figure 14: South African crime trends and population size, 1994–2016
Source: SAPS data, as presented on ISS Crime Hub, https://issafrica.org/crimehub/facts-and-figures/national-crime

Using the murder rate as a proxy for general levels of crime, South Africa's lowest murder rate, 30,2 homicides per 100 000 people, occurred in 2011/12 and has subsequently increased to 34 homicides (see Figure 15).[10] The most recent murder rates per province from the SAPS are given in Table 4.

Table 4: Murder rates per province, 2015/16

Province	Murders per 100 000 people
Eastern Cape	52,8
Western Cape	52
KwaZulu-Natal	36
Free State	35,2
Northern Cape	31,4
Gauteng	29,1
North West	24,5
Mpumalanga	20,1
Limpopo	15,7

Source: SAPS data as presented on ISS Crime Hub, https://issafrica.org/crimehub/facts-and-figures/national-crime

Aggravated robbery (i.e. street robbery, residential robbery, carjacking and kidnapping) has also increased in recent years. Although there have been declines in certain categories, violent crime in South Africa is generally on the increase but has not regressed to the very high levels seen in 1994/95.[11] Drug-related crime, on the other hand, has steadily increased year on year, although there have been signs of a downturn since 2014.

According to the police, an average 55 000 rapes are reported each year. However, given that only an estimated one in 2 525 incidents is recorded, rape, sexual assault and domestic abuse in South Africa are generally far more prevalent than reflected in the police statistics.[12] Indeed, when comparing the police figures with the results from the Victims of Crime surveys conducted by Stats SA, it appears evident that victims of crime are increasingly not reporting incidents to the police. According to the most recent survey, whereas nine in ten vehicle thefts are reported to the police (largely for insurance purposes), only about half of all assaults and home burglaries

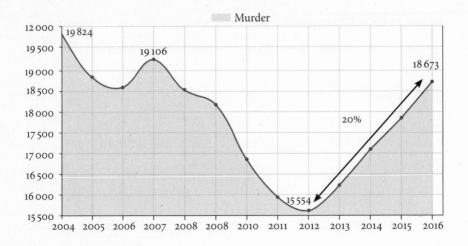

Figure 15: Numbers of murders in South Africa
Source: SAPS data, as presented on ISS Crime Hub, https://issafrica.org/crimehub/facts-and-figures/
national-crime

are reported. Around only a third of stock theft and consumer-fraud incidents, and 55 per cent of street robberies, are reported to the police.[13]

The decline in reporting rates seemingly reflects a lack of trust in the
police. Growing threats of crime and gang warfare in the face of a security
apparatus that is widely perceived as corrupt and incapable, and a justice
system that is under severe strain due to political interference, also play a
role. The police killing of protesting mineworkers at the Marikana mine
in 2012 placed the spotlight squarely on state violence.

According to the Mo Ibrahim Index of African Governance, South
Africa ranks 45th out of 52 African countries in terms of citizens' reported sense of personal safety, a measure that has fallen by 3 per cent
since 2011. This is a staggeringly poor rating when one considers South
Africa's relative wealth and the levels of armed conflict and warfare elsewhere on the continent. It reflects, among others, the rise of vigilantism
and, recently, widespread xenophobia, which suggests that, for the average South African, the overall sense of safety is declining. The 2015/16

results from the Victims of Crime survey show that only 31 per cent of South Africans feel safe walking in their neighbourhood alone after dark, down from 37 per cent in 2011.

It is no coincidence that South Africa has one of the world's largest private security industries.[14] It is often private security firms rather than the police that respond to crime incidents in much of middle- and upper-class suburbia, while local vigilantes enforce community justice in squatter and informal areas, leaving an embattled police force to patrol the rest.

Social instability: riots and protests

After the 1994 elections, the number of protest incidents dropped dramatically as the economy strengthened and South Africans basked in the positive self-image of peaceful reconciliation. However, since 1997, the data points to a steady increase in riots and protests.[15] Data from the SAPS and the ISS Public Violence Monitor indicates that incidents have also become more violent over time. Perhaps it was only natural that the initial euphoria would wear off, exposing the harsh realities that had developed in South Africa and led to the apartheid crisis in the first instance.

In contrast to the apartheid era, contemporary protests in South Africa are not aimed at overthrowing the government. Most protests have been non-violent and motivated by considerations such as frustration with inadequate local government services, such as access to water and electricity, competition over tenders, labour disputes, education and the result of ineffective policing such as when known criminals are not arrested or the police do not deploy in time to prevent the destruction of property after being forewarned.

Protests often appear to be triggered by desperate competition over who controls the allocation of services through tenders. Writing for the *Cape Times* in February 2014, Deputy Minister for Public Works and SACP Deputy General Secretary Jeremy Cronin argued that 'competing ANC factions linked to former councillors and now out of favour small businesses' were behind the 'mobilisation of angry youth'. 'It's not so much the absence of services but desperate competition over who controls their allocation that triggers protest,' said Cronin.[16]

Furthermore, members of politically excluded groups are more likely to mobilise after a change in their relative positions of power.[17] Protests and uprisings tend to occur in contexts that have experienced relative prosperity or growth followed by a sudden decline or reversal. The country therefore is saddled with rising expectations among the recently liberated black population, who have generally experienced extraordinary improvements in living standards in a short space of time and believe that rate of improvement will continue – a sense of aspiration that the state cannot meet, given the low economic growth rates.

From the government's perspective, service delivery protests are ascribed to rising expectations that are fuelled by the government's successes in service delivery. This is a sentiment that has been expressed by Zuma.[18] In reality, however, the opposite appears to be happening. The quality and roll-out of service delivery seem to have waned as the efficiency and capacity of local government have declined. The increasing number of service delivery protests therefore points to widespread anger and growing impatience with local government.

Moreover, being unemployed means that citizens have time on their hands to participate in protests and demonstrations. This was evident in 2016 ahead of the local government elections when the EFF, which presents an electoral message tailored to unemployed poor people, were able to attract a larger audience than any other party.

Much of the literature on the question of how and why protests in South Africa escalate into violence addresses the timing and tactics of police engagement. The question is always, which comes first: violence by the protesters or by the police? This is important because, in highly charged crowd settings, hostility is communicable and spreads rapidly, sometimes via social media or word of mouth, identifying a scapegoat as the focus for its frustration, often the police or security agencies, which are then seen as representing the source of the problem. In such a context, relatively minor incidents can spark off larger and escalating public protests.[19]

The police, through their Incident Registration Information System (IRIS), maintain a database that records all policing activity, including crowd incidents. Incidents are not necessarily protests, however, as IRIS captures only those incidents where the police are involved. After peaking in 2005/06, the number of peaceful incidents recorded within IRIS by the SAPS declined to their lowest point in 2008/09 but increased thereafter.[20] Subsequent analysis published by the ISS would indicate that the decline in incidents from 2006 to 2008 followed the restructuring of the crime-combating units within the SAPS, resulting in a 20% to 40% under-recording of incidents during those years.[21] That said, the general upward trend is clear: South Africa is becoming more turbulent, and more protests are increasingly violent even if population increases are taken into account (see Figure 16).

Ironically, as the number of protest incidents has been increasing, the size of the public-order unit of the police has decreased, largely as part of the disastrous legacy of former police commissioner Jackie Selebi and subsequent political appointments to the position of National Police Commissioner. However, according to the SAPS, the unit will be increased to 8 820 members by 2020. That will bring it back to a size last seen before 2006.[22]

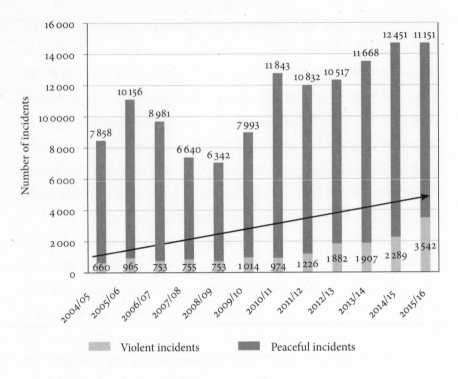

Figure 16: Violent and peaceful public-order incidents
Source: SAPS data, as presented on ISS Crime Hub, https://issafrica.org/crimehub/facts-and-figures/
national-crime

According to police statistics, organised vandalism and organised destruction of public property are not increasing despite highly publicised recent events, such as the burning of schools in Limpopo in 2016.[23]

The #FeesMustFall and the #RhodesMustFall campaigns, which began in 2015, are other recent examples of violent protest movements.[24] Some of the most active campuses have been the University of Cape Town, the University of the Western Cape and the University of Pretoria, but with wide variations in the nature of the grievances and the degrees of violence exhibited at each institution.

A publication by protestors from the University of the Western Cape argues that the nature of the Fees Must Fall protests is indistinguishable from the service delivery protests across the country, in that the student action also calls on government to deliver on its promises: '21 years of democracy should have been enough for the ANC to fulfil these promises [for free education, housing and land] ...'[25] There are widespread accusations of direct involvement by opposition parties, particularly the EFF, in the student protests.[26]

In September 2015, a demonstration of an estimated 10 000 people took place in Pretoria calling for Zuma's resignation. The campaign adopted the slogan #ZumaMustFall and reached over 100 000 users on Twitter alone towards the end of 2015.[27] After the March 2017 Cabinet reshuffle, the Save South Africa campaign and others brought together more than 25 000 people in Pretoria calling for Zuma to step down. ANC politicians trying to speak at the memorial of struggle veteran Ahmed Kathrada were booed off the stage. Meanwhile, public outrage in Cape Town and elsewhere against Zuma was clearly evident as thousands gathered in a hitherto unprecedented show of anger. Then, on 1 May 2017, Zuma was prohibited from speaking at the COSATU annual May Day rally in Bloemfontein by sustained booing – and the event was subsequently aborted.

Those happened to be non-violent demonstrations, but, in the eyes of many South African protesters, violence is, first, a medium through which to communicate frustration about inadequate services or poor local or national leadership, and to force a response from government. Many instances of violent protests have followed protracted efforts at engaging with government using legitimate and non-violent methods. When protests become violent, it generally reflects a failure of politicians to engage with their communities.

Second, violence is used to compete for resources in an environment where the rule of law is regularly flouted. A recent study suggests that a key motive behind violent forms of protest is to oust leaders and occupy positions of power.[28] Protests and violent demonstrations do not occur without instigation and some form of organisation and leadership. They are rarely spontaneous. Political actors, such as ousted councillors or local businessmen or women who have lost out on tenders, often serve as mobilisers, organisers or aggravators of popular protests. They create the opportunity for confrontation.

Adding to the frustration of citizens, there are few effective and open platforms for public participation in local political issues, despite decentralisation, local wards and *izimbizos* (local meetings). Councillors are seen to lack willingness or show no concern to engage with citizens, in part because they are often appointed because of their political loyalty rather than their ability or competence.

Given the high dependence of the poor on public services, there is clearly a relationship between poor governance and instability. For example, over 75 per cent of municipalities across the country failed to receive clean audits, and lacked qualified personnel serving as chief financial officers or in key technical and managerial positions. Subsequent inadequate public-sector productivity adversely affects the poor, worsens impoverishment and heightens social frustration. While the state should be credited for providing welfare payments to the most needy, it is this segment of society that also bears the brunt of inefficient and poor public services. A 2010 ad hoc committee on coordinated oversight documented weakness in local government and confirmed that many communities had unacceptably poor levels of service provision – a trigger for instability.

Vigilantism and xenophobia

Since 2013, incidents of vigilantism have become the third most common form of public violence. Of a total of 199 acts of vigilantism recorded in the media to the end of 2016, 98 per cent were violent.[29] The townships and informal settlements in the greater Cape Town metropolitan area see the most incidents of this form of violence in the country, with Johannesburg in second place.

The roots and cultural context for this type of violence are complex. Some aspects of vigilantism can be traced back to apartheid, when communities relied on their own forms of security to assert local control.[30] Gang-related violence of the sort seen in the former Coloured townships of Cape Town also has origins in this expression of territorial control and in the city's illicit drug markets.[31]

Xenophobic attacks and protests against foreign migrant communities have been a regular feature of South Africa's culture of violence for several years. Such incidents are apparently motivated by a 'hatred or fear of foreigners or strangers',[32] and more specifically by the belief that foreign nationals take jobs from South Africans.[33] Either way, xenophobia reflects the acute leadership deficit in the country.[34]

Xenophobia is not a recent phenomenon, however. The first reported assaults on foreign immigrants by armed gangs were in Alexandra in the mid-1990s, and several dozen migrants were killed in xenophobic attacks in subsequent years, notably during the highly publicised events of late 2007 and early 2008. One of the worst incidents of xenophobic violence occurred in May 2008 in Gauteng when 62 people were killed and 30 000 displaced.[35] Since then, reported incidents of violent xenophobia decreased, only to flare up again during 2015.

Following these events, South Africa suffered a major international-relations embarrassment when the attacks were placed on the agenda of the AU's Peace and Security Council for discussion. Several countries called for punitive measures against South Africa, including the boycotting of South African businesses and goods.

In February 2017, widespread xenophobic violence broke out again in Pretoria and Johannesburg, soon degenerating into the looting of foreign-owned shops. Nigerians in the capital, Abuja, responded by attacking the premises of South African cellphone giant MTN, and the Nigerian Senate threatened to expel several South African corporations (such as Shoprite and DStv). The South African High Commissioner to Nigeria, Lulu Mnguni, was summoned to the Ministry of Foreign Affairs as the Nigerian Government expressed its outrage over the events.[36] For his part, Zuma tried to massage the issue by claiming South Africans were merely protesting against rising levels of crime committed by non-nationals – despite considerable evidence that points to the contrary.[37]

A 2011 study on community protests and xenophobic attacks in South Africa found that most xenophobic attacks occurred in tandem with community protests. Incidents were largely about the notion of citizenship and happened against a backdrop of the growing gap between the post-apartheid elite (both black and white) and the large underclass of unemployed.[38]

A study by the Southern African Migration Project found that South Africans are less tolerant of migrants from countries further away, such as Nigeria, the DRC and Somalia, than of those from neighbouring countries, such as Zimbabwe and Lesotho.[39] This is undoubtedly influenced by the history of the migrant-labour system. Whereas migrants from these countries are known and apparently deemed slightly more acceptable, the influx of fellow Africans from further afield seems to have elicited a more violent reaction.

Election violence

Until 2004, elections in democratic South Africa were generally peaceful affairs, undoubtedly because of confidence in the integrity and independence of the Independent Electoral Commission, a belief in the democratic system that was put in place in 1994, and the transparency surrounding election processes. Subsequently, however, the trend for election violence has become concerning. Ahead of the 2009 elections, clashes occurred between members of the ANC and those of its splinter group, the Congress of the People. During the 2014 elections, people at several voting stations across the country, and staff members from the Independent Electoral Commission in Alexandra and Tzaneen, were threatened.

The 2016 local government elections (at least on the polling day itself) demonstrated that the South African police and other agencies have the potential and means to provide security when there is sufficient political will and public pressure to do so.[40]

However, there were many incidents of violence in the run-up to the 2016 local elections. There was trouble around voter registration, with the Constitutional Court investigating the Independent Electoral Commission's incomplete voter roll in Tlokwe, in North West. In Tshwane, the ANC announced that it was putting forward former agriculture and land affairs minister Thoko Didiza as mayoral candidate when competing factions could not agree on a compromise. Supporters, as well as those who had benefited from jobs and contracts under the incumbent mayor, Kgosientso 'Sputla' Ramokgopa, then sought to make Tshwane 'ungovernable'.[41]

During the ANC's nomination process months before the 2016 local elections, ANC Secretary-General Gwede Mantashe expressed his concern that nominations had become a life-and-death issue for many – a forecast that was quite literally borne out by subsequent events. Eventually there were 20 political killings between 1 January and 18 July 2016 (13 of them in KwaZulu-Natal alone) and dozens of buses were torched in a fiercely contested battle in the run-up to the elections.[42] Political killings are not new, and in the months ahead of the 2014 elections the ISS Public Violence Monitor recorded 28 politically related deaths.

The state's response to crime and violence

South Africa has had a plethora of plans and initiatives to combat crime. These include the National Crime Prevention Strategy of 1996, the National Crime Combating Strategy (NCCS) of 2000 and the 2016 White Paper on Safety and Security. The National Development Plan also set out a comprehensive framework for a South Africa where people 'feel safe at home, at school and at work, and they enjoy a community life free of fear'.[43] To achieve a crime-free South Africa, the plan lists several priorities, including strengthening the criminal justice system and improving professionalism in the police, among others.

If only government could implement such plans. In reality, the public's sense of safety has actually declined since the National Development Plan was published, as the governing party has generally moved away from the proposals contained in it.

Figure 17 shows the widening gap the over past decade between the number of arrests made by the police and the number of cases finalised by the NPA. From 2006/07 to 2015/16, the police made 410 715 more arrests but the NPA finalised 23 701 fewer cases. This disparity is a good measure of the poor progress made in the state's response to crime. Instead of 'prosecuting without fear, favour and prejudice and working with partners and the public to solve and prevent crime' (the NPA's stated mission), the authority has been used by the Zuma administration for the pursuit of factional politics.

Between 2011 and 2015/16, the public's satisfaction with the police declined from 64,7 per cent to 57 per cent, although the most recent

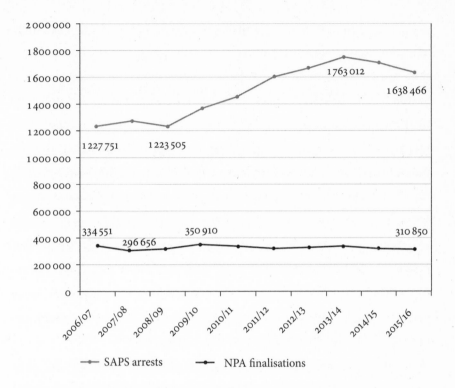

Figure 17: SAPS arrests vs NPA case finalisations
Source: SAPS data, as presented on ISS Crime Hub, https://issafrica.org/crimehub/facts-and-figures/national-crime

survey indicates an improvement of 2 per cent.[44] The rise in civil claims against the police also tells a story of declining levels of trust in the police and increased abuse of power. Such claims rose by 175 per cent from the 2011/12 financial year to 2015/16. The claims related to police involvement in serious crimes, including murder, rape and armed robbery. In the Eastern Cape, for example, almost 60 police officers were fired for serious crimes, and a staggering R51 million was paid out in 781 civil claims in 2015/16. This was almost double the amount in the previous financial year.[45] The number of reported cases of police brutality also increased dramatically between 2001 and 2010.[46]

All of South Africa's security institutions – the police, the defence force and intelligence agencies – suffer from constantly shifting policy direction, poor management and political compromise. The result is a state that is unable to secure public property (such as schools and universities) against destruction, even when provided with ample precedent and warnings. But the efforts at undermining independent investigation go much further than just bad management: elements in the ANC have engaged in deliberate efforts to obstruct justice and have abused the system for political and commercial purposes.

Perhaps the most serious of these were the ANC's efforts to establish political control over the previous independent priority crime investigation unit, the Scorpions. The decision followed the power struggle between Mbeki and Zuma, resulting in what Zuma believed was a politically motivated investigation into his involvement in the arms deal. The Scorpions, which investigated serious crime, was then merged with the police, whose head is appointed by the president.[47] A protracted court battle followed, during which civil society organisations were able to retain a measure of independence for the unit, but Zuma remained steadfast in his belief that the newly named Hawks had to be brought under the authority of the National Police Commissioner.

It soon became clear that the unit would play an important role in factional politics, the most prominent of which was the case against Pravin Gordhan for the purported establishment of a 'rogue' investigation unit while he was head of SARS. Eventually, efforts to prosecute Gordhan by the Hawks and the NPA came to naught, but the unit's exposure to political manoeuvring, as well as its dependence on the police, has had a very negative impact on the organisation's effectiveness.

In April 2017, the High Court in Pretoria confirmed an earlier ruling that the head of the Hawks, Major General Berning Ntlemeza, was dishonest and unfit to lead the crime-fighting unit. Ntlemeza had been irregularly appointed in September 2015, apparently with the sole intent to pursue particular individuals opposed to Zuma.[48]

Under Zuma, the security cluster has steadily become more powerful and there are clear signs of involvement of the security agencies in politics. A stream of bogus intelligence and media reports have claimed the existence of outlandish conspiracies. The Operation Check Mate intelligence report, which was used by Zuma as justification for firing Gordhan and his deputy, is only one in a string of examples.[49]

Although the risk of being a victim of crime has decreased since 1994, much more can and should be done. According to the SAPS, 83 per cent of crimes are reported to the police; that means only 17 per cent of crimes are detected as a result of direct police action. Crime prevention should therefore be more about intervening in those areas that contribute to the risk of violence, such as investing in at-risk youth and addressing the role of alcohol, guns and drugs in crime.[50] In combating crime, the role of government, particularly the Department of Social Development, and interventions in high-risk communities are much more important than efforts that seek to improve efficiency in the police, important as that may be.

Although the picture sketched out in this chapter is concerning, it is important to retain perspective when considering the situation in which South Africa finds itself in 2017. The country does not face anything comparable to the violent events that unfolded during the Soweto protests of 1976 and their aftermath. Ours is a crime-ridden and turbulent society, but it is not primed for violent revolution. However, in the run-up to 2019 there may be a propensity for increased violent political contestation. With good planning and appropriate preparation, the security agencies should, however, be able to contain the situation.

At the same time, it is important to acknowledge that, since 2012, violent crime, labour and service-delivery-related protests have increased, as have the frequency and intensity of student protests and, most recently, demonstrations demanding the president's resignation. Political assassinations and factional violence within the ANC are also on an upward trend, as the ruling party struggles to cope with a host of challenges ranging from corruption to allegations of state capture, leadership and ethical issues, as well as the weakening of its key ally, COSATU. Prominent ANC leaders, including Gwede Mantashe, Chief Whip Jackson Mthembu and human settlements minister Lindiwe Sisulu, have received death threats for daring to question Zuma during internal meetings.[51]

The ISS can attest to the existence of a Zuma-aligned goon squad. For example, in April 2005 the ISS published a study on the campaign for moral regeneration in South Africa, which was, ironically, led by the then deputy president, Jacob Zuma.[52] The study was critical of the leadership and content of what can at best be described as a strange effort of the Mbeki administration. Even before the monograph was published, the ISS was inundated by intimidating and defamatory text and email messages from a wide array of trolls, with clear hints at linkages to the intelligence and broader security community. And when Paul Holden and Hennie van Vuuren (then at the ISS Cape Town office) were completing their groundbreaking study, 'The devil in the detail: How the arms deal changed everything', in 2010, our Cape Town offices were broken into. Nothing was taken in the end, but it was a clear instance of seeking information on the background research.[53]

Future prospects

It is very likely that the ANC will again experience significant levels of internal violence and that the country will see further instability in the period running up to the party's conference in December 2017. The violence within the ANC is also spilling over and affecting other parties. In April 2017, for instance, the images of a man appearing to point a gun at Solly Mapaila, second deputy general secretary of the SACP (which had called for Zuma to step down), at an event commemorating the death of struggle icon Chris Hani were widely circulated on social media. And the leader of the DA, Mmusi Maimane, has taken to wearing a bulletproof vest during marches against Zuma.[54]

This instability will manifest itself in the form of inter- and intra-party violence: there are likely to be political assassinations and orchestrated violent protests as factions and local politicians fight for access to resources and political opportunities. There could also be events orchestrated by the EFF as it seeks to destabilise the ANC, and vice versa. A number of ANC politicians have reported death threats.[55]

Such an environment is potentially very worrisome, as declining public confidence, coupled with growing economic uncertainty and the security sector's uneven track record in responding to violence could feed off one another.

KwaZulu-Natal has consistently experienced more political murders than the other provinces, a trend expected to intensify in the months ahead of the December conference. Since it is the largest single voting block within the party and split between supporters of Nkosazana Dlamini-Zuma and Cyril Ramaphosa, competition will be particularly intense.[56]

After the conference, intra-ANC violence will most likely be replaced by violence between rival political parties in the run-up to the national elections in 2019. The loss of an ANC national majority in those elections (the Nation Divided scenario) could see violence spread and intensify.

In light of South Africa's downgrade to junk status, citizens will also face increased economic pressure, which could well add fuel to our already violent society. We are likely to see repeat cycles of xenophobia and other types of crowd and mob violence in the context of the economic futures set out in both the Bafana Bafana and Nation Divided scenarios.

At the same time, there has been a steady attrition in the capacity of the security agencies, all of which have suffered from regular changes in their senior management and from declining professionalism. Some, the intelligence agencies in particular, seem to have been dragged into internal factional fights. The most public fallout was the forced resignations of Jeff Maqetuka, director general of the State Security Agency, head of foreign intelligence Moe Shaik and head of domestic intelligence Gibson Njenje at the end of 2011 following sustained pressure from Zuma to abandon a project to monitor the influence of the Guptas on government.[57] Consequently, their ability to objectively tackle violence has been compromised. Only the Mandela Magic scenario envisions a positive change in the management and oversight of the security agencies.

Violence and instability occur against the backdrop of economic stagnation and extreme levels of inequality – trends that will continue under the Bafana Bafana and Nation Divided scenarios. Other chapters have reflected on the extent to which South Africa is trapped at low growth levels, which is also likely to exacerbate social turbulence, at least until 2019 or 2020 – and possibly even until 2034 under the two most likely scenarios, Bafana Bafana and Nation Divided. Furthermore, South Africa's fiscal deficit and debt indicators signal that there is limited scope to spend more to achieve greater redistribution, meaning current government spending on social welfare may prove to be unsustainable after the recent credit downgrade.

The Bafana Bafana scenario could see the ANC's national electoral support dip and the DA gain the largest share of support in Gauteng, while retaining its tight control of the Western Cape. At this point, South

Africa would already have entered an era of coalition politics at local- and provincial level, so it is conceivable that the 2024 elections could be heavily contested and therefore particularly violent.

Liberation parties elsewhere in Africa have not readily ceded power, and South Africa is unlikely to be an exception. Under Zuma's leadership, 'a whole parallel state is developing' where organisations such as the Hawks are used for factional purposes, the State Security Agency spies on politicians and decisions are taken outside of Cabinet. This is all taking place in an atmosphere of growing authoritarianism, where political assassinations are on the rise. Jeremy Cronin described what he sees as a 'nostalgia' for militarism; the intimidation of those who speak out against government, such as former social development official Zane Dangor; and the rise of 'provincial goon squads'. 'It is very, very concerning,' he says.[58]

Organisations such as the Independent Electoral Commission will come under increased pressure and its integrity will be questioned. It is also likely that populist policies could incite increased urban violence as city dwellers react to being more marginalised than their rural peers, the main support base of the ANC.

South Africa therefore faces fluctuating but relatively high levels of instability over the forecast horizon to 2034, although the situation is worst in the Nation Divided scenario.

Violence in South Africa will escalate unless the country is able to choose a leader who respects its Constitution, behaves ethically and places the country ahead of personal interest. South Africa then needs to generate and sustain much more rapid and inclusive growth than it has in recent years, restore a capable and engaged government that is more effective and less corrupt, and change its style of policing so as to build mutual respect between its citizenry and law enforcement agencies.[59]

CHAPTER 9

South Africa in a comparative context

*If we are to develop our economy and create jobs on the scale
required, we need to attract businesses that can invest anywhere
in the world, and not just in what lies beneath our soil.*

– Nicky Oppenheimer[1]

South Africa is undoubtedly a leader in Africa, but its influence becomes
contested the further north one travels. Egypt and Algeria, for example,
are much more influential in North Africa, while Nigeria is the undis-
puted heavyweight in the west.[2]

Power, or 'one's ability to affect the behavior of others to get what
one wants',[3] evolves over time and is a function of many factors, including leadership (compare, for example, the impact of Nelson Mandela,
Thabo Mbeki and Jacob Zuma on how South Africa is perceived), alliances (such as our partners in Africa and relationships within the BRICS
grouping), the nature of governance (internal strife constrains the ability
to project power) and economic growth (a larger economy translates into
more power).

This chapter first places South Africa's recent economic growth in a
comparative international perspective and then compares its population

with those of other countries before comparing economic forecasts under the three scenarios. It reviews trade and the evolution of foreign policy since the Mandela era and concludes by presenting South Africa's national interests in a post-Zuma era.

Every year, the World Bank issues its classification of countries on a range from low to high income. In the most recent of these, released in July 2016, South Africa is classified as one of only nine upper-middle-income countries in Africa. Yet it has only half the average income required to graduate to the next level, the high-income bracket, where most wealthy, developed countries find themselves.[4]

After the growth spurt that followed GEAR, South Africa has on average been getting poorer. Following year-on-year improvements since 2002, South Africa's average levels of income per person peaked at USD7 640 in 2012 and have subsequently declined each year. This is because the economy is not growing fast enough when one takes population growth into account. Our high levels of inequality and the backlog in the provision of services to a large segment of the population mean that the effects of economic growth are not trickling down.

It is for these reasons – a growing population and high levels of inequality – that the National Development Plan set an ambitious average growth target of 5,4 per cent to 2030. It is also why South Africa has a highly progressive tax system and spends significant amounts of money on alleviating poverty through welfare schemes. Government has to use the tools available for redistribution and mediate inequality without killing off the economic goose (largely the private sector) that lays the golden eggs.

When comparing the differences between South Africa and other countries on the continent in terms of population size, Tanzania is a good starting point. Tanzania has a much younger population, but currently has a similar number of people – around 55 million. By 2034, however, the size of Tanzania's population is expected to be around 90 million; South Africa's will be around 64,5 million.

The size of the South African working-age population (15 to 64) is steadily growing as a proportion of the total population (which, as mentioned earlier, is good news if the economy can create more jobs for this segment). At the moment, that segment is 66 per cent and will slowly increase to 69 per cent by 2034. By contrast, only 52 per cent of Tanzania's population is currently of working age, and by 2034 the figure will be 57 per cent.

So, relative to the size of its total population, Tanzanians of working age have to support many more dependants (particularly more children), despite the fact that Tanzania is also a much poorer country than South Africa. In countries with a more mature population structure, such as Taiwan, South Korea and China, the percentage of the working-age population has peaked at levels as high as 72 per cent, which was a large factor in the rapid economic growth rates of these countries.

Although South Africa has a relatively young population by global standards, this is not the case when compared with the rest of sub-Saharan Africa. The median age in South Africa is about 26 years; in Tanzania it is just over 17. In Africa, only Mauritius, Seychelles and some North African countries have median ages higher than South Africa's.

These figures reflect the fact that South Africa is further along in the demographic transition from high birth and death rates to low birth and death rates than most other African countries. That transition is an important part of the journey in moving from subsistence economic conditions to a modern, industrialised economy with higher levels of human development for its citizenry.

If we take the average income per person, South Africans have the eighth-highest income levels in Africa and the country is likely to retain this position for the foreseeable future. Only Botswana has a higher average level of income per person in the southern African region, and the gap between the two countries is likely to increase as Botswana's economy is expected to grow more rapidly. Our average income per capita places South Africa at 88th in the world and, under the Bafana Bafana scenario, we will steadily fall down the global rankings to 95th by 2034. Under the worst-case scenario (Nation Divided), Namibia's average income level will overtake that of South Africa by 2032.

Some of these figures should raise eyebrows. For example, South Africa has the 29th-largest economy in the world and the 25th-largest population. But when one compares income levels per person, we are much lower, at 88th. As explained earlier, this is because wealth in South Africa is concentrated in a very small portion of the population. It is not for nothing that we are considered the most unequal country in the world when using measures of inequality such as the Gini coefficient.[5]

After 1960, when Africa was in the midst of decolonisation, South Africa tended to grow more rapidly than most other countries on the continent, but that trend started to change in the late 1980s. The commodity supercycle, rapid population growth and the rise of China have meant that much of the rest of Africa now grows more rapidly than South Africa, although off a lower base.[6] Since the beginning of this century, Africa's average growth rate has been almost 2 per cent higher than that of South Africa, and this trend is unlikely to change. But, although we will be growing more slowly, in part because our economy is more mature and therefore more complex, high growth rates in the rest of Africa will present South Africans with significant business opportunities.

Currently, South Africa is the second-largest economy in Africa, with Nigeria the largest. Table 5 summarises the prospects in terms of the size of the economy by 2034, as well as the expected average levels of income. Average income levels will be affected by the different growth rates in each scenario.

Table 5: South Africa's economic prospects – three scenarios

	Nation Divided	Bafana Bafana	Mandela Magic
Size of SA economy by 2034 in market exchange rates	USD630 billion or R5 505 billion	USD718 billion or R6 280 billion	USD868 billion or R7 593 billion
Economic size ranking globally and in Africa	37th and 3rd	33rd and 2nd	29th and 2nd
Average income by 2034 in purchasing power parity	USD14 300 or R125 000	USD15 700 or R137 000	USD17 800 or R155 700
Income ranking globally and in Africa	100th and 37th	95th and 8th	85th and 7th

In the Bafana Bafana scenario (with a forecast average annual growth rate of 2,3 per cent to 2034), our relative position in Africa will slowly decline, although South Africa should continue to be an economic and industrial giant in the southern African region for many years. By 2034 the size of South Africa's GDP should be around USD718 billion and the country is then likely to be ranked 33rd globally, with an economy slightly smaller than that of Norway and Thailand at that point. We would, at these rates, still contribute about 0,5 per cent of the total global economy and 13 per cent of the African economy, down from 18 per cent in 2017. By 2034 South Africa would still be the second-largest economy in Africa.

In Nation Divided, South Africa's economy will be around USD630 billion and Egypt would have surpassed us, making us the third-largest economy on the continent. In the Mandela Magic scenario, South Africa would have improved its relative global ranking to the 29th-largest economy.

Nigeria is the only African country that has the long-term potential to become globally significant. Nigeria's economy is expected to increase its 20 per cent share of the total African economy. Yet, despite its larger economy, it is unlikely that average income levels in Nigeria will catch up with those of South Africa despite the fact that its economy is set to grow much more rapidly. This is because the Nigerian economy is much less sophisticated than South Africa's and singularly dependent on oil, with all the associated negative implications of a single-commodity export economy. Therefore, as South Africa will struggle to become a high-income economy, Nigeria will struggle to become an upper-middle-income economy.[7]

Other than economic growth, there are many further examples of South Africa's relative size and sophistication compared to its African peers. For example, South Africa has diplomatic missions in a remarkable 122 countries, including 47 African countries, and it hosts embassies from 134 countries, making Pretoria a large diplomatic centre by global standards, although the country has recently been losing some of this influence to Addis Ababa as the African Union steadily ramps up in importance. Only Egypt rivals South Africa in terms of the number of the embassies it has globally; Egypt also enjoys close relations within the Group of 77 developing countries, the Non-Aligned Movement and others. Despite all its domestic and leadership problems, South Africa is still currently Africa's diplomatic heavyweight.

At more than USD182 billion market capitalisation, the Johannesburg Stock Exchange is more than ten times bigger than any other African stock exchange and represents 80 per cent of Africa's entire equity capital markets. The JSE has an average daily trading value more than 200 times greater than Nigeria's stock exchange.[8] If Gauteng (South Africa's richest province) were a country, its economy would rank as the fourth-largest in Africa, with KwaZulu-Natal and the Western Cape the eighth- and ninth-largest, respectively. For this reason, South Africa will remain a major economic player in Africa.

So, in absolute terms, South Africa is an important country in Africa and, depending on future growth prospects, it will remain so for years to come, although the extent of that importance varies quite markedly between the scenarios.

Trade with countries outside the continent

South Africa is deeply embedded in the international economic system and our future prosperity will be determined by what happens with its trade relations both globally and its trade with Africa. It is for this reason that foolish talk about radical economic restructuring and nationalisation is bad for the country.

After a general increase in trade, recent years have seen a slowdown. The global economic recession and declines in commodity prices have hit South Africa hard. Although South Africa accounts for only a 1,3 per cent share of total EU trade, the EU is South Africa's largest trading partner – a relationship that is unlikely to change in the foreseeable future despite the decision by the UK (a major trading partner for South Africa in its own right) to exit from the EU in 2019. In 2015, the value of EU/South Africa trade was almost double that of its trade with China. South Africa and the EU signed a Trade, Development and Cooperation Agreement in 1999, which entered into force in 2004. South Africa is one of the ten strategic partners of the EU, with more than 2 000 European companies active in South Africa. Europe accounts for 77 per cent of foreign direct investment in South Africa (compared to 4 per cent from China).[9]

Apart from the dominance in trade with the EU, the most noticeable trend in South Africa's trade is the surge in imports from China since 2009 and the subsequent fall-off since 2013. South Africa's trade relations with China track those of Africa-Chinese relations. In 2009, China overtook the US to become Africa's single largest trading partner (although trade with the EU group is much larger) and trade grew in leaps and bounds thereafter. However, in 2015 China–Africa trade declined by 19 per cent on the previous year and in 2016 it was set for a further 13 per cent year-on-year decline.[10]

Trade between the EU and South Africa, and between the US and South Africa has also declined. The importance of the North American Free Trade Area/NAFTA (consisting of the US, Canada and Mexico) as a trade partner of South Africa since 2011 has declined, despite the US unilateral concession to provide market access to Africa for 6 400 products in the primary and beneficiated goods category under the African Growth and Opportunity Act (AGOA). AGOA was extended to 2025 under the Obama presidency and presents South African exports with opportunities not available in trade with the EU or China, although the associated compliance costs are considerable.

South Africa's trade relations with India have grown significantly since the mid-2000s. Imports from India peaked in 2013 at nearly USD5,4 billion and then fell by 35 per cent to 2015, while exports to India peaked at nearly USD3,8 billion in 2014, and then decreased by 22 per cent to 2015.

South Africa has a regular, large trade deficit with most regions. In 2015, the South African Reserve Bank recorded a current-account deficit of around 4,4 per cent of the country's GDP. This is because we have a large import bill, low savings and high levels of personal consumption as a percentage of disposable income.

South Africa finances its current-account shortfall through capital inflows from foreign investors who buy local bonds and acquire equity in local companies. Therefore, when foreign investors and speculators lose confidence in the country – often as a result of domestic developments, such as the replacement of the Minister of Finance with someone who is unknown in financial circles and with a questionable relationship with the Gupta family, as happened at the end of 2015 – the value of the rand plummets. The impact of the Cabinet reshuffle in March 2017 was luckily muted by the general positive sentiment towards emerging markets at that point.

Forecasting in which direction trade relations will go is difficult, but it would be reasonable to expect that South Africa's financial and logistic systems will allow it to serve as a gateway to a rapidly growing southern Africa region in the Mandela Magic scenario, and that investors will largely avoid South Africa in the Nation Divided scenario.

Africa's importance for South Africa, and vice versa
South Africa's future growth is tied to demand from Africa, the region where it has some advantages over competitors such as China, but also to Europe and North America. Africa is therefore the most important foreign-policy priority for South Africa given the importance of the continent to our economic, security and political future.

An examination of the consolidated government expenditure budget for 2016/17 reveals that DIRCO gets around R2 892,9 million out of a total government budget of R1,46 trillion. Almost a third of that budget goes to engagement with Africa, which, in straight monetary terms, is larger than the budget for Europe, North America or Asia. Also, South Africa has spent large sums of money trying to stabilise the DRC, such as funding elections and the costs of peacekeeping efforts – and these figures are not included in the DIRCO budget.

Africa is the only region with which South Africa has a consistent trade surplus – a sharp contrast to the annual trade deficits that we have with the rest of the world (see Figure 18). Furthermore, most of South Africa's exports to Africa consist of value-added manufactured products, including refined petroleum, trucks and motor vehicles, diamonds and electricity. To put this in perspective, in 2015 South Africa recorded its biggest trade deficits with China, Germany, Nigeria (due to oil imports), Saudi Arabia, Thailand, France, Italy and India, and its biggest trade surpluses with Botswana, Namibia, Zambia, Zimbabwe, Mozambique, Belgium and Japan. South Africa's export markets are concentrated in SADC. Beyond that region, only Kenya features in the top ten markets for South Africa's exports.

Trade within the Southern African Customs Union (SACU), an economic trading bloc consisting of South Africa, Botswana, Namibia, Lesotho and Swaziland, is highly asymmetric, with South Africa dominating imports and exports while the others are largely dependent on the revenues that they get from South Africa through SACU. Consistent with the global trade slowdown and the reductions in commodity prices, South African exports to the SACU countries peaked in 2012 and have since declined while Namibia and Botswana, with their more rapidly growing economies, have seen their exports to SACU increase.[11]

South Africa's mining, retail, construction, financial services, telecommunications, tourism and retail sectors have all expanded into the continent. Yet, generally, intra-African trade is very low, at roughly 15 per cent. Compare this with East Asia, where trade within the region is over 50 per cent, and Europe, where trade among countries in the continent is over 60 per cent of total trade.[12]

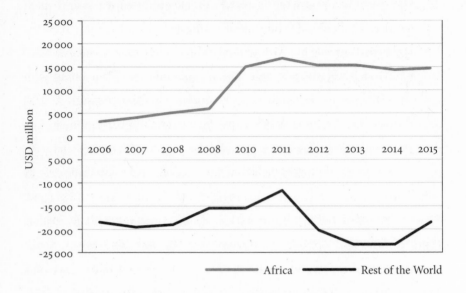

Figure 18: South Africa's trade balance, Africa vs rest of world
Source: TRALAC trade data analysis, https://www.tralac.org/resources/trade-data-analysis.html

So, there is massive potential to develop trade-related infrastructure and the exchange of goods between South Africa and sub-Saharan Africa. South African imports from SADC have already increased since the launch of the SADC free trade agreement, helping to balance relations that are heavily skewed in our favour.

The possibilities are virtually endless – if the Chinese and the Indians don't beat us to it. It is for this reason that the Industrial Policy Action Plan argues for an expanding Trade Invest Africa, as a one-stop shop to provide support to South African businesses doing business in the rest of Africa. And it is why Minister of Trade and Industry Rob Davies speaks of the importance of regional integration and building regional value chains as a tool to further South Africa's industrial development. In Davies's words:

> Our overriding priority is to work to promote African regional in-
> tegration … Practically, this means taking steps to enlarge the free
> trade areas existing in SADC and other regional economic commu-
> nities into larger more expansive FTAs [free trade areas], but also to
> complement this with active cooperation to address infrastructure
> deficiencies. The aim of this is to promote more intra-African trade
> and support industrialisation through the creation of large regional
> markets that can support the development of regional value chains.[13]

If Africa is important for South Africa, the converse is also true, in that South African growth and stability are also important for Africa.

According to consultancy firm Ernst & Young's estimates, if foreign investments into South Africa are removed from the picture, South Africa was the largest investor in Africa in 2012, bigger than China and the US.[14] This is reflected in the changes to South Africa's import foot-print in Africa in the past two decades. Whereas in 2000 only 2 per cent of total imports originated from the rest of Africa, this increased to 12 per cent by 2013, declining moderately thereafter.[15]

South Africa has also invested heavily in the pursuit of peace and security in the continent – in Burundi, the Central African Republic, the DRC, Côte d'Ivoire, Zimbabwe, Madagascar, Lesotho, Libya and others. As well as in its efforts at conflict resolution (most recently in Lesotho), South Africa has been a major contributor to peacekeeping in Africa, although it does not have the military means to continue at the pace of its previous efforts at peacekeeping without a comprehensive rethink.

Major peacekeeping deployments on the continent began in 2002 when 650 troops were sent to Burundi and 1 270 to the DRC the following year. Additional deployments to Sudan, Côte d'Ivoire, Eritrea, Ethiopia, Sudan and other countries followed.

Even at a lowly 1,05 per cent of its GDP, South Africa still wields the largest military budget in Africa after Algeria and Angola, but spending is set to decline to 0,98 per cent of GDP by 2017/18. At their current rates of growth, Morocco and Nigeria's defence expenditure will shortly overtake South Africa's. Angola will eventually play a leading military role in central Africa and possibly in southern Africa if it is able to manage the imminent leadership transition from the aged and sickly José Eduardo dos Santos.[16]

As is the case with many other government departments, the Department of Defence has dug itself into a big hole and keeps on digging. The department has not achieved the first two of its five milestones for the 2015 Defence Review: to 'arrest the decline in critical capabilities through immediate and directed interventions' and to 'recognize and re-balance the Defence Force as the foundation for future growth'. South Africa has already scaled down its contribution to peacekeeping in recent years and it is likely that this trend will continue, reducing our influence in, and contribution to stability on, the continent.

By all accounts, the DRC has been the biggest recipient of South African foreign development assistance for the past twenty years, on top of the deployment of significant peacekeeping efforts in the east of the country. Between 2001 and 2015, South Africa contributed over USD1 billion in overseas-development-assistance activities in the DRC, peaking at USD181 million in 2008, which made South Africa the third-biggest development partner to the DRC that year.[17] With this level of expenditure, South Africa, a small middle-income economy, therefore finds itself in the same league as large rich countries like the UK, France and others, which have large bureaucracies and considerable expertise in the provision and management of aid – capacities not evident in South Africa.

Currently, South Africa does not have a coherent and coordinated approach to its development cooperation. It provides development aid in a fragmented way through a range of different government departments and agencies, as well as non-state and private actors. Several years after it was first unveiled, the much vaunted South African Development Partnership Agency – the vehicle through which DIRCO would manage and channel its development assistance – remains an entity only on paper, as all attention is soaked up by dealing with the fracturing within the ruling party, as well as in a department that appears to be struggling with its internal management systems.

The lack of information and inconsistencies in the way in which South Africa provides development assistance limit the extent to which it can exert its 'soft power' in regional and global development platforms. In the Nation Divided scenario, South Africa will inevitably lose influence globally, whereas in the less likely Mandela Magic scenario the country serves as a compelling example for others to follow.

Foreign policy from Mandela to Zuma

Under the Mandela and Mbeki presidencies, South Africa punched above its weight internationally, but for different reasons. Under Zuma, South Africa's membership of BRICS has potentially elevated its global standing, but, at the same time, the country has been losing ground in Africa.

Mandela's iconic status bestowed the country with great moral clout internationally, even if his foreign minister (Alfred Nzo) lacked dynamism and vision, and the new government was inexperienced and inevitably preoccupied with the domestic imperatives of national reconciliation.

Mbeki, on the other hand, brought unprecedented coherence and energy to foreign policy, premised on idealism, internationalism and an emancipatory orientation. Under his influence, South Africa managed the inevitable tensions between ideology and pragmatism. South Africa played an important role in the 1995 indefinite extension of the Nuclear Non-Proliferation Treaty, the 1997 Ottawa Process (which banned anti-personnel landmines), the 1988 adoption of the Rome Statute to set up the International Criminal Court (which South Africa now intends to withdraw from) and the Kimberley Process to regulate so-called conflict diamonds.

South Africa often played in the premier diplomatic league in Africa and sometimes beyond. In many of these roles, the country served as an intermediary between the industrialised and developing worlds, but consistently proclaimed solidarity with the rest of Africa as the cornerstone of its efforts.

South Africa under Mbeki championed the establishment of the New Partnership for Africa's Development (NEPAD) and the African Peer Review Mechanism, hosting the secretariats for both in Midrand. Mbeki also played an important role in the transition from the Organisation of African Unity to the African Union from 2000 to 2002 and the country hosts the (largely ineffectual) Pan-African Parliament, also in Midrand.

Those were heady days. South Africa was the only African country to be invited to the top table of the G20 meeting of central bank governors in 1999. Following the global financial crisis and the recognition that emerging countries were not adequately represented at the core of global economic discussion, President George W Bush hosted the first G20 heads of state summit in November 2008 in Washington, DC. Since then, the G20 has met annually at the level of heads of state and central bankers, and is steadily establishing itself as the dominant forum for global economic coordination and prioritisation in place of the G7 industrialised nations.

South Africa enhanced its soft power by, among others, holding a series of high-profile events, such as the ninth UN Conference on Trade and Development in 1996, the World Conference against Racism in 2001 and the World Summit on Sustainable Development in 2002.

As a legacy of Mandela's heroic image and Mbeki's activism, South Africa has gained membership to an alphabet soup of international organisations, initiatives and clubs, including the Commonwealth, the India, Brazil and South Africa Dialogue Forum and the African Caribbean and Pacific Group of States. South Africa is also one of the EU's ten strategic partners. And there are many others.

Mbeki's ousting by Zuma in 2008 upended many things, particularly South Africa's courting of the G7 and their engagement with Africa, and South Africa's relationship with China. Foreign policy would subsequently take a back-seat role to other matters.

Instead of a foreign policy run tightly from the Union Buildings, which was the hallmark of the Mbeki administration, the renamed Department of International Relations and Cooperation (DIRCO) under Zuma vigorously pursued membership of the BRIC group. For the rest, DIRCO was given much greater leeway to pursue South–South solidarity and continue broadly the prioritisation of Africa. Zuma does not share Mbeki's keen sense of international politics or passion for the upliftment of Africa. He nominally chairs the AU/NEPAD Presidential Infrastructure Championing Initiative[18] but pays little more than lip service to NEPAD and the African Peer Review Mechanism, both the brainchild of Mbeki.

Whereas Mbeki presented his ideas on the African Renaissance and NEPAD first to the G8 (the G7 plus Russia), Zuma leans unashamedly towards China and Russia. Writing in the prestigious journal *Commonwealth & Comparative Politics*, Chris Alden and Yu-Shan Wu[19] note that:

> South Africa's relationship with China ... is viewed in some circles
> as emblematic of an overall re-orientation of post-apartheid South

African foreign policy away from Western-based humanistic values
to one aligned with the developmental pragmatism, if not the authoritarian agenda, of the strongest member of the BRICS configuration.

BRICS has served as a global disrupter, for it has recalibrated the stark
developed–underdeveloped world divides and helped to level global po-
litical and trading. In the words of Simon Freemantle from Standard Bank:
'The BRICS have unambiguously contributed towards a repositioning
of Africa's long-term commercial promise.'[20] From 2000 to 2014, writes
Garth le Pere, 'BRICS-Africa trade has increased from USD28 billion to
USD377 billion (a rise of 1250 per cent). The "ICS" of India, China, and
South Africa accounted for 91 per cent of this trade in 2015.'[21]

Originally, the BRICS grouping appeared intent on reshaping global
power relationships away from a Western, neoliberal and free-market-
type framework, informed by the requirement for individual rights, free
trade, democracy and the like, to a focus on the importance of national
sovereignty (i.e. non-interference in others' domestic affairs) and the importance of a strong, developmental state.

The ANC under Zuma has embarked upon a wide-ranging social and
cultural initiative to shift thinking and orientations away from the West
and to build people-to-people contact with Chinese, Russians and, to a
lesser extent, Indians and Brazilians, second only to the efforts to support
and build relations with Cuba. Students are sent to study in these countries and language courses have been developed in Mandarin, among
other initiatives. Over time, the courting of China and Russia has become single-minded and obsessive.[22] During April 2017, for example, a
host of national activities were organised to this end. Perhaps most important is that Chinese priorities are shifting towards the One Belt One
Road initiative, an ambitious series of infrastructure projects connecting

more than 60 countries, with China at its centre. This is where Chinese trade is going and where the country will apply its excess capacity. A few countries in East Africa are a small part of the initiative and it is diverting attention away from Africa.[23]

BRICS, on the other hand, is not much of a trading bloc, and its future is unclear. Trade among the BRICS nations comes to less than 5 per cent of their total global trade – about USD300 billion out of USD6,5 trillion.[24] Whereas the leadership in India and Brazil was left-leaning at the time of the establishment of the grouping, current leaders are from conservative or centrist parties.

While Russia, China and India vie for influence within the group, South Africa and Brazil lag behind. Recently China endorsed the idea of a BRICS Plus idea, aimed at an outreach with other developing countries.

Without China, BRICS does not amount to much. To put this into perspective, the Chinese socialist market economy adds the total size of the South African economy to its GDP every eight months.

The contribution of the BRICS group to the global economy should, in about twenty years' time, overtake the share of the G7 countries. The BRICS countries already have more than four times the population of the G7, and their total defence expenditure will overtake that of the G7 shortly after 2030. Nothing is assured, of course, and events in China, Russia or the EU may readily upset the best attempts at foretelling the future.

But, in the interim, the establishment of BRICS has led to greater flexibility within the global financial system and opens the potential for greater balance. Change is always disruptive, however, and the relative decline of the US on the world stage has contributed to the rise of the politics of fear there and elsewhere, reflected most evidently in the election of Donald Trump.

The elevation of China's importance to Africa and South Africa as a trading partner has largely occurred on the back of exports of commodities to China, and at considerable expense to South Africa's manufacturing sector. Mbeki's concerns about this, which he expressed in a widely publicised speech in December 2006, have now come back to haunt Zuma: 'In its relationship with China,' Mbeki argued, 'Africa must guard against merely becoming a supplier of raw materials in exchange for manufactured goods.'[25]

The penny has dropped now, but only after significant damage to the South African manufacturing base. South Africa has suffered from the impact of dumping of Chinese steel and other products, and from intense competition with China in the African markets. More recently, slower growth in China has severely curbed demand for South African exports, especially for iron ore and concentrates, chromium ore, ferro-alloys, platinum and manganese, which together account for more than 60 per cent of South African exports.

Having hitched its fortunes to the BRIC countries, South Africa can benefit from healthy growth in India and China, two very large economies, although Russia and Brazil are growing much more slowly. This growth is expected to remain much more robust in the medium to long term than growth rates in Europe and North America.

South Africa is currently seeking to leverage Chinese financial resources in pursuit of South Africa's industrialisation, and Chinese capital investment into South Africa has increased in recent years.

Ministers such Ebrahim Patel and Rob Davies have worked hard in their respective but overlapping ministries at constraining the steady attrition of the South African manufacturing sector, but they faced an uphill battle in the absence of a team effort in the Cabinet and leadership from the Presidency.

In the most recent effort to find practical benefit from BRICS, South Africa has seized upon the opportunities offered by the New Development Bank (the BRICS Bank). This was established partly in response to the slow pace of reform in existing global financial institutions, such as the World Bank and IMF, and to better reflect the current political and economic realities, which differ starkly from the situation when these bodies were created after World War II. Although there is a huge global savings glut, estimated at USD17 trillion in 2012, this is not being accessed, and the argument that ways need to be found to invest these resources in Africa informed the founding of the New Development Bank.

The bank is particularly germane to relieving Africa's infrastructure financing deficit, estimated to be USD100 billion a year, and to addressing what is perceived to be a lack of appetite to lend in developing countries. Lack of investment in energy, transport and water infrastructure presents a significant barrier to economic growth and development.

Seeking to be a hegemon

Whereas Mbeki was at pains to downplay South Africa's regional hegemonic role, Zuma is much more willing to seek an African leadership role and to pursue specific objectives, sometimes at a cost to the country's standing on the continent. The clear expression of a 'South Africa first' policy under Zuma stands in some contrast to the 2011 White Paper on Foreign Policy, Building a Better World: The Diplomacy of Ubuntu, which states (in language more reminiscent of Mbeki than Zuma) that the two key tenets that inform South Africa's international engagement are Pan-Africanism and South–South solidarity.[26] For example, South Africa has been quite insistent in its proposals for how peacekeeping should be done in Africa.[27]

The government has also eagerly pursued a permanent seat on the UN Security Council, now an explicit goal of the 2011 White Paper on Foreign Policy. This despite our stated commitment to the common African position on UN reform, known as the Ezulwini Consensus, and the view that the African Union is responsible for selecting Africa's representative who will decide on the associated criteria for the selection of African members only once that opportunity actually presents itself.

A series of blunders under Zuma have eroded South Africa's standing in Africa. For example, despite severe competition, South Africa managed to ensure the election of its candidate, Nkosazana Dlamini-Zuma, as chair of the Commission of the African Union in 2012 – against the expectations of most analysts, and in the face of opposition from Nigeria and its allies in West Africa.

Then, after a mixed-result single term, during which she spent a significant amount of her time in South Africa, Dlamini-Zuma announced that she would not seek to run for a second term in 2016. It was clear that her domestic ambitions took precedence: a shot at the presidency of the ANC (and likely South Africa too) at the ANC's 2017 conference. Both her election to the African Union chair and the manner in which she subsequently stepped down damaged South Africa's reputation among its peers in Africa.

Inchoate policies under Zuma – as evidenced by the debacle over introducing a requirement for unabridged birth certificates and visas, and the detrimental effect these decisions had on migration and tourism – have also had negative impact on South Africa's regional and international standing, as have issues around Zuma's personal life and efforts at state capture.

But the most serious setback to South Africa's stature in Africa has been the impact of the embarrassing outbreaks of xenophobic violence (as discussed in Chapter 8). Although it has historical roots, xenophobia reflects South Africa's employment and economic crisis, as well as its deep leadership deficit. The vision of Mbeki's African Renaissance has given way to cries for help from fellow Africans as they are beaten up across South Africa.

It is in this context that the decision to allow the Sudanese president, Omar al-Bashir, to attend the 2015 African Union summit in Johannesburg should be viewed. The invitation was extended despite the fact that Bashir is sought by the International Criminal Court. It was largely an effort to demonstrate that South Africa 'stands with Africa' irrespective of the consequences, and to counter the hugely negative impact that the xenophobic riots had had on the country's image. It is highly unlikely that the Cabinet were unaware that their decision to invite Bashir to South Africa was in contravention of the Constitution and South Africa's legal commitments to the Rome Statute. Therefore, a government purportedly committed to a constitutional state and the rule of law effectively chose to undermine its own Constitution and conspire against the judicial system.

Forecasting South Africa's power potential

Africa has been peripheral in approaches to international relations that have sought to quantify or measure power potential.[28] These have tended to focus on so-called great powers, or the 'states that make the most difference', particularly the US, the UK, France, the former Soviet Union, China and India.[29] Changes in the global distribution of power will influence Africa's and South Africa's agency – the ability to potentially shape outcomes.

Chapter 4 introduced the International Futures forecasting tool, which is used to generate the forecasts associated with the political scenarios in this book. In 2015, together with colleagues Julia Schünemann-Bello and Jonathan Moyer, I published a paper that looked at the distribution of power in Africa, particularly as it affects key states, such as South Africa, Nigeria, Algeria, Egypt and Ethiopia.[30]

There are many ways to conceptualise and measure power potential, and the results therefore depend on how much weight is allocated to the various subsidiary components. Traditional measures of power that were popular during the Cold War were military expenditure, number of military personnel, energy consumption, iron and steel production, urban population and total population. These measures provided a means to measure a state's capabilities. Recent measures place greater emphasis on share of trade and share of aid; they also include nuclear weapons and replace total population with working-age population above the poverty line.

Here I update the forecasts developed in that paper, using the Global Power Index within IFs. The index is an attempt to measure power potential in the 21st century. It allocates the following weights to five sub-components, which, collectively, attempt to measure power potential: international interactions, consisting of share of foreign aid plus a diplomatic power index (20 per cent); technology, consisting of share of global research and development spend plus share of ICT stock (10 per cent); share of the global economy, trade, foreign investment and energy exports (35 per cent); share of global military expenditure, including share of global nuclear weapons (25 per cent); and the global share of working-age population above the poverty line (10 per cent).[31] This type of power calculation, I hasten to add, advantages rich, developed countries and penalises poorer countries with larger populations, such as Nigeria which, by 2050, is forecast to increase from its current size of 191 million to 398 million people.

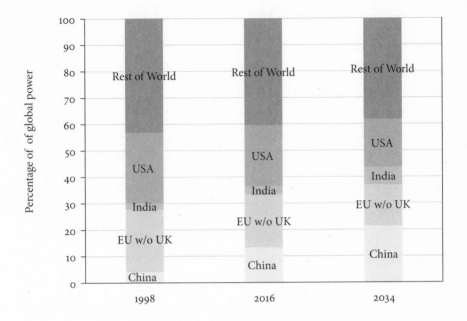

Figure 19: Comparing power potential, 1998, 2016 and 2034
Source: IFs v 7.28

In the long term, it is clear that the world will, by mid-century, consist of three great powers, the US, China and eventually India. This is irrespective of how one measures power potential. Using the Global Power Index, these three countries will collectively have 50 per cent or more of global power potential. The EU (without the UK) could by then constitute an additional 13 per cent of global power. Therefore, around two-thirds of global power could be located in just these three countries plus the EU. The remaining 27 per cent will be divided between the other 200 or so countries, of which only France, the UK, Russia, Germany and Japan will have more than 2 per cent of global power each. Figure 19 presents the distribution of global power when looking back to 1998 and forward to 2034, the forecast horizon for this book. In addition to the rise of China, the decline of the power of the EU (shown without the UK), the other

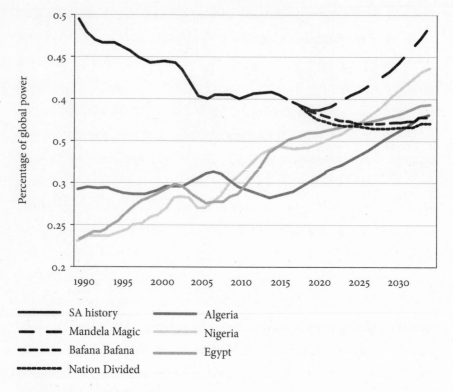

Figure 20: Global Power Index, top four African countries (five-year moving average)
Source: IFs v 7.28

trends are the relative decline of the US, which is overtaken by China in 2029 and the recent momentum seen in India.

The top four powerhouses of Africa – for the foreseeable future – are South Africa, Algeria, Nigeria and Egypt. Figure 20 gives a general picture of how national power may be shifting over time in Africa and includes the impact of the three scenarios on South Africa's power potential. Whereas South Africa loses influence in Bafana Bafana and Nation Divided, it retains its leadership position in the Mandela Magic scenario. The reason for South Africa's relatively large power potential is because the Global Power Index favours more developed countries over poorer countries with larger populations. The use of more traditional measurements of power that place greater weight on population size, for example, would produce a different result.

Under the disastrous leadership of Jacob Zuma, South Africa has made its choice clear. Despite the continued strength of economic, social and cultural ties with many countries in the West, when it comes to 'high politics' South Africa sides with the BRIC countries, specifically China and Russia, and has largely abandoned the idea of an alliance of democratic developing countries, never mind an association with traditional middle powers.

Gone are the days of seeking ways in which the country could play a bridging role between the global North and South, and could shift the debates and discussions within the G7/8 to look at trade, aid and debt relief, or could align with other mid-sized countries (the Nordics in particular) to develop progressive alliances to advance global governance.

Since the Zuma presidency is a product of intense intra-party politics and compromises within the Tripartite Alliance, and as Zuma has been embroiled in numerous internal challenges himself since assuming office, foreign policy has become less coherent and has been relegated to a lower priority. The substantial ideological and intellectual impetus in South Africa's foreign policy evident during the Mbeki administration is not seen today. The result is a country whose commitment to the continent is being questioned and one that seems to have lost its way.

The most obvious practical problem with the way South Africa now conducts its foreign policy is the extent to which it is often at odds with key values espoused in the Constitution and the basis of the historic settlement from 1990 to 1994. These values reflect those of a liberal democracy, a respect for human rights and a positive internationalism.

Human rights, sustainable development, a rules-based global system, equity and fairness should be understood for the global goods that they are, not as constructs of the West. Every survey that the Afrobarometer project conducts in Africa confirms the demand of the majority of African citizens for democracy as their best guarantor to free them from the scourge of bad governance and exploitation at the hands of the big men of Africa (women are generally not allowed in the club).

South Africa's enthusiastic membership of BRICS as an alternative framework to Western dominance has meant that the country is often not even-handed in its engagement with international developments. In the process, South Africa is undermining international rule of law to its own long-term detriment. Instead of adopting an approach that is in accordance with customary international law, the precedents that are being set will come back to haunt South Africa down the line. Small countries need the rule of law.

Once we factor in trade and economic relations, South Africa retains its attachment to its global-North partners, the UK, the EU and, in a more complicated sense, the US. Even if these Western partners have gradually lost profile and traction with successive ANC governments, and although it receives much less attention from the Union Buildings, the EU is nevertheless still South Africa's largest trade and investment partner by a significant margin.

This dichotomous relationship is well captured in the distinction between high and low politics. Whereas South Africa's high politics is avowedly pro-China and pro-Russia, the low politics of trade, investment and aid relations tells a more complex story, one in which the EU, the UK and others continue to play an important role. South Africa therefore has something of a split personality. Some factions in government and the business community agitate for better relations with the West, and others for better relations with China. On face value, the South African Constitution and many of its governance practices emulate those of key European countries, but the ANC looks determinedly east.

Foreign policy is an extension of domestic policy, and the success of economic diplomacy is probably the most vital pillar of South Africa's international interactions – yet it receives the least attention in a department that is largely concerned with placing the steady stream of disgraced politicians from the Zuma presidency in diplomatic positions abroad instead of promoting trade and investment. Foreign trade will help determine whether South Africa is able to deliver the urgently needed domestic economic upliftment to all its people. In the context of the economic and security cluster of the Cabinet, DIRCO and other departments should actively focus on how foreign policy can facilitate economic growth, create jobs, reduce inequality at home, maintain good relations with all our important trading and investment partners (and not only the BRICS countries) and advance a rules-based system. South Africa should actively pursue regional integration in Africa and the development of regional value chains as its most important foreign-policy priority. Africa is and should remain the focus of our foreign and economic policy, for our development and security depends on a stable and growing southern Africa.

Membership of BRICS may have been a smart, pragmatic move to encompass changing geopolitical and economic realities, but we should not abandon other important trading partners nor have illusions about the nature of the Russian or Chinese states, which have both been adept at instrumentalising South Africa in their national interests.

The welcome reality of Africa's rise from a very low base will, over the coming decades, undo some of the damage done during the 1970s and 1980s, when the continent largely went backwards in developmental terms. Africa is rising, but slowly and not for all of its peoples. Development takes a long time and the story of an African Renaissance is at best a multi-generational one.

Today the world is experiencing greater turbulence, and, although it is more connected than before, it is also less multilateral in key aspects. The result is a brittle global system that has less adherence to global norms on the use of force, among others. Greater multipolarity does not imply instability, but global transitions, such as those experienced currently, are inherently disruptive. An increasingly hot, flat and crowded world needs effective and legitimate structures to confront and manage common global threats, and a relatively small country such as South Africa needs to tread carefully as it positions itself to go up the knowledge ladder, as it is only through increased knowledge production that the country will prosper.

CHAPTER 10

Towards meaningful radical economic transformation

The global economy can in many ways be seen as a pyramid scheme of sorts – a hierarchy of knowledge – where those who continually invest in innovation remain at the apex of welfare.

– Erik S Reinert[1]

South Africa in 2017 is an infinitely better place than it was in 1990, when negotiations for the future started between the National Party and the ANC and others. The last decade, however, has been wasted. Things have not been getting better fast enough to allow us to move ahead in terms of key development indicators, such as levels of extreme poverty, employment rates and reductions in inequality.

For things to improve, South Africa will need to grow its economy much more rapidly and it will need to channel that growth into improvements in income and the living standards of poor people, while reducing the gap between the various income classes. Only sustained higher levels of employment can achieve this goal.

The country needs to make a choice between its current strategy of high-wage, high-productivity over labour-intensive job creation. As economist Nicoli Nattrass writes, 'Post-apartheid development strategies [have] contributed to an economic growth path that benefitted insiders (those with jobs), exacerbated unemployment and thereby undermined inclusive development.' This, she argues, 'reflects the power of organized labour (to determine labour policy), economic constraints on government policy (notably the need to avoid a debt crisis) and the political appeal of a growth path premised on "decent" jobs.'[2]

For South Africa, labour-intensive growth would constitute meaningful radical economic restructuring.

In preparation for its national policy conference in June 2017, while this book was going to print, the ANC circulated a series of discussion documents, including reports on economic transformation, according to which,

> ... radical economic transformation is about fundamentally changing the structure of South Africa's economy from an exploitative exporter of raw materials, to one which is based on beneficiation and manufacturing, in which our people's full potential can be realized. In addition to ensuring increased economic participation by black people in the commanding heights of the economy, radical economic transformation must have a mass character. A clear objective of radical economic transformation must be to reduce racial, gender and class inequalities in South Africa through ensuring more equity with regards to incomes, ownership of assets and access to economic opportunities. An effective democratic developmental state and efficiently run public services and public companies are necessary instruments for widening the reach of radical economic transformation, enabling the process to touch the lives of ordinary people.[3]

Few South Africans will disagree with this understanding of the need for change. But here, like elsewhere, the focus is on the potential impact of trickle-down economics – the belief that the creation of a small black, moneyed elite (like the sprinklings of chocolate on a cappuccino) will filter down below.

Our national soccer team, Bafana Bafana, has had 22 coaches since 1992 but it has not succeeded because we have not created a pipeline of talent that feeds and sustains the team. The ANC wants instant gratification. However, it takes more than throwing money at the coach to build a successful team. It takes sustained investment over decades by an entire system geared towards excellence.

The need for a bold, reformist ANC

Without a generational and a policy revolution, the ANC will not prosper and South Africans will suffer, because it is likely that the party will govern until the 2024 elections – and possibly for longer – as part of a coalition (although, as we have seen in the forecasts, it is likely to lose Gauteng in 2019). If knowledge and knowledge flows are the key to our future well-being, South Africa needs policies and approaches that will equip the country for a Mandela Magic future – and ones that allow the economy to gain momentum over time, for this is a long road that needs to endure beyond even the 2034 time horizon set out in this book.

'The economy has to walk on two legs,' argues UCT economist Anthony Black in *Towards Employment-intensive Growth in South Africa*, 'with massive growth in employment at the low end, accompanied by increased dynamism in the "advanced" sector. More rapid growth in the labour-intensive sectors will create new sources of demand, upgrade skills and produce new, small firms. All of this will galvanise the "advanced" sector.'[4]

Much more decisive steps are needed to change the country's current mediocre growth and employment prospects. The extent of unemployment in South Africa is severe; it is disempowering and debilitating. It will destroy us if we do not confront this challenge. More than any other problem, it points to the need for innovation in thinking about the country's economic future, the courage to implement policies and to hold one another accountable. We need meaningful radical economic reform.

Current approaches that lock a relatively small number of unionised employees into the formal economy and, through inflexibility, raises the bar for the entry of others into employment while keeping skilled foreigners at bay simply will not do, as one of many examples. Only significantly higher levels of employment can reduce inequality in South Africa,[5] and only significantly higher levels of employment can reduce poverty. None of this is possible without growth.

In its current factional and confused ideological configuration, the ANC is an obstacle to inclusive growth and its most likely future configuration – i.e. increasingly black nationalist, populist and ruralist in orientation – will compound that challenge. Getting to the Mandela Magic pathway will require:

❏ Modernising the ANC and reversing its current rural and traditionalist mindset, replacing it with one that is appropriate for the two economic legs that Anthony Black refers to.

❏ Dealing with education, particularly the hold that the South African Democratic Teachers' Union has on schools and on the Department of Basic Education. Senior government officials simply cannot serve both the union and government. We must make a choice.

❏ A partnership with the private sector where the state is responsible for regulation and redistribution, and the private sector for growth and employment, necessitating a smaller, more capable civil service and a positive partnership with business.

❏ Focusing on growing small and medium-sized business as the main employment and wealth creators, and reducing the capital intensity of the economy in favour of labour intensity. This can only be achieved by moving towards a more flexible labour market and embarking on a new partnership with labour and business.

❏ Governing for all South Africans – whether they are black, white, poor or wealthy – by adopting an inclusive, non-racial, class-based interpretation of society. Class, and not race, should determine our analysis if South Africa is to find an appropriate theoretical framework that sits comfortably within its Constitution and Bill of Rights, and that will support economic progress.

The question is, who within the party can provide this quality of leadership?

Ahead of the 1994 elections, the ANC was dependent on COSATU to provide it with a national election machine. Ever since then, labour has effectively framed South Africa's broad economic policies and options to the detriment of employment creation. Although COSATU in 2017 is a mere shadow of its former self, it is unlikely that the ANC will break the stranglehold that organised labour continues to exert over economic and migration policy unless COSATU itself also changes. The most likely presidential candidate on the Reformist side, Cyril Ramaphosa, is dependent on the active support of organised labour for his presidential campaign – the organisation that first came out in support of him. But only 28 per cent of workers belong to unions.[6]

The other likely candidate, Nkosazana Dlamini-Zuma, is not handcuffed to labour in this way, but she has her own issues. She has earned respect for being technically proficient, although she is publicly uninspiring as a leader. However, she is tainted by her association with the Traditionalist faction, the Premier League and the close association that they have with the Guptas and their efforts at state capture. Generally considered hostile towards the private sector, she is essentially a black nationalist and ideologically not orientated towards growth and enterprise.

A highly political labour movement serves to protect those in employment but at the cost of growing employment more broadly. This trend can be reversed only by a shift in vision or by ending the hold that organised labour has on government economic policies. Recent years have seen an expansion of employment in the public sector to an extent where the associated wage bill is squeezing out capital investment in infrastructure. Meanwhile, the private sector, which accounts for 80 per cent of production and employs 86 per cent of the 13,5 million of the country's working population, has largely lost confidence and does not invest domestically despite their large, positive balance sheets.

Eventually only two political options present themselves. The first is the break-up of the Tripartite Alliance or the complete implosion of COSATU, essentially freeing up a Reformist ANC to pursue employment-intensive growth. The second is the transformation of COSATU into a union federation that mobilises and champions poor people, stepping away from its current focus on middle-class government employees as the bulwark of its membership. But, even then, the ANC would need leadership that will take South Africa forward, not backward.

The employment compact that Anthony Black and his co-authors write about is to be built on three pillars: strong pro-employment policies, including subsidies and direct state support, macroeconomic stability and limited labour reform. Black offers four examples of employment-intensive growth:[7]

1. Large-scale employment incentives for unskilled workers subsidised through tax breaks or a wage subsidy.

2. An aggressive strategy aimed at rapid expansion of labour-intensive light manufacturing as an explicit policy and pillar of industrial strategy. This, he warns, will require specific interventions and subsidies, and much more than merely deregulating markets. It would also require competition on the basis of wages.

3. Expanding labour-intensive tradeables (such as in the garment sector) by exploiting regional variations in wages, as well as making a concerted effort to deal with the non-labour costs of private-sector employment, such as transport, training, workers' housing and infrastructure.

4. Employment creation in labour-intensive crops in the agricultural sector as well as the processing of these for domestic and international markets. This, he argues, requires stepped-up support to reverse the decline in spending on research and development in the agricultural sector, and fast-tracking infrastructure, such as irrigation.

To this we can add a fifth point: to ascend the value chain, South Africa must significantly increase state spending on research and development (which is a large driver of growth) from the current level of 0,71 per cent of GDP to 3 or 4 per cent. This should include renewed investment and support for a domestic arms industry, which is often the incubator for technological innovation, and is exempted from requirements for trade liberalisation.

There are many things that can and should become possible under new leadership, such as greater efforts at import substitution and to 'buy South African' – both of which should be pursued to the maximum extent possible that is compatible with our international legal obligations. For example, the Buy Back South Africa campaign, launched as a private-public partnership, helps to impress upon consumers and others the importance of purchasing locally manufactured goods.[8] This needs to become dogma.

There is no magic solution to employment creation and there have been some efforts by government, such as the Jobs Fund, that have been able to make headway despite the difficult circumstances.[9] But efforts to improve employment in the longer term will succeed only if South Africa manages to consistently grow the private sector over successive decades.[10]

Growth in the private sector requires business confidence and a facilitating investment climate. The potential for such investment was recently illustrated with the successive rounds of private-sector investment in the renewable-energy sector that had been forced upon a reluctant government by its previous delays before belatedly investing in electricity production capacity.

Implementing the (updated) National Development Plan

South Africa will not prosper without policy clarity, stability and a clear direction. The analysis of what needs to be done and why is largely reflected in the numerous recommendations of the National Development Plan – although the plan does not place employment creation and growth sufficiently at the core of its recommendations.

It is now time to update the National Development Plan and to implement it. The National Development Plan should be converted into a living document that is less a fixed-term blueprint and more of a continually evolving 20-year running vision for the country, to which all in government, labour and the private sector should commit. To translate strategy into implementation, the plan must be converted into national and departmental action plans that are monitored and measured regularly, with commitments and agreements between government, the private sector and labour.

The plan should be formally updated, with a new time horizon at least every five years. An update is now long overdue. The plan was launched in 2011, so that by 2017 the targets set for 2030 have become seriously out of date and unrealistic, as demonstrated by the revised population forecasts included in Chapter 5 of this book. Instead of separate White Papers for various departments that are often at odds with one another and lack coherence, these policy documents should all form part of the National Development Plan and be integrated into its single framework.

The single and overarching job of the next ANC president must be to drive the implementation of the National Development Plan through Cabinet. This will require reinvigorating the work of the National Planning Commission, who should monitor, research and advise on the restoration of a long-term strategic planning capacity within the Presidency and help strengthen the Department of Planning, Monitoring and Evaluation.

The responsibility for driving and producing the National Spatial Development Framework function should be embedded in the National Planning Commission and the offices of the provincial premiers. This will empower the commission to determine what aspects of the National Development Plan will happen where and when.

At the moment, compliance and detailed planning, including cross-departmental collaboration, are uneven and sometimes lacking. There can be only one overarching plan for South Africa, and progress made in implementing it must be measured in Parliament, in the Cabinet, by the

Presidency, in the Treasury and by public reporting on progress by the Department of Planning, Monitoring and Evaluation.

If it is to be effectively implemented, the Presidency must continually address accountability failures and the service-delivery crisis in the public service, and provide clarity on the blurred boundaries between local, provincial and national spheres of government. This way, the various special economic zones in each province will cohere and momentum will be restored to the Presidential Infrastructure Coordinating Commission, the National Infrastructure Plan, strategic integrated projects and their coordination structures at the national, provincial and local level. We need accountability.

Focus on employment-intensive growth

Only an economy where employment is placed at the centre of economic policymaking will work for South Africa. This will require a complete shift in mindset. To achieve rapid growth, South Africa needs foreign and domestic investment, and that requires confidence in the future, which, in turn, requires stability and political coherence. It needs the involvement of all sectors of our society, rural and urban, rich and poor.

That means increasing the supply of skilled workers through improved education and by encouraging inward migration of skilled people and a more flexible labour market, as well as by investing in healthcare and infrastructure, so that we can increase the productivity of the South African worker. We should not, of course, abandon our efforts at global change through our membership of BRICS and other clubs, but evolution is much more likely than revolution, and economic diplomacy is not well served by constantly criticising some of our major trading partners while remaining silent on the excesses of others.

Of these objectives, finding a way to create a more flexible labour market remains the least likely, but an environment needs to be created in which employers are willing to take on new entrants to the labour market so that they can accumulate the required work experience to make them valuable and productive employees. This will happen only if employers can also terminate employment contracts under reasonable circumstances.

On a practical level, South Africa need look no further than the 18 million South Africans still living in the former homelands who are locked into poverty. In line with the approach advanced by Peruvian economist Hernando de Soto Polar, the transfer of communal to individual private-property rights in these areas will empower a large portion of rural South Africans. This way, dead capital will become bankable assets. Most of the land in these areas belongs to government, and not to the communal leaders. The transfer of land to individual ownership is a prerequisite for rural transformation and growth.

Such change requires a modernist government committed to economic growth as a priority, not to the traditionalist policies and 'big man' leadership of yesteryear. It requires an ANC that is willing to step back from its growing partnership with traditional leadership. This will take courage, but the party may find that rural citizens who benefit from these policies could reward them at the polls.

No growth path will succeed if improvements in productivity do not outpace wage increases. The National Development Plan, explains Nattrass, proposes to compensate workers for their wage restraint 'by lowering their cost of living (notably by keeping inflation and import tariffs low) whilst continuing to support skill development and productivity growth in dynamic economic sectors where there is more space for wages to grow without undermining employment or profitability'.

She argues that this is unrealistic given the national minimum wage and commitment to 'decent jobs'. 'As things stand,' she says, 'the counter-narrative about higher wages necessarily being good for productivity and economic growth is standing in the way of any kind of employment-promoting class compromise in South Africa.'[11]

A growth-orientated, employment-intensive pathway inevitably means reviewing and cutting back on the 700 or so state-owned enterprises that give a miserly 2,9 per cent average return on investment. Government would probably get at least three times that return if they were to sell the state-owned businesses and invest the money in a bank. A first step could be to ensure that all state-owned enterprises have proper boards of directors, with the relevant commercial and other expertise, that are able to run them in a financially responsible manner. These companies should also be subject to comprehensive and independent performance audits, including tender processes and risk-management frameworks. The results should be made public and form the basis for the newly constituted boards of directors to take things forward.

There are instances where state control and leadership are needed, such as investment in strategic manufacturing sectors, state support of research and development, and so on. But state-owned enterprises in the mainstream economy, such as South African Airways, that perennially underperform should be self-sustaining or be sold off. It means ending the subsidies whereby Cuban engineers and medical doctors are imported at great cost to the taxpayer instead of employing South Africans or encouraging skilled inward migration, which is free. It means cutting back on perks for government ministers and officials, whose earnings generally exceed those in the private sector. It means a state that is committed to quality.

South Africa generally has a higher cost structure than most other countries at comparative levels of development. Government consumption in South Africa is 30 per cent of GDP, roughly double the global average for upper-middle-income countries and some 8 per cent higher than the average for high-income countries. Admittedly, some of this expenditure is due to social-grant payments, but, nevertheless, the management of South Africa is too expensive.

Our overhead costs are too high; there are too many unproductive senior officials and too few at lower levels who actually do things like teaching, policing and providing healthcare. We have far too many rules and regulations that seek to bend the market. The costs of maintaining this huge edifice squeeze out productive spending on infrastructure, healthcare and education.

We need a strong, capable state as a regulator of a much larger private sector, as an investor in key sectors to spur innovation, to direct much more research and development funding, and, above all, to channel resources in a manner that deals with the historical legacy of apartheid. But a strong state does not need to be a big state, and the current trend that has seen the steady increase in the size of the civil service needs while actually outsourcing core government functions to a network of patronage clients needs to be reversed.

There are many reforms that could derive greater efficiency from government and reduce corruption. For example, amendments to laws and the Constitution to remove the powers of the president to appoint directors general (often against the wishes of ministers) and the requirement for merit-based appointments (including Cabinet appointments) based on minimum education qualifications would be obvious starting points. A second reform would be limiting the pervasive practice of cadre deployment, and instead appointing and promoting senior managers and officials based on merit and qualifications.

Then there is the obvious need to reduce the size of Cabinet to probably half its current number, to consolidate ministries and departments, and do away with most deputy ministers (there were 37 at the last count).

Other obvious reforms would be to strengthen the legal powers of the Auditor General to allow for the enforcement of its recommendations. This would help to rein in South Africa's 35 national government departments, nine provinces, 278 municipalities and more than 120 state entities. Although the Auditor General enjoys relative freedom in South Africa, institutions are not compelled to heed his audit findings. This too needs to change.

The prospects for greater economic inclusion

There are many ways to build economic inclusiveness, such as making it obligatory for companies to include nominees from its workers on the board or to allow them to own a minimum stake in the business. However, current efforts to improve relations between business, labour and government through structures such as NEDLAC have not improved the adversarial relationship between these three parties, which detracts from growth. Only when South Africa has built inclusive systems in its economy will inclusion drive sustained, faster growth.

Changing the distribution patterns in society takes time, but, with the investments made in education, preferential procurement and other areas since 1994, the country is set on an inevitable path of massive transfers of wealth to its black majority. Unfortunately, it appears that this transfer is often limited to certain well-connected individuals and families. Insufficient attention is being paid to the challenge of opportunity creation in an open economy where the emphasis is on facilitating self-help and entrepreneurialism, which would allow for the creation and distribution of wealth within the broader community.

The use of government procurement should be the primary means of black economic advancement. This means setting realistic long-term targets in each sector that reward excellence, not symbolism, and then sticking to these targets and rewarding achievers, not chopping and changing the goals – as has recently occurred in the mining sector, where poor foresight has given way to acrimony over the once-empowered, always-empowered principle. This can, however, happen only if many of the other, more onerous empowerment regulations, are watered down or scrapped.

South Africa needs to establish economic growth coalitions at every level of our society where companies enter into a partnership with their communities, by paying for additional teachers or topping up their salaries, and providing employees with housing and school bursaries, etc.

This is a future where corporate empowerment strategies actually empower ordinary employees and communities. It is a South Africa that invests in the mass training of artisans such as plumbers and electricians, and where the focus is on building small businesses that are sustainable (if perhaps with lower profit margins).

At the individual level, this means 'giving something back': retired professionals, such as teachers, can provide their services teaching maths and science in black schools (as indeed advocated by the EFF). It means accepting the mentorship of a township child, paying for the education of the children of domestic workers, investing in providing domestic workers with practical skills, such as driving, reading, writing, first aid and personal finance. It means that wealthy South Africans adopt a township family and help them.

Fixing education

The best way to achieve and maintain equal opportunity is through quality education that targets the majority of poor South Africans and subsequently offers them the means to gain experience and advance their prospects in a substantial way. Only high-quality, relevant education can provide profound, long-term empowerment. Education should be a top priority for South Africa because education is truly transformational in ways that palliative measures, including black economic empowerment and affirmative action, can never match.

Education transforms and equalises opportunity, and there is an important role for both the state (as regulator and provider of public education) and the private sector (to complement the provision of education services) to play. Belatedly, there does appear to be progress.

Today, the essential challenge when it comes to fixing our education system is political rather than practical. The first requirement is for the governing party to either break the stranglehold of the South African Democratic Teachers' Union on the educational sector or find a way to turn obstruction into positive cooperation. Government should fully implement the 16 recommendations from the May 2016 report of the Ministerial Task Team appointed by Minister of Basic Education Angie Motshekga to investigate allegations into the selling of posts of educators by members of teachers' unions. Some of the key recommendations of this report are:

> Recommendation 4: That the Department of Basic Education (DBE) regain control of administering the education system in all Provinces so that clear distinctions are established between the roles and functions of the DBE and the concerns of Teacher Unions.
>
> Recommendation 7: Principals should be selected by means of

panels which have the resources to evaluate the competence and suitability of the candidates for their leadership, management as well as their academic, experiential and professional abilities.

Recommendation 9: That the observer status of Unions be renegotiated with respect to the recruitment process.

Recommendation 10: That both school- and office-based educators cease to be office-bearers of political parties and that educators in management posts (including school principals) be prohibited from occupying leadership positions in Teacher unions.

Recommendation 12: That measures be put in place to ensure that the practice of cadre deployment into DBE offices and schools ceases entirely.

Recommendation 13: Those who are appointed to Districts and provincial offices should be required to demonstrate their capacity to carry out the job for which they have applied. There should be no political appointments nor cadre deployments.

Recommendation 15: That the South African Council of Educators be reconceptualised and freed from Union and political domination.

Since the South African Democratic Teachers' Union is an important member of COSATU, and therefore in alliance with the ANC, these recommendations will not be easy to implement. But South Africa has already lost more than two decades in reconfiguring its education system – a failure in policy and implementation that has contributed to the exclusion of many potential employees from a labour market that rewards technical skills and entrepreneurship.

Money is not the problem. As a percentage of government expenditure, South Africa spends 2 per cent more on education than the average for upper-middle-income countries globally, although less than Botswana and Namibia. The problem is bad management, lack of accountability and absence of stability.

Government should also encourage, support and positively regulate the development of an expansive system of private education to relieve the burden on the public component of the system. The Centre for Development and Enterprise in Johannesburg has carried out a number of studies that point to the potential complementary role that the private sector can play in this regard.[12] At the moment, South Africa has 12,5 million children in school, so the potential for growth for the private sector in the education system is very large, with lower fee levels than those of many traditional private schools – although their fee structure needs to be regulated.

Private universities can also play an important role. The Fees Must Fall campaign has highlighted the pressure on the public tertiary education system. Currently, 50 000 grade 12 school-leavers who qualify for university cannot get a place in the country's public universities. If properly managed, private universities can help to fill that gap. Government should facilitate this process by supporting the Council for Higher Education, which is responsible for the accreditation of both public and private higher-education institutions. A major obstacle here is that the Higher Education Act precludes any institution from calling itself a university without permission from the minister. This has not been granted as yet to any private institutions.

A key reform must be the adoption and advancement of a single language (English) as the medium for secondary and tertiary education, and of formal communication in all sectors and in all public-funded education institutions, and indeed in government. Those efforts to expand the languages of instruction at secondary, tertiary and other educational institutions need to be resisted and, in my view, reversed, as should the efforts to establish culturally homogeneous institutions, such as at Stellenbosch University and the Potchefstroom campus of the North-West University. Institutions that wish to pursue a second language for teaching and education should be free to do so, and we should, for the next decade, have to provide translation and language services, but we should work towards an associated constitutional amendment to this effect, with a single secondary language allowed per province for a limited period of time.

The focus of education should be on the natural and practical sciences as far as is possible. To complement this shift in focus, the emphasis of the South African education system after grade 8 should include vocational training and skills that align education with the knowledge and skills needed for an economy that has an expanding manufacturing and services sector. These recommendations form part of the National Development Plan. In its policy document, which was discussed at the national policy conference, the ANC aligns itself with the 2014 White Paper on post-school education and training (discussed in Chapter 6). We need to massively increase access to vocational training and apprenticeship programmes. Vocational training must be proclaimed as the official 'developmental mandate' of all large state-owned companies, and government, business and labour must create at least 1 million internships in order to bring more young people into the labour market.

School dropout rates tell the story. Nationally, the dropout rate between grades 10 and 12 is 44,6 per cent – or 490 000 young South Africans who give up. Only 30,2 per cent of pupils who registered for grade 10 in 2014 passed grade 12 in 2016. Vocational training should be the major career path for the majority of South Africans in secondary education.[13]

Finally, in 2015 first the #RhodesMustFall and then the #FeesMustFall movements highlighted the challenges in the tertiary space. Looking to the future, Adam Habib, the vice-chancellor of the University of the Witwatersrand, punts the development of a flexible but differentiated higher education system that would allow some universities to play a bigger role in the teaching of undergraduate students and the production of professionals, and others to focus on postgraduate students and undertake high-level research, which are both essential if the country is to develop a knowledge-based economy for the 21st century. Drawing on the example of Finland, which has such a system, he argues that this differentiation should not be seen as a status hierarchy or translate into a differentiated allocation of funding. He also argues in favour of a higher-education system that has a TVET sector comprising colleges focused on producing graduates with vocational and applied skills.[14] At the moment, government is underfunding colleges. A mere 2 per cent of students entering the TVET colleges qualify in the minimum period of three years after the 152 small technical colleges were merged into 50 TVET colleges, placing a huge strain on their management structures. Just one-third graduate, and many of those who do, wait years for their certificates. Most are already funded by bursaries from the government-funded National Student Financial Aid Scheme, which they do not have to repay.[15]

These reforms to the education system will allow South Africa to make the best use of its human capital.

Free up the economy and reduce concentration

Government should benchmark itself against the various indices that measure the ease of doing business to measure progress. For different reasons, the Mbeki and Zuma administrations created a much larger, more corrupt and incapable state through the weight of regulations, the expansion of the civil service and measures such as black economic empowerment that distort value for money and inhibit foreign investment. The ANC has repeatedly made accountability and effectiveness a priority, such as in the policy documents discussed in June 2017, which call for government to conduct an audit of the policy and regulatory constraints to investment and set a clear timeframe for addressing them, linked to ministers' performance contracts. The practice has been the exact opposite.

In addition, the market power of large companies harms South Africa's development, and low-income groups in particular. This is the real face of big capital that needs to be confronted in South Africa. The South African economy needs to remove the barriers to entry that result in higher prices, lower levels of innovation and a less competitive economy. From a business and regulatory perspective, South Africa presents a host of hurdles, with increased uncertainty in terms of tax legislation and regulatory requirements.[16]

Therefore, Parliament should enact a process whereby it examines current legislation with a view to reducing red tape and bureaucracy, and simplifying the regulations that govern black economic empowerment and other restrictions on economic flexibility that constrain business. Small and medium-sized companies employ three-quarters of all workers and almost half of the country's entire workforce are employed by companies with fewer than ten people.

It is for this reason that a decision to invest in nuclear power generation is not in South Africa's best interests, for it will increase the capital intensity of the economy and is therefore likely to increase poverty, inequality and unemployment in the longer term. South Africa is trapped in a centralised, industrial state mentality when it comes to electricity and should recognise the value of a decentralised, distributed system in which much greater focus is placed on a so-called smart grid than on the silo-like electricity production favoured by Eskom and the Department of Energy.

South Africa needs to break the monopoly of its vertically integrated electricity industry. In line with the 1998 energy White Paper, which also envisioned increased private-sector participation in the electricity supply industry, government needs to separate power generation from the management of the transmission system, but do so in phased and structured manner. As Anton Eberhard writes in *Business Day*,[17] what South Africa needs now is a separate state-owned market and transmission operator that takes care of electricity planning, power procurement and contracting, system operation and balancing, and transmission.

Finally, the large gap in remuneration between workers and executives in South Africa is excessive even by international comparative standards. This breeds resentment and undermines the potential for social compacts. Take the example of mining-sector pay. In the run-up to the August 2012 massacre of mineworkers near Lonmin's Marikana mine by the police, a Lonmin rock-drill operator received a gross income of R8 124 a month with a take-home pay of R5 600, or about R67 000 per annum. At that time, the chief executive officer earned about 230 times more, or R15.3 million.[18] At this extreme level of inequality, 'those at the bottom do not feel that they have a stake in society and start pursuing their economic objectives outside of the mainstream'.[19]

Executive remuneration in South Africa has grown substantially over the past two or three decades. The differential between the highest paid and the lowest paid among the 20 'worst offenders' on the Johannesburg Stock Exchange ranges from 95 to 725, according to Jannie Rossouw, head of the School of Economics at Wits University.[20]

Under these conditions of rank social injustice, annual wage negotiations in the mining sector, among others, rapidly degenerate into acrimony, and often violence. South Africa needs to find a way to cap the excessive remuneration in the private sector and to achieve wage restraint in the public sector. Government and the private sector need to lead from the front on this issue.

Changing the narrative

Many South Africans continue to believe that the vision of a Rainbow Nation in the form of a social compact will somehow unlock growth and development. The reality is that ours is a divided society composed of 'different worlds that are willing to coexist and cooperate but remain separated by different experiences, interests, histories and, ultimately, political affiliations'.[21]

The introductory pages of this book recounted how the various efforts at achieving such a social compact, including the National Development Plan, are foundational to the future of South Africa. Considerable academic research supports the view that greater inclusion leads to sustained higher growth rates over long time horizons.

Populism and fake news have come to South Africa in a big way, the former in the establishment of the EFF and the latter in the form of media companies like ANN7 and *The New Age*, which promote the most outrageous half-truths, with funding indirectly provided by the South African taxpayer. They are part of a deliberate effort to create an alternative public narrative along the lines of news agencies such as RT in Moscow and Breitbart in the US, preaching and inciting confrontation, and peddling division.

The Free Market Foundation and the South African Institute of Race Relations are two of the ANC's most determined ideological opponents in the public domain and unlikely sources from which to draw inspiration for the party or government. Yet both have pointed to the strange reality whereby the ANC refuses to acknowledge progress made in the remarkable, if uneven, transfer of opportunity, wealth and power from white to black hands.

Ahead of the February 2017 state of the nation address, the Institute of Race Relations released a report, *The Silver Lining*, pointing to the progress made in various measurements relating to education, living standards, economic transformation and the like.[22] The number of people dependent on employed persons has markedly declined, the institute noted: whereas in 1995 there were 380 people dependent on every 100 employed people, by 2016 only 250 people were dependent on every 100 employed people. This is a ratio that will continue to improve to 2034. This positive development contributes to social cohesion over time, expanding the tax base and contributing positively to growth and stability.

Organisations such as exclusively black business lobby groups that have the ear (if not the pocket) of the ANC have a vested interest in perpetuating a story of the need for greater preferential treatment in their own financial interests. They and other parties who depend on a similar storyline of land theft and the need for the transfer of assets without compensation and the like have no interest in presenting a balanced story.

South Africa in 2017 is very different from South Africa in 1994. We have come a long way. But much still needs to change if we wish to aspire to a Mandela Magic future. It's time to get our house in order if we want to avoid muddling along like Bafana Bafana while facing the real threat of a blowout, such as in a Nation Divided.

APPENDIX

International Futures and interventions

International Futures is large-scale, long-term, integrated modelling software housed at the Frederick S Pardee Center for International Futures at the Josef Korbel School of International Studies, University of Denver. The Pardee Center is in partnership with the ISS through the African Futures project, and the partners have published a series of papers on various aspects relating to the implementation of South Africa's National Development Plan and African development (see www.issafrica.org).

The IFs system allows researchers to see past relationships between variables, and how they have developed and interacted over time. The base-case forecast represents where the world seems to be heading given our history and current circumstances and policies. The potential to undertake scenario analysis augments this base case by exploring the leverage that policymakers have to push the systems towards more desirable outcomes.

The IFs software consists of 12 main modules: demographics, economics, education, health, environment, energy, infrastructure, technology, agriculture, governance, government finance and international politics. Each module is closely connected with the others, creating dynamic relationships among variables across the entire system.

The full model is available at pardee.du.edu/access-ifs. The forecasts for this book were done using IFs version 7.28.

The data in IFs consists in excess of 3 500 datasets and is collected from a host of international organisations, such as the IMF, the World Development Institute, the Food and Agriculture Organization, and others – all organisations that invest in ensuring comparability and quality. In the case of South Africa, these organisations mostly obtain their data from Statistics South Africa (Stats SA) and subsequently standardise the data across time to ensure that it is compatible with the data from other sources and for other countries. In addition, in preparation for the analysis used in this book, the African Futures and Innovation team at the ISS compared the most important data within IFs on key dimensions and made minor adjustments to four important series (as part of a project data file), namely, infant mortality, life expectancy, household transfers and migration rates, to ensure that our analysis would be consistent with the latest data from Stats SA.

In addition to the changes in inward migration (which leads to a larger population) and the introduction of a carbon tax, which is included in all three scenarios, the Bafana Bafana scenario includes lower government effectiveness and quality of government regulations, in line with the analysis presented in previous chapters, that attest to incoherence in planning, execution and roll-out of various services. Bafana Bafana also includes a modest nuclear build, consisting of two additional nuclear power stations as a reasonable estimate of ANC plans in this scenario, both completed by 2034, as well as increased use of gas (by simulating moderate fracking as well as increased gas imports from Mozambique).

The Nation Divided scenario moderately expands social transfers and simulates a much larger nuclear-build programme (a fleet of six nuclear power stations), all completed by 2034. Government effectiveness and regulatory quality are significantly lower in the Nation Divided scenario than in the others, and corruption increases. The quality of democracy is also lower, while levels of social turbulence are adjusted upward, making South Africa slightly more unstable, which, in turn, requires moderately higher levels of defence expenditure. Levels of economic freedom are reduced in this scenario as government adopts a state-led model of development that constrains the role of the private sector and reduces innovation. In this future, fracking for gas in the Karoo is minimal, since it is unlikely that foreign investors will be prepared to carry the associated burden of black economic ownership and government freehold requirements. Foreign direct investment in South Africa is lower in this scenario than in any other.

In the Mandela Magic scenario, all of South Africa's future electricity requirements come from renewables and gas, and there is no nuclear build, but even these choices require significant infrastructure investment. Generally, government effectiveness and the quality of government regulations improve, corruption lessens, democracy improves and economic freedom increases. Foreign direct investment and portfolio inflows moderately increase, and levels of violence decrease. Military expenditure is slightly down but government is able to expand its social-grants programme, and increase spending on research and development.

Notes

Introduction: Scenarios past and present

1 *The Eighteenth Brumaire of Louis Bonaparte*, 1852.
2 JK Cilliers, Counter-insurgency in Rhodesia, Routledge Library Editions: *Terrorism and Insurgency*, volume 4, second edition, 2015.
3 JK Cilliers, Collective political violence in the PWV (Pretoria, Witwatersrand and Vereeniging) and Cape Peninsula from 1976 to 1984: Origins and development, unpublished DLitt et Phil, University of South Africa, 1987.
4 In South Africa, futures forecasting has been pioneered by Stellenbosch University's Institute for Futures Research by Philip Spies and subsequently by Andre Roux. Perhaps the best-known South African futurologist is Clem Sunter, who gained a large following when, at Anglo American, he undertook work on the concept of a high road and a low road for South Africa, which was made publicly available in 1986. It was presented to both the banned ANC and the National Party's all-white Cabinet.
5 Art Kleiner, The Man Who Saw the Future, *Strategy and Business*, 12 February 2003, issue 30, https://www.strategy-business.com/article/8220?gko=0d07f.
6 A key component of those scenarios was how the country could 'change gears' to transform both the economy and social environment to accompany the political negotiations. The three components of the Change of Gears scenario were outwardly oriented manufacturing, investment in the black community and the importance of social compacts. South Africa was in many ways a different country then. Presentations of the Nedcor/Old Mutual material were given to some 45 000 South Africans from January 1991 to June 1992, including President FW de Klerk and the National Executive Committee of the ANC.
7 This was part of the now infamous arms deal, whereby South Africa purchased, at huge expense, a number of aircraft, ships and submarines that were largely superfluous to its needs but proved lucrative to people such as Fana Hlongwane and others closely associated with Modise, and apparently also to him personally. In the end, the arms deal was, to my mind, less about grand corruption and much more simply about a liberation party that was just not up to the task of governing South Africa and managing complex procurement. It was a harbinger of even bigger things to come.

8 For more details, see http://www.montfleur.co.za/about/scenarios.html.

9 The scenarios are available at http://www.cosatu.org.za/show.php?ID=2148.

10 See http://www.gov.za/sites/www.gov.za/files/sascenarios2025_0.pdf.

11 They are available at http://www.dinokengscenarios.co.za/.

12 See http://www.dinokengscenarios.co.za/over_process.php.

13 IMF, *South Africa 2013 Article IV Consultation*, IMF Country Report no. 13/303, October 2013, 2, http://www.imf.org/external/pubs/ft/scr/2013/cr13303.pdf.

14 IMF, IMF Executive Board concludes 2016 Article IV consultation with South Africa, http://www.imf.org/external/np/sec/pr/2016/pr16322.htm?hootPostID=fa4c61ad05a8d29 b70767d1b3a7661b6.

Chapter 1: Zuma and the future of the ANC

1 Hanna Ziady, Nicky Newton-King warns that withholding tax will disadvantage the poor, *Business Day*, 6 April 2017, https://www.businesslive.co.za/bd/ business-and-economy/2017-04-06-nicky-newton-king-warns-that-withholding-tax-will-disadvantage-the-poor/.

2 Sipho Pityana, the businessman behind the Save South Africa campaign, describes state capture as follows: 'Our view is that the president of the ANC is corrupt and the president of the country is corrupt. He is working with – in our view – very organised professional criminals who are seeking to undermine our state system. They have penetrated our intelligence system, they have penetrated institutions of state, they are crippling them and they are facilitating dysfunctionality of the state because that kind of environment enables corruption to thrive. They have a presence through people that they appoint to state-owned entities, whether these are security structures or these are state-owned corporates and other institutions. They have penetrated cabinet institutions. This is a capture of the state. They basically have undermined the democratic project ...' Interview with Siki Mgabadeli, Winds of change hit the SABC, Pityana tells national radio: Zuma is corrupt, BizNews.com, 28 April 2017, http://www.biznews.com/interviews/2017/04/28/winds-of-change-hit-the-sabc-pityana-tells-national-radio-zuma-is-corrupt/?utm_source=BizNews. com&utm_campaign=3760852e12-dailyinsider&utm_medium=email&utm_term=0_ d5e2e8a496-3760852e12-100572145. These views were subsequently corroborated with the release of the academic report on state capture. See Haroon Bhorat, Mbongiseni Buthelezi, Ivor Chipkin, Sikhulekile Duma, Lumkile Mondi, Camaren Peter, Mzukisi Qobo, Mark Swilling and Hannah Friedenstein, *Betrayal of the Promise: How South Africa is Being Stolen,* Public Affairs Research Institute, May 2017, http://pari.org. za/betrayal-promise-report/. At the end of May, the ANC announced that it was accepting the proposal 'for the establishment of a Judicial Commission of Enquiry into allegations of state capture without delay. The terms of reference of such Commission of Enquiry must be broad enough to uncover the influence of business on the state. The NEC expressed its desire to see all processes of reviewing the Public Protector's State of Capture report accelerated so that they are not an obstacle to the speedy establishment of the Judicial Commission into State Capture.' This leaves the details of the commission to the president, who is at the centre of the allegations. African National Congress, Statement of the National Executive Committee following the meeting held on 26–28 May 2017, 29 May 2017, http://www.anc.org.za/content/ statement-national-executive-committee-following-meeting-held-26th-28th-may-2017.

3 Colin Bundy, Introduction, in Daniel Plaatjies, Margaret Chitiga-Mabugu, Charles Hongoro, Thenjiwe Meyiwa, Muxe Nkondo and Francis Nyamnjoh (eds), *State of the Nation*, Pretoria, HSRC Press, 2016, xviii.

4 Legislatively, this was achieved when Parliament passed the Traditional Leadership and Governance Framework Act in November 2003 and the Communal Land Rights Act in February 2004.

5 Nick Branson, Land, law and traditional leadership in South Africa, Africa Research Institute, Briefing Note 1 604, June 2016, 2.

6 Tebogo Monama and Jennifer Jordaan, Zuma wants six months as a dictator, Independent Online, 21 July 2016, http://www.iol.co.za/news/politics/zuma-wants-six-months-as-a-dictator-2047740.

7 South African Government, President Jacob Zuma appeals Gauteng North High Court decision, 24 May 2016, www.gov.za/speeches/president-zuma-appeals-gauteng-north-high-court-decision-24-may-2016-0000; ConCourt refuses to hear NPA appeal on Zuma corruption charges, News24, 7 October 2016, http://m.news24.com/news24/SouthAfrica/News/concourt-refuses-to-hear-npa-appeal-on-zuma-corruption-charges-da-20161007.

8 On 6 April 2009, the former head of the NPA, Mokotedi Mpshe, said transcripts of telephone conversations between then Scorpions boss Leonard McCarthy and former NPA boss Bulelani Ngcuka showed political interference in the decision to charge Zuma.

9 Johan Burger, No-man's-land: The uncertain existence of SAPS specialised investigative units, ISS Paper 283, August 2015, www.issafrica.org/uploads/Paper283V2.pdf.

10 Gareth van Onselen, Zuma's 11 Cabinet reshuffles: all the graphic details, *Business Day*, 31 March 2017, https://www.businesslive.co.za/bd/national/2017-03-31-zumas-11-cabinet-reshuffles-all-the-graphic-details/. For every additional government Cabinet change per year, the annual growth rate of African countries decreases by 2.39 percentage points. A Aisen and FJ Veiga, How does political instability affect economic growth?, IMF Working Paper, January 2011, www.imf.org/external/pubs/ft/wp/2011/wp1112.pdf.

11 The World Bank Group, Promoting faster growth and poverty alleviation through competition, South Africa Economic Update, Edition 8, February 2016, 11. (This publication provides a summary of the most concerning contradictions.)

12 Pieter-Louis Myburgh, *The Republic of Gupta: A Story of State Capture*, Cape Town, Penguin Random House South Africa, 2017, 88-89.

13 Did Ajay Gupta make Duduzane Zuma a billionaire? *The Citizen*, 16 October 2016, http://citizen.co.za/news/news-national/1315940/did-ajay-gupta-make-duduzane-zuma-a-billionaire/. See also Franz Wild, Millionaire Gupta family seen as symbol of Zuma's failing rule, Moneyweb, 17 December 2015, https://www.moneyweb.co.za/news/south-africa/millionaire-gupta-family-seen-as-symbol-of-zumas-failing-rule/.

14 Tshidi Madia, Gigaba will do Guptas' bidding – SACP, News24, 31 March 2017, http://www.news24.com/SouthAfrica/News/gigaba-will-do-guptas-bidding-sacp-20170331.

15 Franz Wild, Millionaire Gupta family seen as symbol of Zuma's failing rule, Moneyweb, 17 December 2015, https://www.moneyweb.co.za/news/south-africa/millionaire-gupta-family-seen-as-symbol-of-zumas-failing-rule/.

16 Roger Southall, Family and favour at the court of Jacob Zuma, *Review of African Political Economy*, 28, 130, 30 November 2011, 617–626; and amaBhungane, Guptas 'backed' Maine's R140k-a-month bond, amaBungane Centre for Investigative Journalism, 1 May 2016, http://amabhungane.co.za/article/2016-05-01-00guptas-backed-gross-r140k-a-month-bond.

17 This was revealed during an uncharacteristically robust ad hoc parliamentary committee of inquiry that released its report in early 2017. The title *New Age* was suggested by Essop

Pahad and taken from a struggle-era publication. See Myburgh, *The Republic of Gupta*, 97.

18 Thanduxolo Jika and Qaanitah Hunter, Mantashe 'ignored' spy report on Guptas' influence, *Sunday Times*, 5 June 2016, http://www.timeslive.co.za/sundaytimes/ stnews/2016/06/05/Mantashe-ignored-spy-report-on-Guptas-influence1. Myburgh, *The Republic of Gupta*, 87-93

19 Six days before Nene was fired, Dudu Myeni – chair of SAA and of the Jacob Zuma Foundation – wrote to Zuma asking him to intervene, as Nene had refused the SAA board permission to allow a leasing company to lease aircraft to SAA, and instead had ordered the SAA board to ratify a Treasury-approved swap transaction deal between SAA and Airbus.

20 ANC, Organisational report to conference, 26–28 June 2016, http://www.anc.org.za/docs/ reps/2015/Provincial%20Conference%202015.doc-%20PSl.pdf, 2.

21 Statement of the National Executive Committee on the occasion of the 105th anniversary of the African National Congress, 8 January 2017, Orlando, Soweto, http://www.anc. org.za/content/statement-national-executive-committee-occasion-105th-anniversary- african-national-congress.

22 Susan Booysen, *Twenty Years of South African Democracy – Citizen Views of Human Rights, Governance and the Political System*, Freedom House, http://www.freedomhouse. org/report/special-reports/twenty-years-south-african-democracy.

23 Constitutional Court of South Africa, *Economic Freedom Fighters* v *Speaker of the National Assembly and Others* and *Democratic Alliance* v *Speaker of the National Assembly and Others*, 31 March 2016, http://cdn.24.co.za/files/Cms/General/d/3834/24efe 59744c642a1a02360235f4d026b.pdf.

24 Constitution of the Republic of South Africa (Act 108 of 1996) as amended, Section 89.

25 Julius Malema, Zuma is an illegitimate president, *Daily Maverick*, 15 February 2017, https:// www.dailymaverick.co.za/opinionista/2017-02-15-zuma-is-an-illegitimate -president/.

26 Ranjeni Munusamy, South Africa's explosive political cocktail: Fear, loathing, conspiracy, paranoia, *Daily Maverick*, 19 April 2017, https://www.dailymaverick.co.za/article/2017- 04-19-south-africas-explosive-political-cocktail-fear-loathing-conspiracy-paranoia/.

27 South Africa's membership of FATF followed significant work done by the ISS and others, mostly under the leadership of Peter Gastrow.

28 See Financial Action Task Force, http://www.fatf-gafi.org/about/whoweare/#d.en.11232.

29 All banks have to report transactions of R25 000 and above to the Financial Intelligence Centre. Failure to do so may result in imprisonment of up to 15 years or a fine of up to R100 million. See News24Wire, Gordhan drops Gupta bomb, exposing R6.8 billion in 'suspicious' payments, BusinessTech, 15 October 2016, https://businesstech.co.za/ news/finance/140213/gordhan-drops-gupta-bomb-exposing-r6-8-billion-in-suspicious- payments/. The Gupta family disputed the transactions as based on flawed analysis and containing factual errors in a subsequent affidavit, arguing that the decision by the banks to close their accounts stemmed from a meeting that took place between the institutions and Gordhan in January 2016. See Ziyanda Ngcobo, Treasury labels Guptas' answering affidavit 'sensational', Eyewitness News, 21 January 2017, http://ewn.co.za/2017/01/21/ treasury-labels-guptas-answering-affidavit-sensational; National Treasury, Treasury welcomes FATF outcome of plenary discussion on South Africa's 12th Mutual Evaluation Follow-up report, 27 February 2017, http://www.gov.za/speeches/treasury-welcomes-fatf- outcome-plenary-discussion-south-africa%E2%80%99s-12th-mutual-evaluation.

30 Emsie Ferreira, Manyi: Fica bill is a bid to bankrupt the ANC, Independent Online, 25 January 2017, http://www.iol.co.za/news/politics/ manyi-fica-bill-is-a-bid-to-bankrupt-the-anc-7504495.

31 Magda Wierzycka, Where is the FICA Bill, Mr President?, *Daily Maverick*, 16 April 2017, https://www.dailymaverick.co.za/article/2017-04-12-op-ed-where-is-the-fica-bill-mr= president/.

32 Rene Vollgraaff, We raised 'lots of issues' with Jacob Zuma, Telkom's Jabu Mabuza says, *Business Day*, 4 May 2017.

33 Molefe stepped down as CEO of Eskom in November 2016 after Madonsela revealed the extent to which Eskom had been providing preferential treatment and terms to the Gupta family's firm Tegeta Resources & Energy. However, in May 2017 the Eskom Board and public enterprises minister Lynne Brown sought to have him reappointed as CEO. She claimed his reappointment was a better option than paying him the R30 million pension payout he had been promised by Eskom. The matter was before the courts at the time that this book went to print, but on 29 May 2017 the NEC directed that the decision to reappoint Molefe be rescinded, not waiting for a court decision in this regard. See Verashni Pillay, The rise and fall and rise again of Brian Molefe, *The Huffington Post*, 20 February 2017, http://www.huffingtonpost.co.za/2017/02/20/the-rise-and-fall-and-rise-again-of-brian-molefe/; and ANC, Statement of the National Executive Committee following the meeting held on 26–28 May 2017, http://www.anc.org.za/content/statement-national-executive-committee-following-meeting-held-26th-28th-may-2017.

34 Tshidi Madia, Gigaba will do Guptas' bidding – SACP, News24, 31 March 2017, http://www.news24.com/SouthAfrica/News/gigaba-will-do-guptas-bidding-sacp-20170331. See also Myburgh, *The Republic of Gupta*, 82–83.

35 Top ANC leaders apologise for criticising Zuma, *Daily Maverick*, 7 April 2017, https://www.dailymaverick.co.za/article/2017-04-05-top-anc-leaders-apologise-for-criticising-zuma/. See also Stephen Grootes, Analysis: A closer look at the ANC NWC's statement reveals not so Zuma-friendly side, *Daily Maverick*, 6 April 2017, https://www.dailymaverick.co.za/article/2017-04-06-analysis-a-closer-look-at-the-anc-nwcs-statement-reveals-not-so-zuma-friendly-side/.

36 Lizeka Tandwa, Zuma dodges bullet from ANC's integrity commission News24, 5 April 2017, http://www.news24.com/SouthAfrica/News/zuma-dodges-bullet-from-ancs-integrity-commission-20170405.

37 Asha Speckman, Business seeks talks with Zuma, *Business Day*, 18 April 2017, 2.

38 Rob Rose, Why execs iced Gigaba, *Business Day*, 26 April 2017.

39 In addition to the 86 elected members, the NEC includes the following *ex officio* members: the chairperson and secretary of each elected ANC Provincial Executive Committee; the president and the secretary-general of the ANC's Women's League, the Youth League and the ANC Umkhonto we Sizwe Veterans League, plus up to five additional members. See http://www.anc.org.za/officials/national-executive-committee-0.

40 See paragraph 53 from the resolutions of the 52nd national conference, 20 December 2007, www.anc.org.za/show.php?id=2536.

41 Clement Manyathela, Zuma says he's not available for third ANC term, Eyewitness News, 12 January 2017, http://ewn.co.za/2017/01/12/zuma-says-he-s-not-available-for-third-anc-term.

42 Ranjeni Munusamy, Who wants to be a president? A dummy's guide to the 2017 ANC leadership race, *Daily Maverick*, 26 April 2017, https://www.dailymaverick.co.za/article/2017-04-26-who-wants-to-be-a-president-a-dummys-guide-to-the-2017-anc-leadership-race/#.WQSxgon5iX0.

43 As well as the concerns of King Goodwill Zwelithini, Xhosa monarch King Mpendulo Zwelonke Sigcawu recently said that 'South Africa is not yet ready to be led by a woman president'. See Sithandiwe Velaphi, Xhosa royalty says no to woman president,

Independent Online, 7 February 2017, http://www.iol.co.za/capetimes/news/
xhosa-royalty-says-no-to-woman-president-7657474.

44 In 2015, Mandonsela won the same award. Pieter-Louis Myburgh notes that the
close relationship between Dlamini-Zuma and the Guptas was investigated by the
State Security Agency as from 2009 – an investigation that was halted when three
top intelligence officials were forced to resign in an apparent effort to terminate the
investigation. See Myburgh, *The Republic of Gupta*, 88.

45 Ranjeni Munusamy, Cyril Ramaphosa: The true betrayal, *Daily Maverick*, 27 October
2012, https://www.dailymaverick.co.za/article/2012-10-27-cyril-ramaphosa-the-true-
betrayal/#.WPJ5YlP5iX0.

Chapter 2: The Republic of No Consequences

1 Richard Calland, *Make or Break: How the Next Three Years Will Shape South Africa's Next
Three Decades*, Johannesburg, Penguin Random House, 2016, 144.

2 Daron Acemoğlu and James A Robinson, *Why Nations Fail: The Origins of Power,
Prosperity, and Poverty*, London, Profile Books, 2013.

3 Ibid., 427.

4 Heribert Adam, Frederik van Zyl Slabbert and Kogila Moodley, *Comrades in Business: Post-
Liberation Politics in South Africa*, Cape Town, Tafelberg, 1997, 5.

5 Adam Habib, *South Africa's Suspended Revolution: Hopes and Prospects*, Johannesburg, Wits
University Press, 2013, 12.

6 Jeremy Cronin, Lessons from the Reconstruction and Development Programme, in Ben
Turok (ed.), *Changing the Colour of Capital: Essays in Politics and Economics*, Cape Town,
David Philip, 2015, 44–45.

7 Ibid., 47 (as quoted by Cronin).

8 Dot Keet, South Africa's official position and role in promoting the WTO, 4, https://www.
tni.org/files/WTOpositions%20and%20role%20of%20SouthAfrica.pdf.

9 Jeffrey Herbst and Greg Mills, *How South Africa Works: And Must Do Better*, London,
Hurst, 2016, 46.

10 This was certainly the view of Mbeki. See Habib, *South Africa's Suspended Revolution*, 90.

11 Jeremy Seekings and Nicoli Nattrass, *Poverty, Politics and Policy in South Africa: Why Has
Poverty Persisted After Apartheid?*, Johannesburg, Jacana, 2016, 9.

12 Cronin, Lessons from the Reconstruction and Development Programme, p 50.

13 Lesetja Kganyago, The impact of the Eurozone and global financial crisis on South Africa,
South African Reserve Bank, 1 March 2012, https://www.resbank.co.za/lists/speeches/
attachments/337/speech_lesetja%20kganyago.pdf.

14 Statistics South Africa, *Poverty Trends in South Africa: An Examination of Absolute
Poverty Between 2006 and 2011*, 6 March 2014, https://www.statssa.gov.za/publications/
Report-03-10-06/Report-03-10-06March2014.pdf.

15 Richard Calland, *The Zuma Years: South Africa's Changing Face of Power*, Cape Town,
Random House Struik, 2014, 3.

16 At the height of its dizzy appeal leading up to COPE's national convention on 1 November
2008 and its congress (held in Bloemfontein on 16 December 2008), the speculation was
that COPE would have polled at least double that number of votes, such was the discontent
with the Polokwane conference and the manner in which Mbeki had been ousted.

17 See http://www.gov.za/issues/national-development-plan-2030.

18 See http://www.gov.za/issues/national-development-plan-2030 and National Planning Commission, National Development Plan 2030: Our future – make it work, 27.

19 Jakkie Cilliers and Hanna Camp, Highway or byway? The National Development Plan 2030, African Futures Paper no. 6, ISS, July 2013, 1.

20 Ibid.

21 Chris Alden and Yu-Shan Wu, South African foreign policy and China: Converging vision, competing interests, contested identities, *Commonwealth & Comparative Politics*, Routledge, 42, 2, 2016, 209.

22 Ibid., 209, 216.

23 The Supreme Court of Appeal of South Africa, Judgment in the matter between the *Minister of Justice and Constitutional Development and others* v *the Southern Africa Litigation Centre and others*, case no 867/15, delivered on 15 March 2016, http://www.saflii.org/za/cases/ZASCA/2016/17.pdf.

24 Statement on the Cabinet meeting of 1 March 2017, 2 March 2017, http://www.gov.za/st/speeches/statement-cabinet-meeting-1-march-2017-2-mar-2017-0000.

25 Nicoli Nattrass, The drowned and the saved: Development strategy since the end of apartheid, in Giovanni Carbone, *South Africa: The need for change*, Milan, Italian Institute for International Political Studies, 57.

26 Keet, South Africa's official position and role in promoting the WTO.

27 Rob Davies, Debate on the state of the nation address, 15 February 2017.

28 Khulekani Magubane, Not a single new business application approved in 2016, *Business Day*, 27 March 2017, https://www.businesslive.co.za/bd/national/2017-03-27-not-a-single-new-business-application-approved-in-2016-gigaba-confirms/.

29 Sheldon Morais, Mantashe unhappy with Zuma's cabinet reshuffle, Eyewitness News, 31 March 2017, http://ewn.co.za/2017/03/31/mantashe-unhappy-with-zuma-s-cabinet-reshuffle.

30 South African Government, President Jacob Zuma: State of the nation address 2015, 12 February 2015, http://www.gov.za/president-jacob-zuma-state-nation-address-2015. See also South African Government, Nine-Point Plan, http://www.gov.za/issues/nine-point-plan.

31 Carol Paton, Nene lays economic problems at SA's door, *Business Day*, 18 March 2015.

Chapter 3: What do recent elections tell us?

1 Collette Schulz-Herzenberg and Roger Southall (eds), *Election 2014*, Johannesburg, Jacana, 2014, 29–31.

2 In 2012, South Africa's trade unions shed more than 300 000 members, representing an 11 per cent decline in union membership to 3 057 772 members in 196 trade unions. See Karl Gernetzky, SA's unions bleed members on 'loss of trust', *Business Day*, 23 October 2012, http://www.bdlive.co.za/national/labour/2013/10/22/sas-unions-bleed-members-on-loss-of-trust. The figures are contained in the Department of Labour's 2012/13 annual labour market bulletin.

3 African National Congress, Political report of the President of the African National Congress Jacob Gedleyihlekisa Zuma to the National General Council, 9 October 2015, www.anc.org.za/show.php?id=11677; see also Ranjeni Munusamy, ANC NGC: Zuma, Mantashe ring alarm bells as membership plunges by 37%, *Daily Maverick*, 9 October 2015.

4 Sizwe Sama Yende, Mabuza vies for top six, News24, 11 September 2016, http://www.news24.com/SouthAfrica/News/mabuza-vies-for-top-six-20160911-2; Pieter du Toit, Here

are the succession slates the ANC is not supposed to have, *Huffington Post*, 12 January 2017, http://www.huffingtonpost.co.za/2017/01/12/here-are-the-succession-slates-the-anc-is-not-supposed-to-have/; and Ranjeni Munusamy, Who wants to be a president? A dummy's guide to the 2017 ANC leadership race, *Daily Maverick*, 26 April 2017, https://www.dailymaverick.co.za/article/2017-04-26-who-wants-to-be-a-president-a-dummys-guide-to-the-2017-anc-leadership-race/#.WQSxgon5iX0.

5 Ranjeni Munusamy, On the chopping block: Why a slashed ANC suits Zuma and the premier league, *Daily Maverick*, 25 May 2016, www.dailymaverick.co.za/article/2016-05-25-on-the-chopping-block-why-a-slashed-anc-suits-zuma-and-the-premier-league/#.Voh9LpP5i1s.

6 Natasha Marrian, Mchunu exit set to deepen KwaZulu-Natal divisions, *Business Day*, 25 May 2016.

7 Afrobarometer, Afrobarometer Round 5 (2010–2012), www.afrobarometer-online-analysis.com/aj/AJBrowserAB.jsp.

8 Rorisang Lekalake, South Africans have lost confidence in Zuma, believe he ignores Parliament and the law, Afrobarometer, 24 November 2015, http://afrobarometer.org/sites/default/files/publications/Dispatches/ab_r6_dispatchno66_south_africa_zuma_trust_and_performance_24112015.pdf.

9 Afrobarometer, News release: South Africans report racial discrimination by employers and courts, 20 April 2016, www.afrobarometer.org/sites/default/files/press-release/south-africa/saf_r6_pr_discrimination_in_south_africa_20042016.pdf.

10 This is if one applies the classic Peter principle of management practice, namely, the tendency in most organisations for a person to rise up the hierarchy until they reach the levels of their respective incompetence.

11 Heribert Adam, Frederik van Zyl Slabbert and Kogila Moodley, *Comrades in Business: Post-Liberation Politics in South Africa*, Tafelberg, 1997, 1.

Chapter 4: Three scenarios for the immediate future and beyond

1 Asha Speckman and Khulekani Magubane, State entity failures signal wider crisis, *Business Day*, 17 November 2016.

2 Net annual FDI has been at an average of USD1,9 billion over the period 1994 to 2012. See Goldman Sachs, *Two Decades of Freedom*, PowerPoint presentation, 2013, slide 15, http://www.goldmansachs.com/our-thinking/archive/colin-coleman-south-africa/20-yrs-of-freedom.pdf.

3 In the run-up to the ANC's National General Council meeting in October 2015, the premiers of three rural provinces, Supra Mahumapelo (North West), Ace Magashule (Free State) and David Mabuza (Mpumalanga), dubbed the Premier League, had called for the alignment of the term of office of the president of the ANC to that of South Africa, implying a two-year extension of Zuma's current term as president of the ANC. See Carien du Plessis, Where to next for the ANC's 'Premier League'?, Eyewitness News, 12 October 2015, http://ewn.co.za/2015/10/12/OPINION-Carien-du-Plessis-Where-to-next-for-the-ANCs-premier-league.

4 We will fight anyone in our party who defends state capture – Gauteng ANC, *Daily Maverick*, 7 April 2017, https://www.dailymaverick.co.za/article/2017-04-04-we-will-fight-anyone-in-our-party-who-defends-state-capture-gauteng-anc.

5 Malema said this during an interview with eNCA in October 2016. See Checkpoint,

Malema wants a political merger, 5 October 2016, http://www.enca.com/south-africa/checkpoint-merger-offer.

6 Mapungubwe Institute for Strategic Reflection, Patronage politics divides us, http://www.mistra.org.za/MediaDocs/overtypercent20Patronagepercent20Executiveper cent20Summarypercent20smaller.pdf.

7 South African Press Association, Minister touts shale gas fracking, 17 May 2012, http://www.news24.com/SciTech/News/Shale-gas-a-gift-from-God-minister-20120517.

8 Hennie van Vuuren and Peter Gastrow of the Institute for Security Studies partnered with the *Mail & Guardian* in exposing Chancellor House. See the *Mail & Guardian*'s special report on Chancellor House, http://mg.co.za/report/chancellor-house.

9 See Steve Hedden, Jonathan Moyer and Jessica Rettig, Fracking for shale gas in South Africa: Blessing or curse? ISS, 6 December 2013, https://issafrica.org/research/papers/fracking-for-shale-gas-in-south-africa-blessing-or-curse. The Blue Bridge scenario explored in that publication provided for an excise tax on the production of natural gas from fracking, in addition to standard energy taxes. The transition tax begins at R0,05 in 2017 and ramps up to R0,30 per million cubic feet of gas produced by 2050. With this tax in place, the annual investments in renewable energy drive up production to over 1,6 billion barrels of oil equivalent by 2050, making it a larger source of South African energy than coal in 2013.

10 Adrian Saville, Wake up, SA – it takes many years to recover from junk status, BizNews.com, 6 April 2017, http://www.biznews.com/asset-management/2017/04/06/adrian-saville-junk-status/.

11 Within IFs these amounts were calculated by removing the 'invm' adjustment used to simulate the downgrade from the run for each scenario.

12 Nazmeera Moola, A guide to ignoring the ratings agencies, *Daily Maverick*, 13 April 2017, https://www.dailymaverick.co.za/opinionista/2017-04-13-a-guide-to-ignoring-the-ratings-agencies/. The South African Index was included in the WGBI only in October 2012 when it became the first African government bond market to be incorporated, based on its size, credit quality and lack of barriers to entry. See Citigroup, South Africa Joins the Citi World Government Bond Index, 25 September 2012, www.citigroup.com/citi/news/2012/121001b.htm.

13 Etienne le Roux and Carmen Nel, Hope is not enough now that SA has felt the pull of the downgrade vortex, *Business Day*, 20 April 2017.

14 Iraj Abedian, Avoiding SA's junk-grade sovereign credit rating, *Journal of the Helen Suzman Foundation*, 78, April 2016, 23, http://hsf.org.za/resource-centre/focus/focus-78-theeconomy-1/focus-final.pdf/view.

15 Ibid., 139.

Chapter 5: Economic and human-development impacts of the scenarios

1 South African Government, Parliament partners with Pardee Center for international futures in USA, 13 March 2017, http://www.gov.za/speeches/parliament-partners-pardee-centre-international-futures-usa-13-mar-2017-0000.

2 The historical data within IFs come from large international programmes and organisations, such as the UN Population Division, the World Bank World Development Indicators, the UN Development Programme, the International Labour Organization, the International Food Policy Research Institute, the International Telecommunications Union, Freedom House, Transparency International, UNESCO, and so on. In South Africa's case,

almost all of the associated data is originally from Statistics South Africa and organisations such as the South African Reserve Bank. The international data provides checks and adjusts the South African data to make sure that the data from different countries are comparable (standardised) before publishing or releasing their combined datasets. As IFs is a global model that forecasts for 186 countries, it needs to use data that are standardised between countries and the various data providers.

3 Like most models of this type, IFs generates a so-called Current Path run (or base-case forecast, sometimes also referred to as a 'business as usual' forecast) as a reasonable analytical starting point. See the appendix for additional information.

4 National Development Plan, 99, http://www.gov.za/sites/www.gov.za/files/devplan_2.pdf.

5 Statistics South Africa, Quarterly Labour Force Survey trends 2008–2015, 2015, www.statssa.gov.za/publications/P0211/P02112ndQuarter2015.pdf.

6 Jame Manyika, Jonathan Woetzel, Richard Dobbs, Jaana Remes, Eric Labaye and Andrew Jordan, *Global Growth: Can Productivity Save the Day in an Aging World?* McKinsey Global Institute, 2015, http://www.mckinsey.com/insights/growth/can_longterm_global_growth_be_saved.

7 C Darrall, Small business can solve youth job crisis, *Business Day*, 8 December 2015, www.bdlive.co.za/opinion/2015/12/08/small-business-can-solve-youth-job-crisis.

8 Statistics South Africa, National and provincial labour market: Youth, Q1 2008–Q1 2015, 29 June 2015, www.statssa.gov.za/publications/P02114.2/P02114.22015.pdf.

9 This issue was examined in depth in Jakkie Cilliers, South African futures 2035: Can Bafana Bafana still score? ISS Paper 282, August 2015, www.issafrica.org/publications/papers/south-african-futures-2035-can-bafana-bafana-still-score, 20.

10 South Africa's youth bulge actually peaked in 1981/82, declined thereafter and, after the impact of HIV/AIDS worked itself through the system, increasing to a lower peak in 2010/11.

11 This is based on the work of Richard P Cincotta, The future out to 2030: According to demography, in Steven Gale and Sarah Jackson (eds), *The Future Can't Wait*, Washington, DC, United States Agency for International Development, 2013.

12 International Monetary Fund, World Economic Outlook Database, October 2016, http://www.imf.org/external/pubs/ft/weo/2016/02/weodata/weorept.aspx?sy=2014&ey=2021&scsm=1&ssd=1&sort=country&ds=.&br=1&pr1.x=40&pr1.y=12&c=199&s=NGDP_RPCH&grp=0&a.

13 South Africa scored 0,666 in 2015 on the HDI; see UNDP, http://hdr.undp.org/en/content/human-development-index-hdi.

14 See, for example, Jack A Goldstone, Robert H Bates, David L Epstein, Ted Robert Gurr, Michael B Lustic, Monty G Marshall, Jay Ulfelder and Mark Woodward, A global model for forecasting political instability, *American Journal of Political Science*, 54, 1, January 2010, 190–208.

15 Statistics South Africa, General Household Survey 2015, Statistical release P0318, May 2017, https://www.statssa.gov.za/publications/P0318/P03182015.pdf.

16 Mary Tomlinson, South Africa's housing conundrum, South African Institute of Race Relations, @*Liberty*, 4, 20, October 2015, http://irr.org.za/reports-and-publications/atLiberty/files/liberty-2013-south-africas-housing-conundrum.

17 Government of South Africa, Strategic Monitoring Branch: Strategy and Business Development, Fact sheet, issue no. 9 of 2015, 30 September 2015. See also Wange Zembe-Mkabile, Social grants: More than just money at stake, News24, 14 March 2017, http://www.news24.com/Columnists/GuestColumn/social-grants-theres-more-than-just-money-at-stake-20170314.

18 Interview with member of Treasury.
19 Marianne Thamm, SassaGate: As dark clouds gather, Bathabile Dlamini fires special adviser Sipho Shezi, *Daily Maverick*, 16 April 2017, https://www.dailymaverick.co.za/article/2017-04-11-sassagate-as-dark-clouds-gather-bathabile-dlamini-fires-special-adviser-sipho-shezi/; Thapelo Maphakela, Sassa needs R6 billion, Dlamini tells Parliament, eNCA, 11 May 2017, http://www.enca.com/south-africa/sassa-needs-r6-billion-dlamini-tells-parliament; and Marianne Merten, Parliament: Two controversies. Two ministers, Dlamini and Brown. One approach: Deflection, *Daily Maverick*, 26 May 2017, https://www.dailymaverick.co.za/article/2017-05-25-parliament-two-controversies.-two-ministers-dlamini-and-brown.-one-approach-deflection/?utm_medium=email&utm_campaign=First%20Thing%2026th%20May%20S27&utm_content=First%20Thing%2026th%20May%20S27+CID_57f1a894d41ac2b7341c6da51a6b2a9a&utm_source=TouchBasePro&utm_term=Parliament%20Two%20controversies%20Two%20ministers%20Dlamini%20and%20Brown%20One%20approach%20Deflection#.WShm_hP5gzY..
20 H Bhorat, B Stanwix and D Yu, Non-income welfare and inclusive growth in South Africa, Development Policy Research Unit Working Paper 201407, December 2014, 19, www.dpru.uct.ac.za/wp-201407-non-income-welfare-and-inclusive-growth-south-africa.

Chapter 6: Our four greatest challenges

1 Frans Cronje, *A Time Traveller's Guide to South Africa in 2030*, Cape Town, Tafelberg, 2017, 190.
2 Adriaan Basson, *Zuma Exposed*, Johannesburg, Jonathan Ball, 2012.
3 Richard Calland, *The Zuma Years: South Africa's Changing Face of Power*, Cape Town, Zebra Press, 2013.
4 Daniel Plaatjies, Margaret Chitiga-Mabugu, Charles Hongoro, Thenjiwe Meyiwa, Muxe Nkondo and Francis Nyamnjoh (eds), *State of the Nation: Who is in Charge?*, Pretoria, HSRC Press, 2016.
5 Adam Habib, *South Africa's Suspended Revolution: Hopes and Prospects*, Johannesburg, Wits University Press, 2013, 3.
6 Alex Boraine, *What's Gone Wrong? On the Brink of a Failed State*, Johannesburg, Jonathan Ball, 2014.
7 Frank Chikane, *The Things that Could Not be Said*, Johannesburg, Picador Africa, 2013.
8 Brian Levy, Alan Hirsch and Ingrid Woolard, Governance and inequality: Benchmarking and interpreting South Africa's evolving political settlement, Effective States and Inclusive Development Research Centre Working Paper no. 51, University of Manchester, July 2015, http://www.effective-states.org.
9 Zachary Donnenfeld, Alex Porter, Jakkie Cilliers, Jonathan D Moyer, Andrew C Scott, Joel Maweni and Ciara Aucoin, Key to the Horn: Ethiopia's prospects to 2030, ISS Research Report, Policy Brief 102, May 2017.
10 South African Government, *Twenty-Year Review South Africa 1994–2014*, 41, http://www.dpme.gov.za/news/Documents/20%20Year%20Review.pdf.
11 Margaret Chitiga-Mabugu, Evans Mupela, Phindile Ngwenya and Precious Zikhali, Inequality, poverty and the state: The case of South Africa 2006–2011, in Daniel Plaatjies, Margaret Chitiga-Mabugu, Charles Hongoro, Thenjiwe Meyiwa, Muxe Nkondo and Francis Nyamnjoh (eds), *State of the Nation, South Africa 2016: Who is in Charge?*, Pretoria, HSRC Press, 2016, 190; see also Imraan Valodia and David Francis, Revealed: If you earn monthly

R12 500, you are classified as 'rich' – Govt. wage research, BizNews.com, http://www.
biznews.com/sa-investing/2016/11/29/wage-research-government-rich/.

12 Ha-Joon Chang, *23 Things They Don't Tell You about Capitalism*, London, Penguin Books,
2010, 146.

13 Edward Webster, Is Zwelinzima Vavi's Saftu a political game-changer? Inside SA's
new trade union federation, BizNews.com, 26 April 2017, http://www.biznews.com/
thought-leaders/2017/04/26/zwelinzima-vavi-saftu/.

14 Ha-Joon Chang, *23 Things They Don't Tell You about Capitalism*, 189

15 Ibid.

16 The Centre for Development and Enterprise, *The Growth Agenda*, 7 April 2015, www.cde.
org.za/insights-and-key-recommendations/.

17 Department of Basic Education, *Report on the Annual National Assessment of 2013
– Grades 1 to 6 and 9*, 5 November 2013, http://www.education.gov.za/LinkClick.
aspx?fileticket=Aiw7HW8ccic %3d&tabid=358&mid=1325.

18 See eNCA, IEB matriculants shine, 30 December 2016, http://www.enca.com/south-africa/
ieb-matriculants-shine.

19 Department of Basic Education, *Report of the Ministerial Task Team Appointed by Minister
Angie Motshekga to Investigate Allegations into the Selling of Posts of Educators by Members
of Teachers' Unions and Departmental Officials in Provincial Education Departments*,
18 May 2016, 17–18, http://www.education.gov.za/Portals/0/Documents/Reports/
MTTJobsReport2016.pdf?ver=2016-05-20-173514-773.

20 South Africa has one of the world's worst education systems, *The Economist*, 7 January
2017, http://www.economist.com/news/middle-east-and-africa/21713858-why-it-bottom-
class-south-africa-has-one-worlds-worst-education.

21 Enrolment rates went up from 22,5 per cent in 1996 to 91 per cent in 2016.

22 SAPA, 2013 matric pass rate: Proof of good education or failing the youth? *Mail &
Guardian*, 7 January 2014, http://mg.co.za/article/2014-01-07-2014-matric-pass-rate-proof-
of-good-education-or-failing-the-youth. The number of people who completed secondary
school rose from 3,5 million in 1996 to 11,9 million in 2016. The number of people aged 25
to 34 with bachelor's degrees doubled from 157 154 in 1996 to 343 116 in 2016. The total
number of people who have completed a bachelor's degree rose from 410 686 in 1996 to
1,2 million in 2016. See Statistics South Africa, Media Release: Community Survey 2016
results, 30 June 2016, http://www.statssa.gov.za/?p=7957.

23 Bekezela Phakathi, Colleges get too little funding, commission warns, *Business Day*, 5 May
2017, https://www.businesslive.co.za/bd/national/education/2017-05-05-colleges-get-too-
little -funding-commission-warns/.

24 TVETC Governors' Council, HET Portfolio committee presentation on DEHT budget vote,
3 May 2017, http://pmg-assets.s3-website-eu-west-1.amazonaws.com/170503TVETC.pdf.

25 Department of Higher Education and Training, White Paper for post-school education and
training, 2014, http://www.gov.za/sites/www.gov.za/files/37229_gon11.pdf.

26 City & Guilds Group, The economic benefits of vocational education and training in
South Africa, January 2016, https://www.brandsouthafrica.com/wp-content/uploads/
mediaclub/2016/01/CG_Global_Case_Study_South_Africa.pdf.

27 Tamar Kahn, Why SA's colleges are missing all the marks, *Business Day*, 8 March 2017, https://
www.businesslive.co.za/bd/opinion/2017-03-08-why-sas-colleges-are-missing-all-the-marks/.

28 Ibid.

29 Goldman Sachs, *Two Decades of Freedom*, PowerPoint presentation, 2013, slide 25, http://
www.goldmansachs.com/our-thinking/archive/colin-coleman-south-africa/20-yrs-of-
freedom.pdf.

31 Statistics South Africa, Quarterly Labour Force Survey, Statistical release P0211, Quarter 4, 2016, 14 February 2017, http://www.statssa.gov.za/publications/P0211/P0214thQuarter2016.pdf.

32 Maarten Mittner, Corporate SA 'stashing cash due to flux', *Business Day*, 10 October 2016, https://www.businesslive.co.za/bd/companies/2016-10-10-corporate-sa-stashing-cash-due-to-flux/.

33 South Africa created 4,3 million jobs in the period 1995 to the global recession of 2008 – an average of 330 000 jobs per year. Thereafter, the country lost almost a million jobs during the 2008/09 recession. Although it managed to claw most of those back, overall employment at the end of 2014 was only 880 000 higher than at the start of 2008. See Industrial Development Corporation, Department of Research and Information, Economic overview, March 2015, www.idc.co.za/images/download-files/economic-overviews/economic_overview_mar_2015.pdf. See also JP Landman, *The Long View: Getting Beyond the Drama of South Africa's Headlines*, Johannesburg, Stonebridge (fourth impression), 2014, 65, 67.

34 This concept was coined by the 19th-century German-American economist Friedrich List.

35 During his March 2017 Cabinet reshuffle, Zuma moved Faith Muthambi from communications to head up the Department of Public Service and Administration. Muthambi had been Minister of Communications, a tenure during which she oversaw the South African Broadcasting Corporation descend into chaos and bungled the migration from analogue to digital broadcasting, so that South Africa missed the deadline. Given her record of bad management and lack of foresight, there is little chance that Muthambi would be able to stand up to the likes of the SADTU and other unions affiliated to COSATU.

36 Moeletsi Mbeki, *Architects of Poverty: Why African Capitalism Needs Changing*, Johannesburg, Picador, 2009.

37 Ibid.

38 A 2015 survey by Afrobarometer and Transparency International recorded that 83 per cent of South Africans believed that corruption was increasing – the highest response among 28 sub-Saharan countries.

39 Michael Marchant, A captured state? Corruption and economic crime, in Giovanni Carbone, *South Africa – the need for change*, Milan, Italian Institute for International Political Studies, 2016, 37.

40 Joel Hellman and Daniel Kaufmann, Confronting the challenge of state capture in transition economies, International Monetary Fund, *Finance and Development*, 38, 3, September 2001, http://www.imf.org/external/pubs/ft/fandd/2001/09/hellman.htm.

41 Ibid.

42 Mosibudi Mangena, Corruption needs to be fought tooth and nail, *Sowetan*, 15 February 2017, 12.

43 In 2015 South Africa was bettered only by New Zealand and Sweden on the index. The Open Budget Index 2015, http://www.internationalbudget.org/wp-content/uploads/OBS2015-OBI-Rankings-English.pdf.

44 Staff reporter, AG's report exposes billions of irregular expenditure by government, SOEs, *Mail & Guardian*, 16 November 2016, https://mg.co.za/article/2016-11-16-government-state-owned-entities-topple-billions-in-irregular-expenditure.

45 This follows the analysis developed by Barry Hughes and others within the IFs forecasting system (see Appendix). Within IFs, the human-capital contribution to multifactor productivity is driven by number of years of education, education expenditures, life expectancy and health expenditure. Social-capital productivity is driven by Freedom House's measure of political freedom (a variable describing democracy), governance

effectiveness, corruption perceptions and economic freedom. Physical-capital productivity is driven by two separate indices of infrastructure: traditional (roads, electricity and water and sanitation) and information and communications technology. Finally, knowledge-capital productivity is driven by research and development expenditures and economic integration. This final component of multifactor productivity represents a measure of connectedness to the global economy.

46 Whereas human capital and knowledge capital contribute positively to multifactor productivity, the contribution of physical-capital productivity is expected to deteriorate over time and eventually also become a drag on growth.

47 World Bank Worldwide Governance Indicators, 19 October 2016, http://data.worldbank.org/data-catalog/worldwide-governance-indicators.

48 Hilary Joffe, Corporate tax take skewed – and falling, *Business Day*, 30 November 2016, 1.

49 Of these, 68 per cent were white, 18 per cent black, 12,4 per cent Coloured and 4 per cent Indian. Lisa Steyn, Earning R1.5 m a year is not rich, *Mail & Guardian*, 12 March 2017.

50 Nomahlubi Jordaan and Karl Gernetzky, Downgrades could cause recession – but we don't really know, says ANC, *Sunday Times*, 10 April 2017.

Chapter 7: Why is our economy not growing?

1 Cited in an interview with CNN. Nomahlubi Jordaan, If the ANC does not do the right thing by the people of SA, it will fail, Gordhan says, *Business Day*, 28 April 2017, https://www.businesslive.co.za/bd/national/2017-04-28-if-the-anc-does-not-do-the-right-thing-by-the-people-of-sa-it-will-fail-gordhan-says/.

2 JP Landman, *The Long View*, 27.

3 These totalled R639 billion between 1994 and 2009. See A Roux, *Everyone's Guide to the South African Economy*, Cape Town, Zebra Press (11th ed.), 2014, 48.

4 JP Landman, *The Long View: Getting Beyond the Drama of South Africa's Headlines*, Johannesburg, Stonebridge (fourth impression), 2014.

5 Mark Allix, Policy contradictions at the root of economic stagnation, *Business Day*, 23 March 2015, 11.

6 World Economic Forum, *The Global Competitiveness Report 2016–2017*, http://www3.weforum.org/docs/GCR2016-2017/05FullReport/TheGlobalCompetitivenessReport2016-2017_FINAL.pdf.

7 Ibid., 4.

8 World Bank, Doing Business, Ease of doing business in South Africa, http://www.doingbusiness.org/data/exploreeconomies/south-africa.

9 South African Government, President Jacob Zuma: Launch of Invest South Africa One Stop Shop, 17 March 2017, http://www.gov.za/speeches/invest-south-africa-one-stop-shop-launch-17-mar-2017-0000.

10 Eli Margolese-Malin, Jonathan D Moyer, Mickey Rafa and Mohammod Irfan, Enterprising Cape: Building an inclusive and vibrant economy, 24 April 2015, www.issafrica.org/futures/policy-brief/enterprising-cape-building-an-inclusive-and-vibrant-economy.

11 Ibid.

12 James-Brent Styan, *Blackout: the ESKOM crisis*, Johannesburg, Jonathan Ball, 2015.

13 Ibid., 3.

14 Ibid., 1.

15 Robert Laing, If electricity consumption equates to economic health, SA is unwell, *Business*

Day, 4 May 2017, https://www.businesslive.co.za/bd/economy/2017-05-04-if-electricity-consumption-equates-to-economic-health-sa-is-unwell/.

16 US Energy Information Administration, Short-term energy and summer fuels outlook, 11 April 2017, http://www.eia.gov/outlooks/steo/.

17 Government Notice, Electricity Regulation Act (4 of 2006), Electricity Regulations on the Integrated Resource Plan 2010–2030, *Government Gazette* no. 34263, 6 May 2011, 11.

18 Ibid.

19 Three days after the release of the request for information, the Department of Energy published an update of its National Energy Efficiency Strategy, which outlines a number of proposals to reduce energy consumption by 20 per cent by 2030 through various efficiency improvements. Price increases have also forced the closure of a number of energy-intensive industries. For example, in the Nation Divided scenario, the economy will be 33 per cent bigger in 2034 than it is in 2017, but will use only 19 per cent more electricity than it did in 2017; in the Bafana Bafana scenario, the economy is 52 per cent bigger in 2034 but will use only 29 per cent more electricity; in the Mandela Magic scenario, the economy is 88 per cent larger but uses only 46 per cent more electricity.

20 News24, Nuke procurement: Cabinet authorises request for proposals, *Mail & Guardian*, 28 December 2015, https://mg.co.za/article/2015-12-28-nuke-procurement-cabinet-authorises-request-for-proposals.

21 Matthew le Cordeur, Cabinet officially approves nuclear plan, News24, 24 December 2015, http://www.fin24.com/Economy/breaking-cabinet-officially-approves-nuclear-plan-20151224. *Government Gazette* no 39541, 21 December 2015.

22 Statement by Gordon Mackay, DA Shadow Minister of Energy, Why did Ben Martins sign the Cabinet approval of nuclear procurement?, Politicsweb, 24 December 2015, http://www.politicsweb.co.za/politics/why-did-ben-martins-sign-the-cabinet-approval-of-nuclear-procurement.

23 Department of Energy, Integrated Energy Plan, 18, https://www.energy.gov.za per cent2Ffiles per cent2FIEP per cent2F2016 per cent2FIntegrated-Energy-Plan-Report.pdf.

24 The government has designated Eskom as the procuring agent for the new nuclear build, in place of the Department of Energy. Thus Eskom would be the owner/operator of any new nuclear plant, entrenching its monopoly.

25 Nuke procurement: Cabinet authorises request for proposals, News24, 28 December 2015, *Mail & Guardian*, https://mg.co.za/article/2015-12-28-nuke-procurement-cabinet-authorises-request-for-proposals.

26 Eskom is looking for what is known as a turnkey project for the first plant, whereby the contractor would build the plant but with increasing local content over time. See Thanduxolo Jika, Nuclear move made as Gordhan exits, *Sunday Times*, 9 April 2017. In an interview, Eskom's chief nuclear officer, David Nicholls, laid out the following economic model for the cost of producing nuclear energy: 'At an overnight capital cost for the early machines in the range of USD4 500 per kW, a reactor construction time of six years, plant economic life of 60 years, and fixed and variable operating and maintenance costs of about R0,27 per kWh, including fuel costs, which is what we are currently achieving at Koeberg in today's money.' See Chris Yelland, Nuclear the only viable option – Eskom's atomic chief, David Nicholls, BizNews.com, 19 January 2017, http://www.biznews.com/energy/2017/01/19/nuclear-eskom-david-nicholls/. Academics and research bodies have called for a restructuring of the electricity supply system by separating out transmission (including system operation) from generation and distribution. In short, the Eskom monopoly, which controls everything, should be unbundled, as proposed by government in its 2008 White Paper.

27 During the March Cabinet, the president discarded Joemat-Pettersson as energy minister and replaced her with Mmamoloko Kubayi. Joemat-Pettersson had served her purpose, having sold South Africa's entire strategic fuel stock of 10,3 million barrels held by the Strategic Fuel Fund in December 2015 at the bottom of the crude oil price cycle – at an average discounted price of $28 per barrel – at a time when the Brent oil price ranged between USD37,22 and USD44,44 a barrel. The sale to three companies, Glencore, Vital and Taleveras Petroleum Trading, was illegal, as it had not been authorised by Treasury (a requirement in terms of the Public Finance Management Act) or indeed the authorisation of the board of the fund. See Linda Ensor, Parliament 'misled' on SA's oil stockpile, *Business Day*, 3 May 2017.

28 The case, brought by Earthlife Africa and the Southern African Faith Communities' Environment Institute against the government, was launched in October 2015. See Linda Ensor, Court rules on nuclear plans, and it is not good news for Eskom, *Business Day*, 26 April 2017, https://www.businesslive.co.za/bd/national/2017-04-26-court-rules-on-nuclear-plans-and-it-is-not-good-news-for-eskom/.

29 After the Chernobyl disaster in 1986, and again after the 9/11 terror attacks in the US, regulators introduced onerous safety requirements. Then came the Fukushima disaster in 2011, which effectively ended the prospects for nuclear as a commercially affordable option for most countries.

30 Many companies, such as Toshiba in Japan, have decided to pull out of constructing new plants overseas. In France, the state-owned company EDF is being pushed to rescue former rival Areva by taking over its struggling reactor business. See Kana Inagaki, Leo Lewis and Ed Crooks, Downfall of Toshiba, a nuclear industry titan, *Financial Times*, 15 February 2017, https://www.ft.com/content/416a2c9c-f2d3-11e6-8758-6876151821a6?emailId=58a7318cdb2c3900045008a9&segmentId=7e94968a-a618-c46d-4d8b-6e2655e68320.

31 Jarrad G Wright, Tobias Bischof-Niemz, Joanne Calitz, Crescent Mushwana, Robbie van Heerden, Mamahloko Senatla, Formal comments on the Integrated Resource Plan (IRP) Update Assumptions, Base Case and Observations 2016, 20170331-CSIR-EC-ESPO-REP-DOE-1.1A Rev 1.1, 3 April 2017, http://www.engineeringnews.co.za/attachment.php?aa_id=68400.

32 How the state capture controversy has influenced South Africa's nuclear build, The Conversation, 26 May 2016, https://theconversation.com/how-the-state-capture-controversy-has-influenced-south-africas-nuclear-build-58879.

33 See, for example, Stuart Graham, Zuma signs secret Russian nuclear deal, *Sunday Times*, 19 September 2016, http://www.thetimes.co.uk/article/zuma-opens-door-to-russian-nuclear-deal-pv6wxxfmm. The academic report on state capture that was released in May 2017 refers to the presence of Russian intelligence within the Presidency to guide the process, as well as the use of Russian funds for the ANC's 2016 local government election campaign. If true, this mirrors the allegation that funds from the arms deal supported the ANC during the 1999 elections. See Haroon Bhorat, Mbongiseni Buthelezi, Ivor Chipkin, Sikhulekile Duma, Lumkile Mondi, Camaren Peter, Mzukisi Qobo, Mark Swilling and Hannah Friedenstein, *Betrayal of the Promise: How South Africa is Being Stolen*, Public Affairs Research Institute, May 2017, 17, http://pari.org.za/betrayal-promise-report/.

34 Qaanitah Hunter, Thanduxolo Jika and Thabo Makone, Isolated Zuma faces revolt over Pravin Gordhan's axing, *Sunday Times*, 2 April 2017, http://www.timeslive.co.za/sundaytimes/stnews/2017/04/02/Isolated-Zuma-faces-revolt-over-Pravin-Gordhans-axing.

35 Long-term mitigation scenarios: Strategic options for South Africa, http://pmg-assets.s3-eu-west-1.amazonaws.com/docs/080610ltms1.pdf.

36 Harald Winkler, Long Term Mitigation Scenarios (LTMS), http://www.enviropaedia.com/

topic/default.php?topic_id=330.

37 ICF International, The future of natural gas in Mozambique: Towards a gas master plan, 20 December 2012, http://www.eisourcebook.org/cms/January%202016/Mozambique%20 Towards%20a%20Natural%20Gas%20Master%20Plan.pdf.

38 S Mkokeli, CC Paton, PP Ndzamela and LL Ensor, Rand crashes after Zuma fires Nene, Business Day Live, 10 December 2015, www.bdlive.co.za/markets/2015/12/10/ rand-crashes-after-zuma-fires-nene.

39 Steve Hedden, Parched prospects II: A revised long-term water supply and demand forecast for South Africa, African Futures Paper 16, 22 March 2016, https://issafrica.org/research/ papers/parched-prospects-ii-a-revised-long-term-water-supply-and-demand-forecast-for-south-africa.

40 Ibid., 18.

41 See http://www.gov.za/issues/national-development-plan-2030 and National Planning Commission, National Development Plan 2030: Our future: Make it work, 219.

42 Matthew Savides, Kingdom holds keys to our taps, *Sunday Times*, 13 November 2016.

43 Sipho Masondo, Nomvula Mokonyane's water department is bankrupt, *City Press*, 12 February 2017.

44 Babalo Ndenze and Thanduxolo Jika, 'Zuma ministers' want Treasury to 'share the cake', *Sunday Times*, 12 February 2017, http://www.timeslive.co.za/sundaytimes/ stnews/2017/02/12/Zuma-ministers-want-Treasury-to-share-the-cake1.

45 Athandiwe Saba, Inquiry 'set to unravel water arrears mystery', *Sunday Times*, 5 March 2017.

Chapter 8: Crime, violence and instability

1 Moeletsi Mbeki and Nobantu Mbeki, *A Manifesto for Social Change: How to Save South Africa*, Johannesburg, Pan Macmillan, 2016, 102.

2 This chapter draws on Jakkie Cilliers and Ciara Aucoin, Economics, governance and instability in South Africa, ISS Paper 293, 19 June 2016, https://issafrica.s3.amazonaws. com/site/uploads/Paper293.pdf.

3 These events are the subject of my PhD thesis, Jakkie Cilliers, Collective political violence in the PWV (Pretoria, Witwatersrand and Vereeniging) and Cape Peninsula from 1976 to 1984: Origins and development, unpublished DLitt et Phil, Unisa, 1986.

4 Rachel Jewkes and Robert Morrell, Gender and sexuality: Emerging perspectives from the heterosexual epidemic in South Africa and implications for HIV risk and prevention, *Journal of the International Aids Society*, 13, 6, 2010, 4.

5 Daniel Conway, *Masculinities, Militarisation and the End Conscription Campaign: War Resistance in Apartheid South Africa*. Manchester, Manchester University Press, 2012.

6 Therese F Azeng and Thierry U Yogo, *Youth unemployment and political instability in selected developing countries*, African Development Bank Working Paper Series no. 171, May 2013.

7 Geoff Harris and Claire Vermaak, Economic inequality as a source of interpersonal violence: Evidence from sub-Saharan Africa and South Africa, *South African Journal of Economic and Management Sciences*, 18, 1, 2015, 45–57, http://dx.doi. org/10.17159/2222-3436/2015/v18n1a4.

8 Ibid.

9 Violence is not just a South African, or even an African, problem. In conflict-ridden countries

in Latin America, for example, an estimated 5,65 per cent of GDP is lost annually as a result of the costs of violence to the job market and healthcare systems.

10 South African Police Service, An analysis of the national crime statistics: Amendment to the Annual Report 2013–2014, 2014, 13, http://www.saps.gov.za/about/stratframework/annual_report/2013_2014/crime_statreport_2014_part1.pdf.

11 See the ISS Crime Hub national statistics page for more, www.issafrica.org/crimehub/national-statisticswww.issafrica.org/crimehub/national-statistics.

12 Harris and Vermaak, Economic inequality as a source of interpersonal violence.

13 Lizette Lancaster, Why are South Africans underreporting on crime? ISS Today, 6 March 2017, https://issafrica.org/iss-today/why-are-south-africans-underreporting-on-crime.

14 Kylie Thomas, The power of naming: 'senseless violence' and violent law in post-apartheid South Africa, Centre for the Study of Violence and Reconciliation and Centre for Humanities Research, University of the Western Cape, http://www.csvr.org.za/index.php/publications/2555-the-power-of-naming-senseless-violence-and-violent-law-in-post-apartheid-south-africa.html.

15 The Armed Conflict Location and Event Data Project uses the term 'riots and protests' to refer to both non-violent and violent forms of protests.

16 Jeremy Cronin, The real, complex reasons behind protests, Cape Times, 26 February 2014, http://www.iol.co.za/news/opinion/the-real-complex-reasons-behind-protests-1653218.

17 Lars-Erik Cederman, Andreas Wimmer and Brian Min, Why do ethnic groups rebel? New data and analysis, World Politics, 62, 1, 2010, 87–119.

18 Cronin, The real complex reasons around protest.

19 Jakkie Cilliers, Crowd dynamics: The value-added approach, South African Journal of Sociology, Routledge, 20, 3, April 1989, 177, http://dx.doi.org/10.1080/02580144.1989.104 32149.

20 The incidents captured by the SAPS should not be equated with protests, which, according to one estimate, constitute only around 43 per cent of incidents. See Peter Alexander, Carin Runciman and Boitumelo Maruping, The use and abuse of police data in protest analysis, South African Crime Quarterly, ISS Paper no. 58, December 2016, http://dx.doi.org/10.17159/2413-3108/2016/von58a1513.

21 Ibid., 13–14.

22 Detail provided by Johan Burger, senior researcher at the ISS.

23 At the time of writing, the number of schools attacked was 24. The 2016 incidents in Vuwani and Lebuvu were apparently motivated by a High Court ruling that the schools would fall under the remit of the newly created Malamulele municipality, a move resisted by affected local politicians (less so by the residents of the Makhado municipality), who were reportedly actively inciting the violence. See Elmon Tshikhudo, More mayhem at Vuwani, Limpopo Mirror, 7 May 2016, http://www.limpopomirror.co.za/articles/news/36759/2016-05-07/more-mayhem-at-vuwani.

24 #FeesMustFall at the University of the Western Cape: Building a living archive of struggle, Africa is a Country, 13 April 2016, http://africasacountry.com/2016/04/more-than-fees-must-fall-building-a-living-archive-of-struggle.

25 University of the Western Cape Fees Must Fall protesters, UWC Fees Will Fall movement intelligence report Part 1, Free education now or never!, 21 March 2016, http://africasacountry.org/posted_docs/Student_Rebellion_Counter_Narrative per cent20UWC_21_March_2016.pdf.

26 Steven Tau, EFF to blame for varsity protests – analyst, The Citizen, 24 February 2016, http://citizen.co.za/1006210/eff-to-blame-for-varsity-protests-analyst/; I Pijoos and J Chabalala, EFF protesters enter closed UFS campus, News24, 23 February 2016, www.

news24.com/SouthAfrica/News/eff-protesters-enter-closed-ufs-campus-20160223.

27 Kyle Findlay, The Twitter world of #ZumaMustFall, *Daily Maverick*, 19 January 2016, www.dailymaverick.co.za/article/2016-01-19-the-twitter-world-of-zumamustfall/#. Vx3XhKNcSkp.

28 Karl von Holdt, Malose Langa, Sepetla Molapo, Nomfundo Mogapi, Kindiza Ngubeni, Jacob Dlamini and Adele Kirsten, The smoke that calls: insurgent citizenship, collective violence and the struggle for a place in the new South Africa, Centre for the Study of Violence and Reconciliation and Society, Work and Development Institute, July 2011, http://www.csvr.org.za/docs/thesmokethatcalls.pdf.

29 Lizette Lancaster, At the heart of discontent: Measuring public violence in South Africa, ISS Paper 292, May 2016, https://issafrica.org/research/papers/at-the-heart-of-discontent-measuring-public-violence-in-south-africa.

30 Gail Super, Twenty years of punishment (and democracy) in South Africa: The pitfalls of governing crime through the community, *SA Crime Quarterly*, 48, June 2014, http://www.issafrica.org/uploads/SACQ48_SuperV2.pdf.

31 Khalil Goga, Eduardo Salcedo-Albaran and Charles Goredema, A network of violence: Mapping a criminal gang network in Cape Town, ISS Paper no. 271, November 2014, http://www.issafrica.org/uploads/Paper271V2.pdf.

32 Simon Bekker, Ilse Eigelaar-Meets, Gary Eva and Caroline Poole, Xenophobia and violence in South Africa: A desktop study of the trends and a scan of explanations offered, University of Stellenbosch, November 2013, http://simonbekker.com/simonsdocs/Full per cent20Xeno per cent20Report per cent20final per cent2020.11.08.doc.

33 Obi Anaydike, South Africa's xenophobia problem: Dispelling the myths, *IRIN*, 21 April 2015, http://www.irinnews.org/analysis/2015/04/21/south-africa per centE2 per cent80 per cent99s-xenophobia-problem-dispelling-myths.

34 Jean Pierre Misago, Xenophobic violence in the 'Rainbow' nation, Al Jazeera, 1 March 2017, http://www.aljazeera.com/indepth/opinion/2017/03/xenophobic-violence-rainbow-nation-170301075103169.html.

35 Andrew Kanyegirire, Less sugar coating for victims of xenophobia in South Africa, ISS Today, 30 June 2008, www.issafrica.org/iss-today/less-sugar-coating-for-victims-of-xenophobia-in-south-africa.

36 Peter Fabricius, Xenophobia again jeopardises South Africa's interests in Africa, ISS Today, 2 March 2017, https://issafrica.org/iss-today/xenophobia-again-jeopardises-south-africas-interests-in-africa.

37 James de Villiers, Govt can't ignore claims about foreigners and crime – Zuma, News24, 24 February 2017, http://www.news24.com/SouthAfrica/News/govt-cant-ignore-claims-about-foreigners-and-crime-zuma-20170224. Said the president: 'We cannot close our eyes to the concerns of the communities that most of the crimes, such as drug dealing, prostitution, and human trafficking, are allegedly perpetrated by foreign nationals.' See Barry Bateman, Crime, feuds, incorrectly called xenophobia attacks, says Zuma, *Eyewitness News*, 1 March 2017, http://ewn.co.za/2017/03/01/incidents-of-crime-feuds-incorrectly-characterised-as-xenophobia-says-zuma.

38 Von Holdt et al. The smoke that calls.

39 Anaydike, South Africa's xenophobia problem.

40 Lizette Lancaster, Public protests cast a shadow over SA voter registration, ISS Today, 5 April 2016, http://www.issafrica.org/crimehub/news/public-protestscast-a-shadow-over-sa-voter-registration; S Chan, *Southern Africa: old treacheries and new deceits,* New Haven, Yale University Press, 2011; and D Bruce, Dictating the local balance of power: Election-related violence in South Africa, *SA Crime Quarterly*, 28, June 2009, http://www.issafrica.org/

uploads/CQ28BRUCE.PDF.

41 Kenny Mudzuli, #TshwaneUnrest plot hatched at hotel, *Independent Online*, 22 June 2016, http://www.iol.co.za/news/crime-courts/tshwaneunrest-plot-hatched-at-hotel-2037071.

42 According to the ISS Public Violence Monitor.

43 National Development Plan, 387.

44 Statistics South Africa, Victims of crime survey 2014/2015, 1 December 2015, www.statssa. gov.za/?p=5937.

45 Angela Daniels, 'Lawless' cops cost province millions, TimesLive, 9 December 2016, www. timeslive.co.za/local/2016/12/09/'Lawless'-cops-cost-province-millions.

46 Johan Burger, ISS Talk, 19 May 2016, ISS.

47 The Directorate for Priority Crime Investigation is responsible for the combating, investigation and prevention of national priority crimes, such as serious organised crime, serious commercial crime and serious corruption in terms of Section 17B and 17D of the South African Police Service Act, 1995 as amended.

48 Karl Gernetzky, Fikile Mbalula to meet Hawks on fired Ntlemeza, *Business Day*, 13 April 2017.

49 Qaanitah Hunter, Zuma to justify Gordhan axing with intelligence report – sources, Sowetan Live, 29 March 2017, http://www.sowetanlive.co.za/news/2017/03/29/zuma-to-justify-gordhan-axing-with-intelligence-report---sources. At the request of the DA, the Inspector General of Intelligence, Sethlomamaru Dintwe, subsequently launched an investigation into the origins of the report.

50 ISS, SA crime stats: Hope amid alarming trends, 2 September 2016, https://issafrica.org/crimehub/analysis/press-releases/sa-crime-stats-hope-amid-alarming-trends.

51 Matuma Letsoalo, Dineo Bendile, Given Sigauqwe, ANC dissenters 'face death threats' *Mail & Guardian*, 7 April 2017, https://mg.co.za/article/2017-04-07-00-anc-dissenters-face death-threats.

52 Janine Rauch, Crime prevention and morality: The campaign for moral regeneration in South Africa, ISS Monograph 114, 1 April 2005, https://issafrica.org/research/monographs/crime-prevention-and-morality-the-campaign-for-moral-regeneration-in-south-africa.

53 Paul Holden and Hennie van Vuuren, *The Devil in the Detail: How the Arms Deal Changed Everything*, Johannesburg, Jonathan Ball, 2011.

54 Stephen Grootes, SACP: Mapaila gun incident an attempt at repeating Hani assassination, *Eyewitness News*, 12 April 2017, http://ewn.co.za/2017/04/12/sacp-mapaila-gun-incident-an-attempt-at-repeating-hani-assassination; Thando Kubheka, Maimane: I wore bulletproof vest because of death threats, *Eyewitness News*, 7 April 2017, http://ewn.co.za/2017/04/07/maimaine-i-wore-bulletproof-vest-because-of-death-threats-1.

55 Report says Lindiwe Sisulu has received death threats for criticising Zuma, *Business Day*, 7 April 2017, https://www.businesslive.co.za/bd/national/2017-04-07-report-says-lindiwe-sisulu-has-received-death-threats-for-criticising-zuma/.

56 Athandiwe Saba, Politics becomes a deadly game, *Mail & Guardian*, 27 May to 2 June 2016.

57 Pieter-Louis Myburgh, *The Republic of Gupta: A Story of State Capture*, Cape Town, Penguin Random House, 2016, 89–90.

58 Rebecca Davis, What's left? Fighters, communists and unionists plot a post-Zuma future, *Daily Maverick*, 20 April 2017, https://www.dailymaverick.co.za/article/2017-04-20-whats-left-fighters-communists-and-unionists-plot-a-post-zuma-future/. This points to the danger should a Gupta company gain access to the information technology systems of the Independent Electoral Commission. These views were subsequently further corroborated with the release of the academic report on state capture. See Haroon Bhorat, Mbongiseni Buthelezi, Ivor Chipkin, Sikhulekile Duma, Lumkile Mondi, Camaren Peter, Mzukisi Qobo, Mark Swilling and Hannah Friedenstein, *Betrayal of the Promise: How South*

Africa is Being Stolen, Public Affairs Research Institute, May 2017, 62, http://pari.org.za/
betrayal-promise-report/.

59 Changing police 'style' may be as important as focusing on police 'substance'. See Lawrence W
Sherman, Denise Gottfredson, Doris MacKenzie, John Eck, Peter Reuter and Shawn Bushway,
Preventing Crime: What Works, What Doesn't, What's Promising, report to the US Congress,
Washington, DC, US Department of Justice, 1997, 655, http://www.ncjrs.gov/works/.

Chapter 9: South Africa in comparative context

1 Nicky Oppenheimer, Foreword to Jeffrey Herbst and Greg Mills, *How South Africa Works:
And Must Do Better*, London, Hurst, 2016, xi.

2 This chapter draws on Jakkie Cilliers, Life beyond the BRICS – South Africa's future foreign
policy interests, Institute for Security Studies, *Southern Africa Report* No. 9, June 2017.

3 Joseph S Nye, Get smart: Combining hard and soft power, *Foreign Affairs*, 88, 4, July/August
2009.

4 According to the World Bank, South Africa's average annual income per person in 2015
was USD6 050. The income range for upper-middle-income countries is a gross national
income per capita of between USD4 036 to USD12 475 a year.

5 According to the World Bank, South Africa's Gini coefficient was 63,4, out of a worst 100, in
2011, the last year for which the bank has published South Africa's coefficient.

6 An exception is the island state of Seychelles, the only country in Africa that the World
Bank classifies as a high-income economy.

7 Converting Nigeria's potential into actual power and influence would also require far-
reaching changes in its current domestic stability, governance capacity and political
leadership, which can only unfold over decades rather than years. The World Bank
considers Nigeria a low-middle-income country and its income per person in 2015 was
USD2 820, less than half of the South African average.

8 Goldman Sachs, *Two Decades of Freedom*, PowerPoint presentation, 2013, slide 14, http://
www.goldmansachs.com/our-thinking/archive/colin-coleman-south-africa/20-yrs-of-
freedom.pdf.

9 Presentation by Bart Van Uythem, Head Economic and Infrastructure Cooperation Section,
Delegation of the European Union to South Africa, Gauteng Economic Indaba, 9 June
2016, https://eeas.europa.eu/sites/eeas/files/160609_en.pdf.

10 Standard Bank, Feeling the pressure: Inside China macro, 15 November 2016, 1, https://
ws15.standardbank.co.za/ResearchPortal/Report?YYY2162_ISRqWkWXsgcSIFSOmyP9nB
YCsFWQDxsdkTmQIxjwILvJv+YLZfPs8UttfSPPajz/xoiITm+eZxvGcE6UxHkpQ==&a=-1.

11 John Stuart, Intra-SACU trading relationship, TRALAC (Trade Law Centre) trade data
analysis, February 2017, 5, https://www.tralac.org/images/docs/11220/intra-sacu-trading-
relationship-synopsis-february-2017.pdf#page=1&zoom=auto,-56,843.

12 Elsie S Kanza, 3 ways to make rich Africa work for poor Africans, World Economic Forum,
https://www.weforum.org/agenda/2017/04/ways-rich-africa-can-work-for-poor-africans/.

13 Rob Davies, Minister of Trade and Industry, in response to the 2017 debate on the state of
the nation address.

14 Ernst & Young, Africa attractiveness survey 2013: Getting down to business, 3, http://www.
ey.com/Publication/vwLUAssets/The_Africa_Attractiveness_Survey_2013/$FILE/Africa_
Attractiveness_Survey_2013_AU1582.pdf.

15 Shireen Darmalingam, *Special Report – Part IV: SA Trade Picture – Africa's Dominant*

Position, 12 August 2013, https://research.standardbank.com/Search#/?Analysts=6856
72D4-6317-4011-BEC4-64B0AB2C949E&Keyword=europe&Page=4&Preview=1671-
1B66E2571B614E4DB6AAA4C71CA493AF. Later figures were calculated from data
available at https://www.tralac.org/resources/our-resources/6364-south-africa-africa-
tradingrelationship.html.

16 This analysis uses data from the Stockholm International Peace Research Institute, https://
www.sipri.org/databases/milex.

17 Niessan Alessandro Besharati, South African Development Partnership Agency: Strategic
aid or development packages for Africa?, SAIIA Report no. 12, South African Institute of
International Affairs, August 2013, http://www.saiia.org.za/research-reports/south-african-
development-partnership-agency-sadpa-strategic-aid-or-development-packages-for-africa.

18 This programme sets out to improve north–south road and rail infrastructure on the
continent under the Programme for Infrastructure Development of Africa.

19 Chris Alden and Yu-Shan Wu, South African foreign policy and China: converging visions,
competing interests, contested identities, *Commonwealth & Comparative Politics*, 54, 2,
2016, DOI:10.1080/14662043.2016.1151170

20 Simon Freemantle, BRICS-Africa: the hype is gone, but much remains, Standard Bank, 8 June
2016, https://research.standardbank.com/ResearchPortal/PDFViewer.action?showPage=.

21 Garth Le Pere, Can Africa truly benefit from global economic governance?, *Global
Policy*, 10 March 2017, http://www.globalpolicyjournal.com/blog/10/03/2017/
can-africa-truly-benefit-global-economic-governance.

22 Thus arts and culture minister Nathi Mthethwa co-chairs a South Africa-China People-
to-People Exchange Mechanism to 'enhance mutual trust, friendship and strategic
partnership and further deepen co-operation between our two countries especially in the
areas of culture, education, communications, health, technology, sports, tourism, women
advancement and youth'. Media statement by Nathi Mthethwa, at the briefing on the
high-level people-to-people exchange mechanism between South Africa and the People's
Republic of China, 20 April 2017, http://www.gov.za/speeches/minister-nathi-mthethwa-
briefing-high-level-people-people-exchange-mechanism-between-south.

23 Jeremy Stevens, OBOR and Africa, Standard Bank, 19 May 2017, https://ws15.
standardbank.co.za/ResearchPortal/Report?YYY2162_FISRqWkWXsjoLNloFp3Zff19eRI
TTl7ZeYATQ8TyLc+WGGamA7Oat6bNCLM7jspT/xoiITm+eZxvGcE6UxHkpQ==&a=-1.

24 According to India's commerce and industry minister, speaking at the October 2016 BRICS
Trade Fair.

25 As quoted by Alden and Yu-Shan Wu, South African foreign policy and China.

26 The White Paper describes South–South solidarity as 'cooperation amongst countries and/
or groupings in the global South aimed at addressing and developing a common stance
on political, economic, social and human rights issues' – all of which are often termed
developmental issues, or issues that must be addressed to overcome the historical legacy of
marginalisation faced by these countries.

27 For example, South Africa has proposed the establishment of the African Capacity for
Immediate Response to Crises, an initiative that seeks to duplicate aspects of the African
Union's African Standby Force. This has confounded and exasperated other African
countries.

28 This is a contested concept in international-relations literature. For the purposes of this
book, however, power potential is the general capacity of a country to influence or impose
its will on others or to shape outcomes.

29 Kenneth Waltz, *Theory of International Politics*, New York, Random House, 1979, 73.

30 Jakkie Cilliers, Julia Schünemann and Jonathan D Moyer, Power and influence in Africa:

Algeria, Egypt, Ethiopia, Nigeria and South Africa, African Futures Paper 14, ISS, March 2015.

31 The exact measures are as follows: 20 per cent global share of military spending at market exchange rate; 5 per cent global share of nuclear weapons (logged); 10 per cent global share of working-age population living above the poverty line; 5 per cent global share of energy exports minus global share of energy imports; 5 per cent global share of external investments; 20 per cent global share of GDP at purchasing power parity; 5 per cent global share of trade; 5 per cent global share of R&D expenditure; 5 per cent global share of ICT stock; 5 per cent global share of foreign aid; and 15 per cent global share of diplomatic power times government revenue. See Jonathan D Moyer, Measuring and forecasting relative national power, University of Denver, 2015, unpublished.

Chapter 10: Towards meaningful radical economic transformation

1 Erik S Reinert, *How Rich Countries Got Rich and Why Poor Countries Stay Poor*, London, Constable, 2010, 148.

2 Nicoli Nattrass, The drowned and the saved: development strategy since the end of apartheid, in Giovanni Carbone, *South Africa: The Need for Change*, Milan, Italian Institute for International Political Studies, 2016, 55.

3 African National Congress, Employment creation, economic growth and structural change: strengthening the programme of radical economic transformation, National Policy Conference discussion documents, 2, http://www.anc.org.za/sites/default/files/National%20Policy%20Conference%202017%20Economic%20Transformation_1.pdf.

4 Anthony Black, Conclusion, in Anthony Black (ed.), *Towards Employment-intensive Growth in South Africa*, Cape Town, UCT Press, 2016, 355.

5 See, for example, Rahul Anand, Siddharth Kothari and Naresh Kumar, South Africa: Labor market dynamics and inequality, IMF Working Paper WP/16/137, July 2016, https://www.imf.org/external/pubs/ft/wp/2016/wp16137.pdf. The paper finds that 'a 10 percentage point reduction in unemployment lowers the Gini coefficient by 3 percent. Achieving a similar reduction solely through transfers would require a 40 percent increase in government transfers.'

6 As reported by Natasha Marrian, New federation gears up for action, *Business Day*, 21 April 2017.

7 Black, Conclusion, in Black (ed.), *Towards Employment-intensive Growth in South Africa*, 356–359.

8 Mark Allix, Buy Back SA campaign pushes urgency of creating jobs, *Business Day*, 20 November 2013, http://www.bdlive.co.za/business/trade/2013/11/20/buy-back-sa-campaign-pushes-urgency-of-creating-jobs.

9 President Zuma announced the Jobs Fund during the February 2011 state of the nation address. It was launched in June 2011 by the Minister of Finance and R9 billion was set aside towards the realisation of the objective, which is to co-finance projects by public, private and non-governmental organisations that will significantly contribute to job creation. It provides public funding through four 'funding windows': enterprise development; infrastructure investment; support for work-seekers, and institutional capacity building. See http://www.jobsfund.org.za/about.aspx.

10 South Africa, Department of Planning, Monitoring and Evaluation, 2014–2019 Medium-Term Strategic Framework, www.thepresidency-dpme.gov.za/keyfocusareas/outcomesSite/Pages/the-Outcomes-Delivery-Agreements.aspx, 6, accessed 7 April 2015.

11 Nattrass, The drowned and the saved, 73–74.

12 Companies like Curro have set a target of having 80 000 children being taught in 200 private schools by 2018. It already has 47 000 children in 127 schools and a turnover of R1,7 billion in 2016. See https://www.curro.co.za/media/10869/curro-interim-results-presentation-2016.pdf.

13 South Africa has a system of Technical and Vocational Education and Training (TVET) colleges and/or universities that aims to provide a technical education in training colleges and through apprenticeships. In 2014, there were 1 037 088 students at universities and 781 378 at TVET colleges. At the moment, students can proceed to TVET after completing grade 9 and if they are 16 or older.

14 Adam Habib, Reimagining the South African university and critically analysing the struggle for its realization, University of the Witwatersrand, 25 January 2016, https://www.wits.ac.za/news/latest-news/in-their-own-words/2016/2016-01/reimagining-the-south-african-university-and-critically-analysing-the-struggle-for-its-realisation.html.

15 Tamar Kahn, Why SA's colleges are missing all the marks, *Business Day*, 8 March 2017, https://www.businesslive.co.za/bd/opinion/2017-03-08-why-sas-colleges-are-missing-all-the-marks/.

16 Amanda Visser, Political stability Africa's biggest stumbling block, says PwC, *Business Day*, 1 October 2013, http://www.bdlive.co.za/africa/africanbusiness/2013/10/01/political-stability-africas-biggest-stumbling-block-says-pwc.

17 Eberhard calls this 'Gridco', an entity that needs to be independent of Eskom generation and the independent power producers, so that it can procure power at the least cost. In this manner, it separates Eskom's generation business from the management of the grid. See Anton Eberhard, SA's power lies in breaking up Eskom's monopoly model, Business Day Live, 21 July 2016, http://www.bdlive.co.za/opinion/2016/07/21/sas-power-lies-in-breaking-up-eskoms-monopoly-model.

18 Greg Marinovich, A tragedy of desperate need, broken promises, *Sunday Times*, 28 June 2015.

19 Ibid.

20 Jannie Roussouw, Investigate executive salaries to close the wage gap, *Mail & Guardian*, 19 June 2015, https://mg.co.za/article/2015-06-18-investigate-executive-salaries-to-close-the-wage-gap.

21 Paolo Magri, Introduction, in Giovanni Carbone, *South Africa: The Need for Change*, Milan, Italian Institute for International Political Studies, 2016, 13.

22 South African Institute of Race Relations, The silver lining 2017, February 2017, http://irr.org.za/reports-and-publications/occasional-reports/files/sona-2017-2013-the-silver-lining.

Acknowledgements

I owe both Gerd Linska and Wolf Krug, previous and current resident representatives of the Hanns Seidel Foundation in South Africa, a debt of gratitude for indulging my desire to always want to look over the horizon. And to my wife, Ulrika, who remains the best source of commentary on my writings.

Others who have contributed in various ways to the original papers and to this book are Julia Bello-Schünemann, Ciara Aucoin, Axel Schimmelpfennig, Iraj Abedian, Ebrahim Fakir, Steven Friedman, Judith February, Sivuyile Maqungo, Gareth Newham, Amanda Lucey, Carien du Plessis, Somadoda Fikeni, Azar Jammine, Ettienne le Roux, Collette Schulz-Herzenberg, Zachary Donnenfeld, Alex Porter, Steve Hedden, Hanna Camp, Joel Maweni, and members of the ANC, the DA and other parties, who prefer to remain anonymous. Ciara was particularly kind to allow me to use portions of a joint paper on violence in South Africa in 2016 as part of Chapter 8.

The scenarios contained in Chapter 4 were first published by the ISS in February 2014 and updated several times, including for this book. They inform the subsequent socio-economic forecasts for which I used the IFs system, which is hosted by the Frederick S Pardee Center for International Futures at the University of Denver (see the Appendix).

The African Futures Project at the ISS has a long-standing partnership with the Pardee Center and I have benefited immensely from our relationship with the former and current directors, Professors Barry Hughes and Jonathan D Moyer. They and their graduates have provided friendship, encouragement and many discussions and disagreements on our many journeys to the future.

Needless to say, the views and analysis presented here do not represent those of the ISS, the Hanns Seidel Foundation or any other partner, including the ISS Board of Trustees or its Advisory Council.

Finally, my thanks to Annie Olivier from Jonathan Ball Publishers, who came up with the idea for the book and who helped to shepherd it to a more rapid conclusion than originally envisaged, and to Mark Ronan, who helped make it all readable.

Index